The Nature of God

Cornell Studies in the Philosophy of Religion

EDITED BY WILLIAM P. ALSTON

God, Time, and Knowledge
  by William Hasker

The Nature of God: An Inquiry into Divine Attributes
  by Edward R. Wierenga

Edward R. Wierenga

The Nature of God

An Inquiry into Divine Attributes

Cornell University Press, Ithaca and London

First published 1989 by Cornell University Press.

International Standard Book Number 0–8014–2212–4
Library of Congress Catalog Card Number 88-47929

Printed in the United States of America

Librarians: Library of Congress cataloging information appears on the last page of the book.

The paper in this book is acid-free and meets the guidelines for permanence and durability of the Committee on Production Guidelines for Book Longevity of the Council on Library Resources.

For Wilma

Contents

Contents

Acknowledgments

I am glad to have the opportunity to acknowledge my indebtedness to the friends, colleagues, and institutions whose help and support have significantly contributed to the existence and improvement of this book.

Thanks are due to Alvin Plantinga for several reasons, but in the first place for his example and influence. His writings have always seemed to me to be a model of philosophical insight and clarity. I refer to, borrow from, or discuss his work in nearly every chapter.

This project was conceived during the term of a Mellon Faculty Fellowship provided by the University of Rochester in 1984. Much of the research and writing was accomplished during the tenure of a Distinguished Scholar Fellowship granted by the Center for Philosophy of Religion of the University of Notre Dame in 1986–87. I am grateful to these institutions for their support and to the members of the Center and its director, Alvin Plantinga, for their hospitality and intellectual stimulation. Thanks also go to my chairman, William Scott Green, who has supported my requests for leave and arranged for favorable teaching schedules.

William P. Alston, the editor of the series in which this book appears, made many suggestions that resulted in improvements, as did an anonymous reader for Cornell University Press. Others who commented on all or parts of the manuscript include Earl Conee, Richard Feldman, Thomas Flint, Alvin Plantinga, Philip Quinn, and Linda Zagzebski. I am grateful to all of these colleagues. Richard Feldman deserves special mention: he has had to read every draft, and philosophical discussion and collaboration with him has long been a source of insight and pleasure.

Chapter 1 derives from "Omnipotence Defined," *Philosophy and Phenomenological Research* 43 (1983):363–375. Chapter 8 incorporates material from "A Defensible Divine Command Theory," *Noûs* 17 (1983):387–407, and "Utilitarianism and the Divine Command Theory," *American Philosophical Quarterly* 21 (1984):311–318. A paper including some paragraphs from Chapters 2 and 6 has appeared as "Omniscience and Knowledge *De Se et De Praesenti*," in David Austin, ed., *Philosophical Analysis: A Defense by Example* (Dordrecht: D. Reidel, 1988), pp. 251–258. I am grateful to the editors of these journals and to Kluwer Academic Publishers for permission to include this material.

Finally, I thank John G. Ackerman and Roger Haydon of Cornell University Press for their help in bringing this book to publication.

Edward R. Wierenga

Rochester, New York

The Nature of God

Introduction

1. Divine Attributes

Western theism, despite great diversity both within and among the traditions of Judaism, Christianity, and Islam, understands God to be, among other things, supremely wise, powerful, and good. Theistic thought on the nature of God derives from several distinct sources which, nevertheless, manifest broad agreement. These sources—scriptural, experiential, and philosophical—concur in attributing wisdom, power, and goodness to God. With somewhat less universality, they also ascribe eternity, immutability, timelessness, and other attributes to God. It is only natural, therefore, that philosophical reflection on the nature of God has focused on the same attributes. The aim of this book is to evaluate and extend this philosophical reflection.

Thus far I have referred to western theism generally, to what Philip Quinn has called—perhaps with a note of disparagement—"generic theism."[1] My own interest and training, however, are primarily in Christian theism. Thus, the historical references I cite are mainly to the work of Christian authors. But I hope that this does not limit the interest of what follows only to Christians or only to those who take an interest in the "philosophical credentials of the

---

1. Philip L. Quinn, "Original Sin in Anselm and Kant" (unpublished).

Christian faith"; for, as I have suggested, Christianity and theism generally agree on many of the attributes of God.

Let us briefly consider some of the sources of views on the nature of God. No doubt the primary source is scriptural. The Bible, of course, ascribes a great many properties to God, some of which, though of utmost religious significance, are presumably not part of God's nature.[2] Christianity places great emphasis on such claims as that God is the Creator of every contingent thing, that he takes an interest in his creation, that he desires his creatures to be in a right relationship with him, that he has a plan for redeeming his creation and restoring the relationship with human beings their sinfulness has destroyed, and that he will grant eternal life with him to those whom he redeems. But these statements are not usually taken as claims about God's nature, perhaps because God could have been different in these respects; he need not have created the world and its inhabitants, or he might not have taken an interest in such creatures, or he might have left them in their misery after they had rebelled against him.

The biblical writers also ascribe to God various attributes that are usually taken to be part of his nature. Here is just a small sampling. God is often described as almighty (e.g., Job 32:8, Ps. 91:1) and his knowledge as unlimited: "God is greater than our conscience and knows all" (1 John 3:20; cf. Ps. 139, Luke 12:6–7). In addition, God is good:—"for the Lord is good and his love is everlasting, his constancy endures to all generations" (Ps. 100:5; cf. Luke 18:19)— and the source of "every perfect gift" (James 1:17).[3]

Another source of ideas about God is human experience and reflection on it. John Calvin, for example, held that "there is within the human mind, and indeed by natural instinct, an awareness of divinity [*divinitatis sensum*]. This we take to be beyond controversy. To prevent anyone from taking refuge in the pretense of ignorance,

---

2. Compare Hendrikus Berkhof: "Many of the attributes which are usually regarded as uniquely divine are definitely not the ones that impress themselves upon us first in the revelational encounters." He adds, however, that the attributes we are studying are "the presuppositions or consequences of such experiences." Berkhof, *Christian Faith*, trans. Sierd Woudstra, (Grand Rapids, Mich.: Eerdmans, 1979), p. 114 (translation of *Christelijk Geloof* [1973]).

3. Unless indicated, all scriptural passages are quoted from the New English Bible.

God has implanted in all men a certain understanding of his divine majesty."[4] Calvin adds that this understanding typically issues in worship. It may not be beyond controversy that all people are instinctively aware of divinity, as Calvin suggests, but it is certainly true that many people find themselves with the conviction that there is a higher being, a being who is worthy of worship. Reflection on what is involved in being worthy of worship can lead to views about God's nature, for no being is worthy of worship unless that being is supremely excellent.

An interesting proposal in this connection comes not from someone convinced of God's existence but from someone who was endeavoring to prove that God does not exist. J. N. Findlay writes:

> Not only is it contrary to the demands and claims inherent in religious attitudes that their object should *exist* "accidentally": it is also contrary to those demands that it should possess its *various excellences* in some merely adventitious manner. It would be quite unsatisfactory from the religious standpoint, if an object merely *happened* to be wise, good, powerful, and so forth, even to a superlative degree, and if other beings had, *as a mere matter of fact*, derived their excellences from this single source. An object of this sort would doubtless deserve respect and admiration, and other quasi-religious attitudes, but it would not deserve the utter self-abandonment peculiar to the religious frame of mind.[5]

Thus, Findlay suggests that a being who is worthy of worship will not merely be omnipotent, omniscient, and so forth but will have these attributes *essentially*.[6]

Another source of ideas about God's nature is philosophical. Some philosophers have given arguments for the existence of a

---

4. John Calvin, *Institutes of the Christian Religion*, I, 3, 1, ed. John T. McNeill (Philadelphia: Westminster Press, 1960), p. 43. I am construing Calvin as holding that the awareness of divinity manifests itself in finding oneself to have either the belief that God exists or some other belief, say, that God has created the world, which self-evidently entails that God exists. By thus emphasizing the experience of one's religious convictions and inclinations I do not mean, of course, to deny the existence or the value of a more passionate or mystical religious experience.

5. J. N. Findlay, "Can God's Existence Be Disproved?" in *New Essays in Philosophical Theology*, ed. Antony Flew and Alasdair MacIntyre (London: SCM Press, 1955), p. 48.

6. I briefly characterize essential properties in Section 4 below.

being they take to be God, and these arguments demand that the being in question possess certain features. For example, Aquinas begins the first part of the *Summa Theologica* with his famous "Five Ways" of proving God's existence; these include arguments for the existence of a first mover and a first cause. In the subsequent discussion of God's nature, Aquinas makes frequent appeals to what a first mover or a first cause must be like in order to justify his claims that God is, for example, simple, perfect, immutable, and eternal.

Leibniz, too, held that there must be a reason or a cause of the world, and he concluded that

> this cause must be intelligent: for this existing world being contingent and an infinity of other worlds being equally possible, and holding, so to say, equal claim to existence with it, the cause of the world must needs have had regard or reference to all these possible worlds in order to fix upon one of them. This regard or relation of an existent substance to simple possibilities can be nothing other than the *understanding* which has the ideas of them, while to fix upon one of them can be nothing other than the act of *will* which chooses. It is the *power* of this substance that renders its will efficacious. Power relates to *being*, wisdom or intelligence to *truth*, and will to *good*. And this intelligent cause ought to be infinite in all ways, and absolutely perfect in *power*, in *wisdom* and in *goodness*, since it relates to all that is possible.[7]

So Leibniz thought that the existence of a first cause required the existence of a being that is omnipotent, omniscient, and perfectly good.[8]

A second philosophical source of views about the nature of God derives from the claim that God is a perfect being or that, in Anselm's phrase, he is a being "than which a greater cannot be conceived." As Anselm employed this idea in his *Proslogion*, he first presented the Ontological Argument, which was supposed to establish the existence of such a being. He then ascribed various properties to God, often appealing to the premiss that "God is whatever it

7. Leibniz, *Theodicy*, I, 7, ed. Diogenes Allen, trans. E. M. Huggard (Indianapolis: Bobbs-Merrill, 1966), pp. 34–35.

8. Cf. Leibniz's remark that God's "GOODNESS prompted him *antecedently* to create and to produce all possible good; but that his WISDOM made the choice and caused him to select the best *consequently*; and finally that his POWER gave him the means to carry out *actually* the great design which he had formed." Ibid., II, 117 (p. 73).

is better to be than not to be." In this way Anselm concluded that God is supremely good, just, happy, perceptive, omnipotent, merciful, and impassible.[9]

Conceiving of God as a perfect being need not require starting with the Ontological Argument; the idea may also grow out of reflection on religious experience. We saw above how what Calvin described as an instinctive sense of divinity can give rise to the belief that there is a being who is worthy of worship. Reflection on what such a being is like might also lead to the conclusion that God is perfect. That is, in thinking about what is involved in being worthy of worship, we may be led "to ponder [God's] nature, and how completely perfect are his righteousness, wisdom, and power."[10]

I have cited these various sources of ideas about God's nature not because I mean to endorse them all as equally legitimate. Rather, I want to make the point that, despite such a variety of approaches, there is substantial agreement about a cluster of divine attributes, including (but not limited to) omniscience, omnipotence, and perfect goodness. But the ascription of these properties to God gives rise to numerous questions. To take just one example, what does it mean to say that God is all-powerful? Are there any limits to what an omnipotent being can do? Some philosophers have even claimed that the concept of omnipotence is incoherent, so that it is not so much as possible that a being be omnipotent. Progress on these issues will require our coming to a better understanding of what omnipotence amounts to and investigating philosophical objections to the coherence of the concept.

My approach to the topic of the divine attributes begins by looking at what such classical theists as Augustine, Anselm, and Aquinas have had to say about the nature of God. I thus concur with Leibniz, who wrote that "the meditations of the theologians and philosophers called Scholastics are not to be totally despised."[11] I shall endeavor to provide an account of some of the divine attributes by

9. Anselm, *Proslogion* V–VI. The quotation is from *St. Anselm's Proslogion,* trans. M. J. Charlesworth (Notre Dame: University of Notre Dame Press, 1979, p. 121. For an exuberant defense of the importance of this idea, see Thomas V. Morris, "Perfect Being Theology," *Noûs* 21 (1987):19–30.

10. Calvin, *Institutes,* I, 1, 2.

11. From Leibniz's summary of the *Discourse* in a letter to the landgrave Ernst von Hessen-Rheinfels, 1–11 February 1686, in *The Leibniz-Arnaud Correspondence,* ed. and trans. H. T. Mason (Manchester: Manchester University Press, 1967), p. 5.

trying, in the first place, to state in contemporary terms what these authors have said about them. This will require, I believe, making generous use of the insights of recent philosophy. Some of the more technical ideas to which I shall appeal are introduced in the balance of this chapter. Then, I examine whether the ascription of these attributes to God can be defended against recent philosophical objections. In short, my aim is to find historically adequate and philosophically defensible formulations of claims about the nature of God.

2. Some Metaphysical Assumptions

This is a book about the divine attributes, and since attributes are *properties*, I assume that there are properties. Examples (in addition to the divine attributes of omnipotence and omniscience) include, for instance, such familiar items as *being a person*, *being red*, and *having six legs*, as well as such more recondite objects as *being unmarried if a bachelor*, *being believed by Plato to be wise*, and *being identical to Socrates*. Some properties, for example, *being red* or *having written the "Critique of Pure Reason,"* are exemplified. Other properties, such as *being a unicorn* or *having read the "Critique of Pure Reason" in a single sitting,* are, as far as I know, not exemplified, but they could have been. One might suppose, then, that a property is something that is possibly exemplified,[12] but that would be a mistake. To see this, we need to introduce some additional assumptions. First, corresponding to each property is its complement, a property exemplified just in case the first is not.[13] And for any two properties there is a property which is the conjunction of those properties, a property exemplified just by those things which exemplify both of the original properties. It follows that for any property *P*, there is the property *P & not-P*, a property that cannot possibly be exemplified.[14] So

12. Cf. Roderick M. Chisholm, *The First Person* (Minneapolis: University of Minnesota Press, 1981), p. 6.

13. Exception: if *self-exemplification* is a property, then on pain of generating a version of the Russell paradox, *non-self-exemplification* is not.

14. Chisholm would not be convinced by this argument, since he denies the conjunction principle that for any two properties there is a property which is their conjunction. There is an alternative argument *ad hominem* against Chisholm for the conclusion that there are impossible properties. According to Chisholm, belief consists in the self-attribution of properties: a person *S* believes that he himself is *F* just

there are even impossible properties, though, of course, nothing could have them.

I shall also assume that there are states of affairs, objects typically expressed in English by such gerundial nominalizations as *Socrates' being wise, Kant's having written the "Critique of Pure Reason,"* or *There being unicorns.* All states of affairs exist, but only some of them *occur* or *obtain.* In the list just given, the first two obtain, but the third does not.[15] In Chapter 1 I argue that omnipotence is best thought of by reference to the ability to bring about certain states of affairs, and I suggest in Chapter 8 that the moral categories of obligation, permissibility, and wrongness may be understood in terms of the obligation, permissibility, and wrongness of bringing about states of affairs.

Closely related to states of affairs are propositions. Thus, corresponding to the state of affairs of Socrates' being wise is the proposition that Socrates is wise. According to Roderick Chisholm the correspondence is identity,[16] but even if the relation is not as close as identity, it is certainly intimate. Propositions are typically thought to be the bearers of truth value as well as the objects of belief. We shall see, when we consider omniscience in Chapter 2, that whether propositions are the only objects of belief is an interesting question. We shall also consider, in connection with our discussion of omniscience and eternity in Chapter 6, the issue of whether propositions have their truth values eternally—whether, that is, they are always true if they ever are.

3. Modality

Some propositions are true and some are false; among those that are true, some *must be true,* whereas others *could have been false.*

---

in case the property of being *F* is such that *S* directly attributes it to *S* (*The First Person*, p. 28). But surely a person can believe that he has a property that, as it turns out, is impossible. For example, *S* might believe that he has squared the circle or that he has proved that there are finitely many prime numbers. Then, according to Chisholm's, view there must be such properties as *having squared the circle* and *having proved that there are finitely many primes*, but these properties are impossible.

15. For a fuller presentation of this view, see Roderick M. Chisholm, *Person and Object* (La Salle, Ill.: Open Court, 1976), chap. 4.

16. See ibid., pp. 122–123. Strictly, Chisholm holds that propositions comprise a subset of states of affairs.

(Among those that are false, some must be false, whereas others could have been true.) Propositions that have to be true include propositions of arithmetic ($2 + 2 = 4$) and logic (*For any propositions p and q, if p is true and q is true then the conjunction of p & q is true*), as well as various conceptual truths (*Anything known to be true is true*). A distinguished tradition holds that *God exists* belongs in this last category.

Propositions that, though true, could have been false include such items as *Reagan is the fortieth President of the United States, There are people*, and *Leeuwarden is the capital of Friesland*. Propositions that have to be ₂rue are *necessarily* true, and propositions that are true but could have been false (or are false but could have true) are *contingent* (possibly true and possibly false). And those propositions which could not have been true are necessarily false or *impossible*. The kind of necessity involved here is often called *broadly logical* or *metaphysical* necessity.[17]

One fascinating feature of the philosophy of religion is that it usually involves issues from other areas of philosophy; advances in the philosophy of religion always seem to require solutions to problems in metaphysics, epistemology, philosophy of language, or philosophical logic. In recent philosophy of religion there is no more outstanding example of this phenomenon than the difference made by a better understanding of the modal notions of necessity and possibility and their kin for progress on the Ontological Argument for God's existence and on the problem of evil.[18] I exploit recent developments in various areas of philosophy in my investigation of the divine attributes, and since modal concepts figure prominently in this project, it will be worthwhile discussing them further. Readers familiar with these concepts may wish to skip to the next chapter.

17. So called in what is essential reading on this topic, Alvin Plantinga's *The Nature of Necessity* (Oxford: Oxford University Press, 1974). Leibniz had used the phrase "the truths whose necessity is logical, metaphysical, or geometrical," in "Preliminary Dissertation on the Conformity of Faith with Reason," 2, *Theodicy* (p. 10).

18. See Alvin Plantinga *The Nature of Necessity*, chaps. 9, 10, as well as *God, Freedom, and Evil* (1974; rpt. Grand Rapids, Mich.: Eerdmans, 1977). On the ontological argument see also David Lewis, "Anselm and Actuality," *Noûs* 4 (1970):175–88.

4. Possible Worlds, Essential Properties, and Essences

It is helpful to think about possibility and necessity in terms of possible worlds. We can approach this topic by noting that a proposition is necessarily true just in case there is no way things could go or could have gone according to which it would have been false. Thus, no matter how things had been different, it would still have been true, for example, that two plus two equals four or that anything known to be true is true. Similarly, a proposition is possibly true (false) just in case there is a way things could have gone which is such that if they had gone that way, the proposition would have been true (false). Thus, the proposition that Leeuwarden is the capital of Friesland is possibly false, since there is a way—in fact, many ways—things could have gone according to which it would have been false. For example, the Frisians could have centered their government in Sneek or Makkum or another of their fine dorps, and if they had, the proposition that Leeuwarden is the capital of Friesland would have been false.

Now a possible world may be thought of as a *complete way* things could have gone. The easiest way to grasp this idea is to think first about everything that is in fact the case (including what has happened and what will happen)—a complete way things *can* go, since it is the complete way things *are* going. Now imagine something having been different. Suppose Walter Mondale had won the 1984 U.S. presidential election. Then the proposition that Ronald Reagan won reelection in 1984 would have been false. In that case, countless other things would have been different as well. Many newspapers have described Reagan as president; if Mondale had won the 1984 election, these newspapers would have printed different articles. The proposition that the president spends a great deal of time with Nancy Reagan was true in 1986; if Mondale had won the election, that proposition would then have been false. So if we imagine a way in which things could have been different, and then we consider all of the other things that would be changed in those circumstances, what we have conceived is a complete way things could be; and that is just a possible world. Of course we are not able to specify another possible world in all its intricate detail, but we can be confident that if, for example, it could have happened that Mondale won the 1984 election, then there is some complete way things could have gone in which he won the election. Among the various complete ways things could go, as we have noted, is the way things really are going; that possible world is the *actual world*.[19]

The concept of a possible world may be given a more rigorous presentation. We have just been speaking of propositions that could have been true. Given the correspondence noted above between propositions and states of affairs, we could also speak of states of affairs that could have obtained. This is perhaps a better way of thinking about these matters, because what is a way things could be if it is not a state of affairs that could obtain? Now we need some technical terms. One state of affairs *includes* another just in case the first could not obtain without the second obtaining as well. And one state of affairs *precludes* another just in case it is not possible that they both obtain. Finally, a state of affairs S is *maximal* just in case for any state of affairs S', S either includes S' or precludes S'. A possible world, then, is a maximal state of affairs that is possible.[20]

We began this section by observing that a proposition is necessary (or necessarily true) just in case there is no way that things could go according to which it would be false, and a proposition is possible (or possibly true) just in case there is a way things could go according to which it would be true. We may now put this point by explicit reference to possible worlds. Necessary propositions are

19. In an interesting passage in his *Studies in Words* (Cambridge: Cambridge University Press, 1960), C. S. Lewis suggests that the word 'world' has what I mean by 'the actual world' as one of its senses. Lewis distinguishes two senses of 'world,' which he calls '*World A*' and '*World B*'. He then writes: "Another way of putting it would be that, just as *World B* is the Region that includes all other regions, so *World A* is the State of Affairs which includes all states of affairs; the over-all human situation, hence the common lot, the way things go. *Things* or *life* would often translate it" (p. 222). Quoted by Peter van Inwagen in "Two Concepts of Possible Worlds," in *Midwest Studies in Philosophy*, XI, ed. Peter French, Theodore Uehling, Jr., and Howard Wettstein, (Minneapolis: University of Minnesota Press, 1986), p. 211.

20. This is the view of possible worlds presented in *The Nature of Necessity*. To accommodate the fact that some states of affairs, say, *Socrates' walking*, occur at some times but not others, Plantinga modifies his account as follows. First, a *temporally invariant* state of affairs is one that, necessarily, either always occurs or never occurs. Then a possible world is a possible state of affairs that is temporally invariant and maximal with respect to temporally invariant states of affairs. See Alvin Plantinga, "Self-Profile," in *Alvin Plantinga*, ed. James Tomberlin and Peter van Inwagen, (Dordrecht: D. Reidel, 1985), esp. pp. 90–91. I am heavily indebted throughout this section to Plantinga's work.

true in every possible world, and possible propositions are true in at least one possible world. (A proposition is true in a possible world if and only if the world includes the state of affairs of that proposition's being true, that is, if it is not possible for that world to obtain or be actual without that proposition being true.)

Two related ideas, both of which can be explained by reference to possible worlds, will also be useful. First, if an individual could not lack a certain property, then that individual has the property *essentially*. More precisely, an object has a property essentially just in case the object could not exist without having that property, that is, just in case the object has that property in every world in which it exists. (An object has a property in a world provided the world *includes* the object's having that property.) If an individual has a property but does not have it essentially, the individual has it *accidentally*. Among the properties that individuals have essentially, some are *trivially essential*, that is, everything has them essentially. Everything is either red or nonred, and everything is unmarried if a bachelor. But individuals can have some properties essentially that not everything has. Ronald Reagan, for example, has the property of being a person essentially; the White House does not have this property at all.

Second, an *individual essence* of a thing is a property that thing has essentially and nothing else could have at all. More precisely, an essence of an individual x is a property E which is such that (i) x has E in every possible world in which x exists and (ii) there is no possible world in which an individual y distinct from x has E. For example, *being identical to Reagan* is an essence of Reagan. (Being identical to Reagan does not require being named "Reagan"; obviously Reagan could have had a different name.)

We shall have several occasions to employ these concepts. In the next chapter, I claim that what an individual's essential properties are places constraints on what the individual must be able to do in order to be omnipotent. And the concept of an individual essence will be utilized in Chapters 2 and 6 to develop some views about the objects of knowledge and the nature of omniscience.

[1]

Omnipotence

1. The Problem

Theists typically hold that God is almighty or all-powerful, that, in some sense, he is able do anything. But theists are usually quick to add that there are many things God *cannot* do. For example, Augustine claims that God is unable to die or be deceived, and he concludes that "it is precisely because He is omnipotent that for Him some things are impossible."[1] Anselm adds that God "cannot be corrupted, or tell lies, or make the true into the false (such as to undo what has been done)."[2] And Aquinas gives a lengthy list of things God cannot do, including moving, failing, tiring, making the past not to have been, making himself not to be, and making what he did not foreknow that he would make.[3]

Moreover, holding that various limitations on ability are compat-

1. Augustine, *City of God,* V, 10, trans. Gerald Walsh et al., ed. Vernon Bourke (Garden City, N.Y.: Image Books, 1958), p. 109.

2. Anselm, *Proslogion,* VII, trans. M. J. Charlesworth (Notre Dame: University of Notre Dame Press, 1979), p. 1979.

3. Aquinas, *Summa contra gentiles*, I, 2, 25. Compare the list offered by an early twentieth-century Dutch theologian: "Scripture . . . teaches that there are certain things which God cannot do: he cannot lie, he cannot repent, he cannot change, he cannot be tempted with evil." Herman Bavinck, *The Doctrine of God* trans. and ed. William Hendriksen (Grand Rapids, Mich.: Baker, 1951), p. 244 (translation of *Gereformeerde Dogmatiek,* vol. 2, 3d ed., 1918).

ible with being omnipotent is not restricted to the Christian tradition. The tenth-century Jewish philosopher Saadiah ben Joseph spoke of "those absurdities that cannot be attributed to divine omnipotence, such as the bringing back of yesterday and causing the number five to be more than ten."[4] And in the twelfth century Moses Maimonides wrote, "that which is impossible has a permanent and constant property, which is not the result of some agent, and cannot in any way change, and consequently we do not ascribe to God the power of doing what is impossible. No thinking man denies the truth of this maxim; none ignore [sic] it, but such as have no idea of Logic. . . . It is impossible that God should produce a being like Himself, or annihilate, corporify, or change himself. The power of God is not assumed to extend to any of these impossibilities."[5]

The diversity of inabilities allegedly compatible with being omnipotent may seem to make the giving of a clear account of omnipotence a hopeless task. As Peter Geach puts it, "When people have tried to read into 'God can do everything' a signification not of Pious Intention but of Philosophical Truth, they have only landed themselves in intractable problems and hopeless confusions; no graspable sense has ever been given to this sentence that did not lead to self-contradiction or at least to conclusions manifestly untenable from the Christian point of view."[6] Geach's animadversions notwithstanding, I think it is possible to give a coherent account of omnipotence without landing in hopeless confusions. My strategy is to begin by categorizing some of the limitations on ability that are compatible with being omnipotent. I then introduce two technical concepts, and in terms of them I formulate a definition of omnipotence. Finally, I show that this definition accords with my initial list

4. Saadiah ben Joseph, *The Book of Beliefs and Opinions,* Treatise VII (variant), chap. 1, trans. Samuel Rosenblatt (New Haven: Yale University Press, 1948), p. 412. Cf. Introductory Treatise, chap. 5, p. 25.

5. Maimonides, *Guide for the Perplexed,* Pt. 1, chap. 15, trans. M. Friedlander (London: George Routledge & Sons, 1904), p. 279.

6. Peter Geach, *Providence and Evil* (Cambridge: Cambridge University Press, 1977), p. 4. The quotation is from chap. 1, previously published as "Omnipotence," *Philosophy* 48 (1973):7–20. Chap. 2 was previously published as "An Irrelevance of Omnipotence," *Philosophy* 48 (1973):327–333. Richard LaCroix has also recently argued that it is impossible to define omnipotence. See his "The Impossibility of Defining 'Omnipotence,'" *Philosophical Studies* 32 (1977):181–190.

of conditions on omnipotence and that it can be defended against objections.

2. Conditions on Omnipotence

An omnipotent being can do anything (subject to the restrictions to be discussed). How is this to be understood? The claim that someone can do anything is a universal claim. Hence, it involves quantifying over entities of some kind. But what kind? An omnipotent being has, according to Anthony Kenny, "every power which it is logically possible to possess."[7] Kenny thus quantifies over *powers*. Some discussions of the Paradox of the Stone, on the other hand, seem to presuppose that an omnipotent being can perform any possible *task*.[8] I confess that I find both powers and tasks somewhat obscure, unless they are to be understood in terms of bringing about states of affairs. But then we might as well speak directly of bringing about states of affairs. Accordingly, I assume that what is required to define omnipotence in a way that takes account of the limitations on ability that are compatible with being omnipotent is a specification of the relevant conditions C in the following schema:

(O) A being x is omnipotent =df for every state of affairs A satisfying conditions C, x is able to bring about A.

My first condition on an adequate definition of omnipotence, then, is that (A) *omnipotence is to be understood in terms of the ability to bring about states of affairs*. On this point there is considerable agreement in recent literature.[9]

7. Anthony Kenny, *The God of the Philosophers* (Oxford: Oxford University Press, 1979), p. 96.
8. For example, C. Wade Savage, "The Paradox of the Stone," *Philosophical Review* 76 (1967):74–79.
9. See George Mavrodes, "Defining Omnipotence," *Philosophical Studies* 32 (1977):191–202; Richard Swinburne, *The Coherence of Theism* (Oxford: Oxford University Press, 1977), chap. 9; Gary Rosenkrantz and Joshua Hoffman, "What an Omnipotent Agent Can Do," *International Journal for Philosophy of Religion* 11 (1980):1–19; Thomas Flint and Alfred Freddoso, "Maximal Power," in *The Existence and Nature of God*, ed. Freddoso (Notre Dame: University of Notre Dame Press, 1983), pp. 81–113; Stephen Davis, *Logic and the Nature of God* (Grand Rapids, Mich.: Eerdmans, 1983), chap. 5; and Edward Wierenga, "Omnipotence Defined," *Philosophy and Phenomenological Research* 43 (1983):363–375, from which the present

In Geach's presentation, God is omnipotent just in case he can do everything, but as the quotation from Maimonides suggests, (B) *God need not be able to do what is logically impossible in order to be omnipotent.* As Aquinas put it, the "phrase, *God can do all things*, is rightly understood to mean that God can do all things that are possible."[10] In the same passage Aquinas goes on to suggest that being able to do anything logically possible is a necessary condition of being omnipotent. He says, "God is called omnipotent because he

---

chapter derives. A rather different sort of definition is given by James F. Ross in *Philosophical Theology* (Indianapolis: Bobbs-Merrill, 1969), p. 211, and in "Creation," *Journal of Philosophy* 77 (1980):614–629.

It would be illuminating, but well beyond the scope of this work, to examine each of these proposals in detail. I merely mention some relevant literature and indicate some broad areas of agreement and disagreement. Mavrodes' definition has been criticized by Richard LaCroix in "Failing to Define Omnipotence," *Philosophical Studies* 34 (1978):219–222, by Joshua Hoffman in "Mavrodes on Defining Omnipotence," *Philosophical Studies* 35 (1979):311–315, and by Bruce Reichenbach in "Mavrodes on Omnipotence," *Philosophical Studies* 37 (1980):211–214. Kenny's definition has been discussed by W. S. Anglin in "Can God Create a Being He Cannot Control?" *Analysis* 40 (1980):220–223. Ross's definition has been criticized by William Mann in "Ross on Omnipotence," *International Journal for Philosophy of Religion* 8 (1977):142–147. I am not persuaded by the published criticism of Mavrodes' definition, but I note an objection to it, as well as to the definitions of Kenny, Swinburne, and Rosenkrantz and Hoffman below. Rosenkrantz and Hoffman attempt to repair their definition in the light of this objection, and they also attack the definitions of Flint and Freddoso and Wierenga in "Omnipotence Redux" (forthcoming). I do not believe, however, that their criticism of my definition is decisive. Davis's proposal is somewhat incomplete, but if the missing details are supplied in the way I recommend, his proposal turns out to be the same as mine. See my review of his book in *Faith and Philosophy* 3 (1986):88–91. The paper by Flint and Freddoso and my paper are remarkably similar, despite their having been produced entirely independently. I attribute that to good sense and the pervasive influence of Alvin Plantinga. Flint and Freddoso think that my definition is subject to the McEar objection, to be discussed below. Their definition appeals to a particular account of accidental necessity which I reject in Chapter 4, Section 2, below, and it does not, I believe, specify a necessary condition of omnipotence.

10. Aquinas, *S.T.*, Ia, 25, 3. The quotation is from *Basic Writings of Saint Thomas Aquinas*, ed. Anton Pegis, vol. 1 (New York: Random House, 1945), p. 261. This restriction is accepted by the authors mentioned in the previous note. Its importance has also been emphasized by George Mavrodes in "Some Puzzles Concerning Omnipotence," *Philosophical Review* 72 (1963):221–223. As is well known, Descartes apparently denied that God is limited to what is possible. See the references in Harry Frankfurt, "The Logic of Omnipotence," *Philosophical Review* 73 (1964):262–263. For a recent discussion of Descartes' views on this topic, see Alvin Plantinga, *Does God Have a Nature?* (Marquette: Marquette University Press, 1980), pp. 95–140.

can do all things that are possible absolutely. . . . A thing is said to be possible or impossible absolutely, according to the relation in which the very terms stand to one another: possible, if the predicate is not incompatible with the subject, as that Socrates sits; and absolutely impossible when the predicate is altogether incompatible with the subject, as, for instance, that a man is an ass."[11] On this suggestion, schema (O) above yields a definition of omnipotence by specifying condition C as the condition of being logically possible. But such a definition would not permit the following additional restrictions on omnipotence, and it does not seem to accord with what Aquinas himself says elsewhere.

Some states of affairs are such that, although they are possible, it is not possible that anyone bring them about. Perhaps the state of affairs of *no one ever bringing anything about* is an example; necessary states of affairs, such as *5 + 7 being equal to 12*, provide a better example. Moreover, some states of affairs are such that, although it is possible that *someone* bring them about, there is no reason to think that an omnipotent being should be able to bring them about, at least not in any strong sense of 'bring about.'[12] Suppose that Claude is essentially nonomnipotent and that A is some action within his power. Then it might be that Claude can freely do A and, hence, bring about the state of affairs of Claude's freely doing A. But it is not possible that an omnipotent being bring about this state of affairs, since if anyone other than Claude were in any strong sense to bring about Claude's doing A, then Claude would not do A freely. I will say more about this claim below, but for now let us, at least tentatively, draw the moral that (C) *an omnipotent being need not be able to bring about a state of affairs which it is impossible that that being bring about.*

A state of affairs that is within the power of an omnipotent being at one time may no longer be within the power of that being at a later time. Several of the philosophers and theologians we quoted in section 1 held that an omnipotent being need not be able to change the past. Perhaps changing the past is just a special case of doing something impossible, but merely noting that changing the past

11. Aquinas, *S.T.*, Ia, 25, 3.
12. By 'bring about in a strong sense' I mean *strongly actualize,* a concept to be introduced in the next section.

is impossible does not explain why, for example, the state of affairs of *Socrates' never engaging in philosophy* can no longer be brought about, not even by an omnipotent being. It is no doubt *possible* that God bring about this state of affairs—there are possible worlds in which he does bring it about. Moreover, at one time God *was* able to bring it about. But he is not able to do so now; it is too late. The moral in this case is that (D) *an omnipotent being need not be able to do something that is incompatible with what has already happened.*[13]

Many theists who believe that God is omnipotent also hold that he is unable to sin; so they apparently think that being unable to sin is compatible with being omnipotent. Aquinas not only held that the two are compatible but also thought that it followed from the claim that God is omnipotent that God cannot sin. Aquinas's argument, however, in which sinning is identified with "falling short in action" and in which it is assumed that "to be able to fall short in action is repugnant to omnipotence,"[14] may leave some unpersuaded. Nevertheless, the weaker claim of compatibility can be made plausible.

To avoid certain theological complexities, let us speak of God's ability to do what is morally wrong rather than of his ability to sin. Since God is typically conceived of as essentially morally perfect, it is reasonable to think that theists who have attributed omnipotence to God have intended a concept which allows that an omnipotent being who is essentially morally perfect need not be able to do what is morally wrong. More generally, (E) *an omnipotent being need not be able to do anything incompatible with its having the essential properties it has.* Doing something incompatible with having the essential properties one has is, of course, merely a special case of doing what is impossible for one to do. So for an essentially morally perfect being, doing what is wrong is just a special case of doing what it is impossi-

13. Several previous attempts to define omnipotence (including those of Kenny, Mavrodes, and Ross) fail to take this condition into account. Swinburne's final definitions [D] and [E] (*Coherence of Theism*, pp. 152, 160) also violate this condition unless we understand his use of the phrase, 'logically contingent state of affairs after *t*' along the lines of his remark that "we must understand here by a state of affairs *x* being a logically possible state of affairs after *t* that *x* be not merely logically possible and after *t* but also that *x* be a state of affairs logically compatible with all that has happened at and before *t*" (p. 151).

14. Aquinas, *S.T.*, Ia, 25, 3, ad 2. See also Nelson Pike, "Omnipotence and God's Ability to Sin," *American Philosophical Quarterly* 6 (1969):208–216.

ble for that being to do. But noting this does not explain why certain states of affairs are not within God's power. For example, God has promised never "to lay waste the earth" with a flood.[15] It surely seems possible that he lay waste the earth with a flood; but given that he has made a sincere promise not to do so and that he is omniscient and morally perfect, God is unable now to do so.[16] But what exactly is the connection between doing wrong and laying waste the earth with a flood? It is not simply that if God were to lay waste the earth with a flood, then he would be doing something wrong; for if he were to lay waste the earth with a flood, he would not have first promised not to. The definition of omnipotence to be proposed below allows for a resolution of this puzzle.[17]

A definition of omnipotence that accords with what theists have actually meant when they have attributed omnipotence to God ought to allow that an omnipotent being can lack the abilities just listed while not allowing that clearly nonomnipotent beings satisfy the definition. I now introduce two technical concepts to be employed in the definition of omnipotence.

3. Initial Segments and Strong Actualization

The first technical concept I employ is that of an *initial segment of a possible world*.[18] It seems clear that two possible worlds could be

15. Gen. 9:11.

16. I am not here endorsing the general claim that God is unable to break promises. For someone who does make this claim, see Geach, *Providence and Evil,* chap. 2, and his "Can God Fail to Keep Promises?" *Philosophy* 52 (1977):93–95.

17. According to Richard La Croix (in "The Impossibility of Defining 'Omnipotence'"), "an omnipotent being is able to bring about . . . a state of affairs which is such that if it is brought about then it has the property of having been brought about by a single being who has *never at any time* been omniscient." Presumably the kind of state of affairs LaCroix has in mind is one that has essentially the property of *having been brought about solely by a nonomniscient being, if brought about at all.* (In "Omnipotence Defined," nn. 10 and 21, I consider several other interpretations of La Croix's contention.) But in the case of an essentially omniscient being, LaCroix's claim violates condition (E). And in the case of a contingently omniscient being, LaCroix's claim violates condition (D). If a being is omniscient, that is a fact that is already the case, and so an omnipotent being need not be able to do something incompatible with that.

18. I borrow the term from Alvin Plantinga, *The Nature of Necessity* (Oxford: Oxford University Press, 1974), pp. 175–176.

alike up to a certain time and then diverge. For example, there might be a pair of worlds W and W' which are alike up until a certain time t, but in W Jones freely commences to mow his lawn at t whereas in W' Jones freely refrains from mowing his lawn at t. Before t, W and W' seem indistinguishable; we can describe them as sharing an initial segment that terminates at t.

The concept of an initial segment is naturally introduced by reference to free action, but this approach is not required. A pair of worlds could be alike up until the time that an indeterministic event occurs: perhaps in one such world a subatomic particle is emitted with a certain spin whereas in the other world it is emitted with opposite spin. Or perhaps two worlds sharing an initial segment are such that determinism is true in one of them, but the other is deterministic only until an event occurs which does not occur in the other world.

I think that the concept of an initial segment is an intuitive one, but it is difficult to make it precise. The reason is that, to continue with our first example, as alike as W and W' are, they do differ in some respects before t. In W, but not in W', it is true before t that Jones will mow his lawn at t; in W, but not in W', Jones has before t the property of being such that he will mow his lawn at t; and in W but not W', someone may correctly believe before t that Jones will mow his lawn at t. Nevertheless, it is possible to be somewhat more explicit about what initial segments are like. First, there is an existence condition:

(1) For every world W and time t, there is a state of affairs $S(W, t)$ which is an initial segment of W terminating at t.

Furthermore, initial segments are complete, in the sense that no world has more than one initial segment terminating at the same time. Thus, we have the following uniqueness condition:

(2) If $S(W, t)$ and $S'(W, t)$ are initial segments, then $S(W, t) = S'(W, t)$.

If two worlds share an initial segment up to a certain time, then they share all their initial segments terminating at earlier times. More formally,

(3) If $S(W, t) = S(W', t)$ then, for every time t' such that t' is earlier than t, $S(W, t') = S(W', t')$.

Thus, if two worlds share an initial segment terminating at a time t, it does not follow that the worlds diverge at t; but if they share an initial segment up to t, then at t or later something happens in the one world that does not happen in the other.

Moreover, if two worlds share an initial segment, then the same things exist in each world prior to the time at which the worlds diverge. That is,

(4) If $S(W, t) = S(W', t)$, then for all x, x exists before t in W if and only if x exists before t in W'.

Finally,

(5) A proposition p is true in an initial segment $S(W, t)$ if and only if it is not possible that $S(W, t)$ obtain and p be false.

An initial segment of a world W, then, is a state of affairs which is included in W and which includes just those states of affairs which obtain in both W and in any world as like W as can be until something happens in the one that does not happen in the other.[19]

The second technical concept I employ is that of *strongly actualizing a state of affairs*.[20] In the previous section I spoke of "bringing about" a state of affairs, but in so doing I ignored an important distinction. Perhaps the primary sense of 'bringing about' is causal; in this sense, to bring about a state of affairs is to cause it to obtain.

19. The concept of an initial segment seems to be related to the concept of accidental necessity, to be discussed in Chapters 3 and 4. It is tempting to think that a proposition p is accidentally necessary at a time t in a world W just in case p is contingent and true in $S(W, t)$. I wish that I were able to give a detailed explanation of initial segments or of accidental necessity, but I know of no completely satisfactory account. Accordingly, rather than have my treatment of omnipotence depend upon a controversial analysis of the concept of an initial segment, I shall assume that our intuitive grasp of this concept is adequate for the purpose of coming to a clearer understanding of omnipotence. Some detailed attempts to explicate the concept of accidental necessity will be examined in Chapter 4.

20. The distinction between strongly actualizing and weakly actualizing a state of affairs is also introduced in Plantinga, *The Nature of Necessity*, pp. 172–173. I take 'strongly actualize' to be a single word (the space is silent). Thus, the phrase 'to strongly actualize' is not a split infinitive.

Finer distinctions can be made here. For example, some of the states of affairs we cause to obtain we cause directly. These are ones we bring about but not by bringing about some other state of affairs; exactly which states of affairs we bring about directly, however, is a matter of some controversy. Roderick Chisholm suggests that "anything an agent brings about directly is a change within himself."[21] In contrast, Donald Davidson holds that "our primitive actions, the ones we do not do by doing something else, are mere movements of the body. . . . We never do more than move our bodies: the rest is up to nature."[22] Both Chisholm and Davidson are concerned with human, nonomnipotent agents; perhaps we need not settle the issues they raise in order to apply the concept of strongly actualizing a state of affairs to candidates for omnipotence. God, after all, is an immaterial spirit, and internal changes (at least if these are changes internal to a body) and bodily movements are both inappropriate to characterize his direct action. Perhaps in God's case, every state of affairs he causes to obtain he brings about directly; he wills that a certain state of affairs obtain, and it does. Let us say that if God causes a state of affairs to obtain, then he strongly actualizes it.[23]

We can often arrange it that some state of affairs obtains without *causing* it to obtain. Sometimes this is due simply to the intimate but noncausal connections that hold between states of affairs.[24] Perhaps, for example, Socrates did not cause *Xanthippe's becoming a widow*, but there is some sense in which by drinking hemlock, he nevertheless brought it about. Another, and for our purposes more interest-

21. Roderick Chisholm, *Person and Object* (La Salle, Ill.: Open Court, 1976), p. 85.

22. Donald Davidson, "Agency," in *Agent, Action, and Reason,* ed. Robert Binkley et al. (Toronto: University of Toronto Press, 1971), p. 23.

23. In his "Self-Profile," Plantinga has a different proposal. There he says that God strongly actualizes a state of affairs S if and only if God causes S and God causes every contingent state of affairs S* such that S includes S*. (Recall that one state of affairs includes another just in case it is not possible that the former obtain without the latter obtaining as well.) As a general account of strong actualization, Plantinga's proposal is too restrictive, since it would follow that I never strongly actualize anything. Any state of affairs I cause to obtain, for example, *my arm's raising* or *my endeavoring to walk*, includes some state of affairs as *my hand's existing* or *my existing* that I do not cause to obtain. See *Alvin Plantinga,* ed. James Tomberlin and Peter van Inwagen, (Dordrecht: D. Reidel, 1985), p. 49.

24. See Jaegwon Kim, "Noncausal Connections," *Noûs* 8 (1974):41–52.

ing, kind of case is that in which a person can arrange it that some state of affairs obtains by inducing someone else to cause it to obtain. Thus, I may be able to bring it about that the window is open by politely asking you to open it. What is common to both of these cases is that there is something the agent can strongly actualize which is such that if the agent were to strongly actualize it, some additional state of affairs would obtain as well. Let us describe this as *weak actualization*, and define it as follows:

> (6) x weakly actualizes a state of affairs S if and only if there is some state of affairs T such that (i) x strongly actualizes T, and (ii) if x were to strongly actualize T, S would be actual.[25]

One consequence of (6) is that any state of affairs an agent strongly actualizes is thereby one the agent weakly actualizes. It will be convenient to have a notion of weak actualization that excludes strong actualization, so let us say that whoever weakly but not strongly actualizes a state of affairs *strictly* weakly actualizes it. Having introduced this cumbersome locution, let us henceforth avoid it and use the term 'weakly actualize' to mean strictly weakly actualize.[26]

Whether an agent can weakly actualize a given state of affairs depends in part upon the truth of those counterfactual conditionals which are the requisite instances of clause (ii) of (6). These counterfactual conditionals cannot themselves be within the direct control of the agent; for if I strongly actualize T, for example, and strongly actualize its being the case that if I were to strongly actualize T then S would obtain (where S is contingent), it follows that I strongly actualize S and, thus, do not weakly actualize it.

Are there any counterfactual conditionals, not within God's direct control, which enable him to weakly actualize some states of affairs? Perhaps ones representing certain noncausal connections between states of affairs are like this. For example, perhaps the conditional *If*

25. Cf. Plantinga, *The Nature of Necessity*, pp. 172–173, and his "Self-Profile," p. 49.

26. Another consequence of (5) is that an agent who can strongly actualize something can weakly actualize necessary truths as well as any proposition that would be true no matter what the agent did. I shall not try to revise (5) to avoid this consequence; I am content to note that weak actualization is a technical concept that might not correspond precisely to any ordinary notion of 'bringing about.'

God were to strongly actualize Jones's having a child then anyone who is a sister of Jones is an aunt, though true, is not one God can cause to be true. If so, by strongly actualizing *Jones's having a child*, God can weakly actualize *anyone who is Jones's sister being an aunt*.

An especially interesting class of counterfactual conditionals is the class of those Plantinga calls "counterfactuals of freedom." These are counterfactual conditionals reporting what an agent would freely do in particular circumstances, that is, they are propositions of the form:

(7) If Jones were in circumstances C, then Jones would freely do action A.

I assume that no agent distinct from Jones can strongly actualize *Jones's freely doing A*. Perhaps someone else could cause Jones to do A, but if someone did, Jones would not do A *freely*. Thus, not even God can strongly actualize Jones's freely doing A. However, if (7) is true and God can strongly actualize *Jones's being in circumstances C*, then God is able to weakly actualize *Jones's freely doing A*. So counterfactuals of freedom provide a second avenue by which God can weakly actualize various states of affairs.

A counterfactual of freedom is typically contingent, that is, it is true in some possible worlds and false in others.[27] Perhaps it is true that

(8) If you were to offer me four hundred dollars for my bicycle I would freely sell it to you.

There are nevertheless other possible worlds in which I would not accept your offer, worlds in which (8) is false. Moreover, pairs of related counterfactuals, for example, (8) and

(9) If you were to offer me ten dollars for my bicycle I would freely sell it to you,

typically are logically independent of each other. That is, there are worlds in which (8) and (9) agree in truth value and worlds in which they do not. An interesting consequence of these features of coun-

27. I defend this assumption against objections in Chapter 5.

terfactuals of freedom is that it can happen that although it is logically possible for an agent to weakly actualize a certain state of
affairs, the agent is unable to do so. This is because it can happen
that all of the counterfactuals required to satisfy the second condition of (6) (for some free action) are contingently false. For example,
it is logically possible that for every state of affairs A you can strongly actualize, the counterfactual,

> (10) If you were to strongly actualize A I would freely sell you
>   my bicycle,

is false. In that case, you would be unable to weakly actualize my
selling you my bicycle, even though it is logically possible that you
do so.

An omnipotent being can be in a similar situation.[28] It is logically
possible (though no doubt monumentally unlikely) that for every
state of affairs A an omnipotent being can strongly actualize, the
proposition

> (11) If anyone were to strongly actualize A I would sell him or
>   her my bicycle

is false. These propositions are all contingent, and they are, for the
most part, logically independent of one another; accordingly, it is
possible that they are all false.[29] But in a world in which every such
instance of (11) is false, an omnipotent agent is unable to weakly
actualize my selling him or her my bicycle. This can be the case even
if there are other worlds in which that omnipotent being *is* able to
weakly actualize this state of affairs. So being able to weakly actualize every state of affairs it is possible for one to actualize is not a
necessary condition of being omnipotent.[30]

---

28. The argument that follows is inspired by Plantinga's argument that there are
possible worlds God cannot actualize. See his *The Nature of Necessity*, pp. 180–184,
and "Self-Profile," pp. 50–52.

29. The qualification that they are *for the most part* independent is required because
there are specifications for 'A' as *my being offered an amount between fifty and one
hundred dollars* and *my being offered seventy-five dollars* such that necessarily, if (11) is
true in the case of the former it is true in the case of the latter. What I claim is that
there is no instance of 'A' which is such that, necessarily, if (11) is false under that
interpretation then it is true under some other interpretation.

30. The fact that an omnipotent being can be unable to weakly actualize certain

The moral I draw from these considerations is that it is the ability to *strongly actualize* states of affairs that is relevant to omnipotence. In the next section I incorporate this idea into a definition of omnipotence.

4. A Definition of Omnipotence

I suggest that omnipotence be understood as follows:

(O*) a being x is omnipotent in a world W at a time t =df In W it is true both that (i) for every state of affairs A, if it is possible that both $S(W, t)$ obtains and that x strongly actualizes A at t, then at t x can strongly actualize A, and (ii) there is some state of affairs which x can strongly actualize at t.

According to (O*), what is required for a being to be omnipotent is that it be able to strongly actualize any state of affairs which is such that that being's strongly actualizing it is compatible with what has already happened. The second clause is added to preclude essentially impotent things, for example, stones, from trivially satisfying the definiens.

It is clear that (O*) satisfies the conditions on omnipotence that we developed in Section 2. It satisfies condition (A) by defining omnipotence in terms of the ability to bring about—or more precisely, the ability to strongly actualize—states of affairs. And it satisfies conditions (B) and (C) by not requiring that an omnipotent being be able to bring about states of affairs that are impossible for it to bring about. If it is compatible with what has happened that an agent strongly actualize a certain state of affairs, it is a fortiori possible that the agent strongly actualize that state of affairs.

According to condition (D) an omnipotent being need not be able to do something that is incompatible with what has already happened; (O*) accords with this by not requiring an omnipotent being to strongly actualize anything at a time such that the agent's strongly actualizing it then is incompatible with the initial segment up to that time. In particular, although it is logically possible that God

states of affairs logically possible for the being to weakly actualize can be used to construct counterexamples to the definitions of omnipotence proposed by Kenny, Mavrodes, Rosenkrantz and Hoffman, and Swinburne.

make it the case that Socrates never engages in philosophy, (O*) does not require that God be able now to bring about this state of affairs in order to qualify as omnipotent. The reason is that S(the actual world, now) ('S(now)' for short) includes Socrates' having engaged in philosophy. Hence it is not possible both that S(now) obtains and that God strongly actualizes *Socrates' never engaging in philosophy*. So (O*) does not require that God be able to bring about this state of affairs in order to be omnipotent. Aquinas, after the passage quoted above, went on to say that "some things . . . were at one time in the realm of possibility, while they were yet to be done, which now fall short of being possible, since they have been done."[31] Aquinas thus appears to hold that a state of affairs can be possible at one time but not at a later time. However, whether a state of affairs is possible does not vary over time; rather, what can vary over time is whether a state of affairs is possible in conjunction with what has already happened, and it is this variability that (O*) is designed to accommodate.

Our final condition, (E), entails that an omnipotent being who is essentially morally perfect need not be able to do what is morally wrong. As we saw, of course, doing something wrong is for an essentially morally perfect being no more than a special case of doing something that it is impossible for that being to do. But laying waste the earth with a flood is not something impossible for God to do, so must God be able to do it in order to be omnipotent? The answer is that if God has promised not to lay waste the earth with a flood, then S(now) includes not only God's being essentially morally perfect but also his having made such a promise and its being wrong to break it. Hence, S(now) is incompatible with God's strongly actualizing the laying waste of the earth with a flood. So (O*) does not require that God must be able to bring about this state of affairs in order for God to be omnipotent.

So (O*) satisfies our conditions on an adequate definition of omnipotence; accordingly, it does not, I believe, require too much of an omnipotent being. It is more difficult to show that (O*) requires enough. In the next section I consider two objections to this definition, both of which allege that beings who are less than omnipotent can satisfy the definiens of (O*).

31. Aquinas, *S. T.*, Ia, 25, 4, *ad* 2.

5. Two Objections

It might be objected that the fact of God's foreknowledge makes trouble for (O*). Let A be some state of affairs that God will strongly actualize at some future time t. Since God is omniscient, he knows before t that he will actualize A at t. So $S(t)$ includes God's knowing before t that he will actualize A at t. But then $S(t)$ is incompatible with God's not actualizing A at t. According to (O*), then, God need not be able to refrain from actualizing A at t in order to be omnipotent. The point can be generalized: since God has foreknowledge of all of his actions, he need not be able to do anything other than what he does do in order to be accounted as omnipotent. Worse, this objection can be generalized further: if God foreknows everything I do, then I need only be able to do what I do in order to be omnipotent; but I am able to do what I do and I am not omnipotent.[32]

My reply is that what God foreknows before t is not included in the initial segment $S(t)$. Recall that I introduced initial segments by suggesting that a pair of worlds would share an initial segment if they were alike up until a time t at which, for example, in one of the worlds Jones freely commences to mow his lawn at t whereas in the other world Jones freely refrains from mowing his lawn at that time. Clearly there could be a pair of worlds like this in which God exists; and in the one God knows before t that Jones will freely commence to mow his lawn at t whereas in the other God knows before t that Jones will freely refrain from mowing his lawn at t. Since God's foreknowledge is not the same in both worlds, it is not part of the initial segment the two worlds share. And since, by (2) above, no world has more than one initial segment terminating at a given time, God's foreknowledge of Jones's action is not a part of some other initial segment (terminating at t) which is a segment of the first world but not the second. More generally, God's foreknowledge at a time of anyone's future free action is not part of the initial segment up to that time.[33]

32. This objection is considered by Aquinas, *S. T.*, Ia, 25, 5, obj. 1.
33. The objection just discussed bears some resemblance to the argument from the accidental necessity of the past for the conclusion that divine foreknowledge is incompatible with human free will. That argument is discussed more fully in Chapters 3 and 4.

A second objection is that essentially limited and hence nonomnipotent beings can satisfy the definiens of (O*). Consider McEar, a man essentially capable only of scratching his left ear.[34] If McEar were merely accidentally capable only of scratching his left ear, then it would be logically possible both that S(now) obtain and that, say, McEar strongly actualize his taking a step. Since McEar is unable to strongly actualize his taking a step, (O*) would have the proper result that McEar is not omnipotent.

But McEar's limitation is alleged to be essential. There is no possible world in which he exists and in which he is capable of doing anything other than scratch his left ear. And since he *is* capable of scratching his left ear, he is able, so the objection goes, to do everything such that his doing it is compatible with what has already happened. Hence, according to (O*), McEar is omnipotent.[35]

The objector presumably does not mean to assert that McEar really exists, for no doubt there is no such unfortunate creature. Rather, the objector holds that it is *possible* that McEar or a similarly essentially limited being exists, and thus concludes that it is possible

---

It is not only God's foreknowledge of future free actions that is excluded from initial segments; his foreknowledge of certain other things is excluded as well. This is because, as we saw above, there are various ways in which worlds can share initial segments and then diverge. In any such case God's foreknowledge of the divergent events is not included in the initial segments that the respective worlds have in common.

34. La Croix, in "The Impossibility of Defining 'Omnipotence,'" p. 187, so dubs a character introduced by Plantinga in *God and Other Minds* (Ithaca: Cornell University Press, 1967), p. 170. It was Mavrodes who called attention to the question of whether the limitation in such cases is *essential*. See his "Defining Omnipotence," p. 280. Flint and Freddoso endorse this objection in "Maximal Power," p. 112, n. 23, as do Hoffman and Rosenkrantz in "Omnipotence Redux."

Though McEar is a recent invention, Flint and Freddoso quote an anonymous note to a manuscript of Ockham's: "Nor is a being said to be omnipotent because he can do all things which are possible for him to do . . . since it would follow that a minimally powerful being is omnipotent. For suppose Socrates performs one action and is not capable of performing any others. Then one argues as follows: 'He is performing every action which it is possible for him to perform, therefore he is omnipotent.'" "Maximal Power," p. 110, n. 4. They cite *Ockham: Opera Theologica,* ed. Gerald Etzkorn and Francis Kelly, vol. 4 (St. Bonaventure, N.Y.: Franciscan Institute, 1979), p. 611.

35. To make the objection fit (O*) more precisely, we would need an assumption such as that McEar is essentially capable only of *strongly actualizing his scratching his ear*. I think we can resolve this objection without stating it in these more cumbersome terms.

that a being satisfy (O*) without being omnipotent. But is it really possible that there be such a being? Necessarily, scratching one's ear takes time. Accordingly, it is necessary that there are infinitely many intervals of time t such that anyone who is able to scratch his ear is also able to scratch his ear throughout t. So if McEar is able to scratch his ear, he is able to do infinitely many things.[36] Moreover, if McEar can scratch his ear, he must be able to do so by moving some other part of his body, perhaps his arm, in the appropriate way. But then McEar can also move his arm, contract his muscles, disturb adjacent air molecules, and do countless other things as well. So it does not seem possible that there be such a being as McEar.

A natural way of strengthening the objection is to claim that it is possible that there is a being with a wide range of abilities who is nevertheless essentially incapable of performing some other action (say, tying a shoe, remembering the second stanza of our national anthem, or creating *ex nihilo*) which an omnipotent being ought to be able to do.[37] But is it really possible that there be a being whose abilities are *essentially* limited in this way? For any agent who is incapable of tying a shoe, it would seem to be at least possible that God confer on the agent greater powers that include the ability to tie a shoe. In that case, it would be possible for any such limited being to do more than it is able to do. So it seems to me that the objection from essentially limited beings is unpersuasive.

6. The Paradox of the Stone

Appealing to (O*) will allow us to give a resolution of the so-called paradox of the stone, a familiar formulation of which, due to C. Wade Savage, is as follows:

(12) Either God can create a stone which he cannot lift, or God cannot create a stone which he cannot lift.

(13) If God can create a stone which he cannot lift, then he is not omnipotent.

---

36. This point, stated in terms of strong actualization, is that if McEar is able to strongly actualize *his scratching his ear,* then he is able to strongly actualize *his strongly actualizing his scratching his ear throughout t,* for infinitely many intervals *t.*

37. Cf. Hoffman and Rosenkrantz, "Omnipotence Redux."

(14) If God cannot create a stone which he cannot lift, then he is
not omnipotent

Therefore,

(15) God is not omnipotent. (12)(13)(14)[38]

Savage remarks that "what the argument really tries to establish is
that the existence of an omnipotent being is logically impossible."[39]
We should therefore examine whether the argument succeeds.

Savage's response is to note, in effect, that the antecedent of (14) is
equivalent to

(14a) If God creates a stone then he can lift it,

and he claims that since (14a) does not express a limitation on ability, it is a mistake to conclude from it that God is not omnipotent.
Thus, Savage holds that (14) is false. However, this reply is inadequate; for if (14a) is true, then there is a state of affairs God cannot
strongly actualize, namely, *his creating a stone which he cannot lift*, and
that is surely some sort of limitation on ability.

George Mavrodes also rejects (14), but on the grounds that, since
God is essentially omnipotent, *creating a stone which God cannot lift* is
logically impossible.[40] As we have seen, God need not be able to do
what is impossible in order to be omnipotent; since (14) assumes
otherwise, it is false. Although this solution has a certain plausibility, several philosophers have accused it of question-begging.
Richard Swinburne, endorsing a point made by Savage, writes that
"the point of the paradox is to show that the concept of omnipotence is incoherent. It is therefore begging the question to assume
that a certain person, if he exists, has that property, whether by
definition or not."[41] It is not entirely clear to me that a theist is not

38. Savage, "The Paradox of the Stone," p. 74. I have deleted the parenthetical
remarks Savage appends to (13) and (14).
39. Ibid., p. 75. Cf. J. L. Mackie, "Evil and Omnipotence," *Mind* 64 (1955):200–
212, who gives a version of the argument (asking whether God can create a being he
cannot control) and who claims that it shows that "we cannot consistently ascribe to
any continuing being omnipotence in an inclusive sense." (p. 212).
40. Mavrodes, "Some Puzzles Concerning Omnipotence."
41. Swinburne, *The Coherence of Theism*, p. 154.

entitled to appeal to his or her views in attempting to defend those views against a charge of inconsistency, but if we can find a solution to the stone paradox that does not make such an appeal, so much the better.

Swinburne's own approach is to deny (13). He claims that if God has the ability to create a stone that he cannot lift, it does not follow that God is not omnipotent unless God exercises that ability. Since Swinburne thinks that God could have this ability without exercising it, he believes that (13) is false. Swinburne thus holds that "the omnipotence of a person at a certain time includes the ability to make himself no longer omnipotent."[42] Now if God has the ability to make himself no longer omnipotent, then it is possible that he make himself not omnipotent, since no one has the ability to do anything impossible. Hence, if God has the ability to make himself no longer omnipotent, then God is not essentially omnipotent. Thus Swinburne's solution involves assuming the denial of Mavrodes' assumption. Many theists think that God *is* essentially omnipotent, however, so Swinburne's solution is not open to them.

Swinburne assumes not only that an omnipotent being need not be essentially omnipotent but also that such a being could *lose* its omnipotence. But is it possible for an omnipotent being to lose its omnipotence? This question is difficult, but perhaps we can give a reply to the argument without answering it. Let us say that an *enduring property* is a property it is not possible to lose. More precisely,

(16) P is an enduring property for x =df (i) it is possible that x has P and (ii) necessarily, for every time t if x has P at t, then x has P at every later time at which x exists.[43]

If a property is essential to a thing, then it is enduring for that thing; any property a given thing cannot possibly lack is a property it cannot possibly lose. But the converse is not true. A property could

---

42. Ibid., p. 158.

43. (16) allows that a property can be enduring for one individual but not another. This is as it should be, since *being as tall as Socrates* is a property that some of Socrates' colleagues may have had but that was enduring only for Socrates. We could say that a property is enduring *simpliciter* if, necessarily, it is enduring for everything that has it.

be enduring for a thing without being essential to it. Each of us has the property of *having been born*, and that is a property we cannot lose; hence, it is enduring for each of us. But it is not essential to us. Presumably we existed before we were born, and, somewhat more controversially, it is possible that God create us as full-grown adults. So it is possible that we exist without having been born. Accordingly, this property is enduring for each of us without being essential to any of us.[44]

Now let us apply some of these ideas to the paradox of the stone. We should first note that for the argument to apply to omnipotence as defined by (O*), the crucial second and third premises should be understood as

(13′) If God can strongly actualize *there being a stone which he cannot lift*, then he is not omnipotent,

and

(14′) If God cannot strongly actualize *there being a stone which he cannot lift*, then he is not omnipotent.

Next, let us ask whether omnipotence is an enduring property or, in particular, whether it is an enduring property for God. If it is not, then for the reasons Swinburne gives, (13′) is false. If omnipotence is not an enduring property for God, it does not count against his omnipotence if he has the ability to do something that results in his losing his omnipotence.

So suppose that omnipotence is enduring for God, and let us call the state of affairs of *there being a stone God cannot lift*, '*T*'. According to (O*), (14′) is true only if God's strongly actualizing *T* is compatible with what has already happened. But on the assumption that omnipotence is enduring for God, God's strongly actualizing *T* is compatible with what has already happened only if God is not now omnipotent. For if God is already omnipotent, his being omnipotent is included in the initial segment up to now, and that segment is not compatible with God's strongly actualizing *T* if omnipotence is

44. Anyone unconvinced by this example may substitute *having been born in a log cabin,* which is surely enduring to anyone who has it but not essential.

enduring for God. So if omnipotence is enduring for God, God's strongly actualizing T is compatible with what has already happened only if God is not now omnipotent. Hence, on the assumption that omnipotence is enduring for God, (14′) is true only if God is not now omnipotent; that is, (14′) by itself presupposes the conclusion of the argument. Thus, without further defense, (14′) is useless for establishing that God is not omnipotent.

In sum, either omnipotence is enduring for God or it is not. If it is not, (13′) is false. If it is, (14′) stands in need of support. Either way, the argument is defective, and we have been able to arrive at this conclusion without either assuming with Mavrodes that God is essentially omnipotent or assuming with Swinburne that omnipotence is not enduring for God.[45]

7. Atemporal Omnipotence

My account of omnipotence has been designed to allow that God's abilities change over time. But an influential tradition within classical theism holds that God is "outside of time." On this view, God does not have differing abilities at different times. We shall discuss a cluster of related ideas, including timelessness, eternality, and immutability, in Chapter 6. For now, however, I want merely to indicate how the ideas we have developed about omnipotence may still apply even if God is not "in time."

A key condition in (O*) is

(17) In W x can strongly actualize A at t.

45. The structure of this response to the argument owes much to the treatment by Plantinga in *God and Other Minds*, pp. 168–173, although he does not consider the question whether it is possible for a being to lose omnipotence. Several others have given disjunctive solutions having to do instead with whether omnipotence is an essential property of whoever has it. They claim that if God is essentially omnipotent then (14′) is false, and if God is not essentially omnipotent then (13′) is false. See Flint and Freddoso, "Maximal Power," p. 99, and Hoffman and Rosenkrantz, "What an Omnipotent Agent Can Do," and "The Omnipotence Paradox, Modality, and Time," *Southern Journal of Philosophy* 18 (1980):473–479. However, this approach does not succeed in identifying a flaw in the argument. In particular, it does not follow from the assumption that God is not essentially omnipotent that (13′) is false; it may be that, although omnipotence is not essential to God, it is nevertheless *enduring* for him. In that case, if God *could* bring it about that there is a stone he cannot lift, it *would* follow that he is not omnipotent.

But a timeless being does not have its abilities *at times*. So the condition specified by (7) would seem not to apply to a timeless being. Our project, then, is to find a way of interpreting (7) in such a way that it applies to a timeless being.

In the tradition which holds that God is outside of time, it is usually held that God performs a single eternal act, which, however, has a vast array of temporal effects.[46] One way to think of the sum of all of these effects is as a very large state of affairs. Let '$T(W)$' designate, for a given world W, the largest state of affairs God strongly actualizes in W. That is, God strongly actualizes $T(W)$ in W, and for any state of affairs A that God strongly actualizes in W, $T(W)$ includes A.[47] So if God is timeless in W, we may think of him as timelessly strongly actualizing $T(W)$.

Now those who think of God as outside of time also usually concede, as indeed they should, that even though it has always been true that God is (timelessly) strongly actualizing $T(\alpha)$ (where α is the actual world), God *could have* done something else. The relevant sense of "could have" here may well need explanation, since on this view there never was a time at which God was faced with a choice between $T(\alpha)$ and some distinct $T(W)$ and at which he decided to embark on $T(\alpha)$. But however this sense of "could have" is to be understood, it is clear that in some sense God could have done something other than what he is doing. So I shall assume that God could have strongly actualized a different state of affairs.

In order to interpret (17) we need to be able to express what it is for God to be able to do something at a time (say, now). It will not do to say that he can do something now just in case it is part of something he could have done, for as we saw in Section 2, some things God could have done it is now too late for him to do. We can capture the right idea, I think, if we introduce a second restriction to initial segments. Thus, I propose interpreting (17) as

(17′) There is a world W' such that (i) $S(W', t) = S(W, t)$, (ii) $T(W')$ includes A's *occurring at t*, and (iii) either God (ten-

46. Sources of the doctrine of divine timelessness are cited in Chapter 6. On the topic of God's eternal act, see, for example, Eleonore Stump and Norman Kretzmann, "Eternity," *Journal of Philosophy* 78 (1981):429–458.

47. This idea and definition are from Plantinga, *The Nature of Necessity*, p. 181; cf. his "Self-Profile," p. 50.

selessly) strongly actualizes $T(W')$ or God could have strongly actualized $T(W')$.

The idea is that whether (in the actual world) God can now strongly actualize, say, *Socrates' coming into existence* should depend on what has already happened and not merely on whether God from his atemporal perspective has (tenselessly) the power to actualize a state of affairs including *Socrates' coming into existence now*. Instantiating clause (i) to the actual world thus specifies a restricted class of worlds that share an initial segment up to now with the actual world. And what God can do now is, roughly, anything he does in any of those worlds. More precisely, he can actualize any state of affairs included in the largest state of affairs he in fact (tenselessly) strongly actualizes $(T(\alpha))$, and he can actualize any state of affairs included in a state of affairs $T(W')$ such that (i) $T(W')$ is the largest state of affairs God strongly actualizes in some world W' sharing an initial segment up to now with the actual world, and (ii) God (tenselessly) could have strongly actualized $T(W')$.

With this interpretation of (17), the hard part of our project is accomplished. There remains the task of incorporating this interpretation into (O*), which I present without further comment:

(O+) a being x is omnipotent in W =df In W it is true both that (i) for every time t and state of affairs A, if it is possible that both $S(W, t)$ obtains and that x strongly actualizes A's *obtaining at t*, then there is a world W' such that (a) $S(W', t) = S(W, t)$, (b) $T(W')$ includes A's *occurring at t*, and (c) either x (tenselessly) strongly actualizes $T(W')$ or x could have strongly actualized $T(W')$, and (ii) there is some state of affairs which x can strongly actualize.

We have seen in this chapter that it is possible to give the concept of omnipotence a relatively clear account that accords with what theists who have attributed omnipotence to God have said and that can be defended against various philosophical objections. Moreover, this account can be modified, if we like, to allow for atemporal omnipotence. In the next chapter we shall turn our attention to the concept of omniscience.

[2]
Omniscience

1. Defining Omniscience

As we have seen, there has been in recent years a lively debate on the topic of defining omnipotence. In contrast, defining omniscience has seemed almost trivial. According to Aquinas, "in God there exists the most perfect knowledge,"[1] and what is the most perfect knowledge except knowledge of all there is to be known? In other words,

> (D1) A being x is omniscient =df For every proposition p, if p is true then x knows p.

Of course, something needs to be said about the *nature* of such knowledge. For example, it is usual to distinguish occurrent from dispositional belief. A person who has an occurrent belief in a proposition actually has that proposition in mind; whereas a person who has a dispositional belief in a proposition is *disposed* to have an occurrent belief in it; that is, roughly, the person would have an occurrent belief in it if he or she were to consider it or to have it in mind.[2]

---

1. Aquinas, *S.T.*, Ia, 14, 1.
2. Roderick Chisholm uses 'judging' for what I have called occurrent belief and 'believing' for what I have called dispositional belief, emphasizing that 'judging' "suggests a mental *act*—an occurrent phenomenon." Roderick M. Chisholm, "Self-Profile," in *Roderick M. Chisholm: A Profile*, ed. Radu Bogdan (Dordrecht: D. Reidel, 1986), p. 15.

Corresponding to these two kinds of belief are two kinds of knowledge: occurrent knowledge and dispositional knowledge. The question then arises as to whether an omniscient being's knowledge is occurrent or dispositional. Aquinas considered this question in his discussion of whether God's knowledge is "discursive." According to Aquinas, "In our knowledge there is a twofold discursion. One is according to succession only, as when we have actually understood anything, we turn ourselves to understand something else; while the other mode of discursion is according to causality, as when through principles we arrive at the knowledge of conclusions."[3] Aquinas holds that God's knowledge is not discursive in either way, but he considered an argument for the conclusion that God's knowledge is discursive in the first way. That argument appealed to the distinction between occurrent and dispositional knowledge, put in Aristotelian terms as the distinction between actual and habitual knowledge: "It seems that the knowledge of God is discursive. For the knowledge of God is not habitual knowledge, but actual knowledge. Now the Philosopher says: *The habitual knowledge may regard many things at once; but actual knowledge regards only one thing at a time.* Therefore as God knows many things, Himself and others, as was shown above, it seems that he does not understand all at once, but proceeds from one to another."[4] Since Aquinas in his reply does not dispute the claim that God's knowledge is actual or occurrent knowledge—Aquinas denies instead that actual knowledge must regard only one thing at a time—I take it to be his view that God's knowledge is occurrent knowledge.

A second feature of God's knowledge, suggested by Aquinas' second mode of discursive knowledge, is that God's knowledge is not inferential. Aquinas thinks that from the claim that God's knowledge is not discursive in the first way it follows that it is not discursive in the second way either, because, as he puts it, "whosoever proceeds from principles to conclusions does not consider both at once." This argument is puzzling, since, as we have just seen, Aquinas denies that knowledge must regard only one thing at a time. Why, then, could not someone "proceed from principles to conclusions" and end up with occurrent knowledge of

3. Aquinas, *S.T.*, Ia, 14, 7.
4. Ibid., Ia, 14, 7, obj. 1. The quotation from Aristotle is from *Topics*, II 10 (114b 34).

both? Of course, someone who did so would not be omniscient at the outset, but does knowing all true propositions preclude having learned some of them? On the other hand, Aquinas is specifically talking about *God's* knowledge, and God, according to Aquinas, has always been omniscient; God, therefore, does not arrive at additional items of knowledge by deduction from prior knowledge.[5] Nor, presumably, is his knowledge inferential, in the sense that some of his beliefs are based on or derived from others. For any propositions p and q, if p entails q then God knows that p entails q; but if p is true, God's belief in q is not based on his inferring it from p.[6]

2. Some Complications

We began with the suggestion that omniscience could easily be defined, as in (D1), as knowledge of all true propositions. Matters are not quite this simple, however. We examine in this chapter some of the complications that arise in formulating a definition of omniscience. Perhaps some of them call for only relatively minor emendations of (D1); still, the way in which they are treated has important implications for how omniscience is best understood.

Some philosophers think that (D1) is incomplete. They think it should be supplemented by the condition that an omniscient being believes no falsehoods. Thus, they advocate

(D1′) A being x is omniscient =df For every proposition p, if p is true then x knows p and if p is false then x does not believe p.[7]

5. Moreover, some of the more abstruse propositions an omniscient being must know cannot be known inferentially. According to the Halting Problem Theorem, there is no algorithm or computer program for deciding with respect to an arbitrary program P and input i whether P halts with input i (that is, whether P completes its computation and produces an output or whether instead P continues to compute indefinitely). Thus, there are indefinitely many true propositions of the form *program P halts with input i* which an omniscient being must know but which cannot be arrived at by inference or calculation.

6. For the contrary view that all of God's knowledge is inferential, see George Mavrodes, "How Does God Know the Things He Knows?" (unpublished).

7. Alvin Plantinga writes, "If God is omniscient, then He is unlimited in knowledge; He knows every true proposition and believes none that are false." *God, Freedom, and Evil* (1974; rpt. Grand Rapids, Mich.: Eerdmans, 1977), p. 68. It is not

No doubt it should be a consequence of the definition of omniscience that an omniscient being believes no falsehoods. The only question is whether this condition needs to be an explicit part of the definition.

I am inclined to accept

(1) Necessarily, for any being S if S knows every true proposition then S believes no false proposition,

but the only considerations in its favor of which I am aware are some unusual consequences of rejecting it, which does not consititute a proof. A being who knew all truths and who nevertheless believed some falsehood, p, would know that he or she believed p while knowing it to be false. It is difficult to conceive how anyone could be in this situation. Moreover, anyone who believes all true propositions would seem to be unlimited in deductive powers; thus, such a being can be expected to believe the deductive consequences of his or her beliefs. But the deductive consequences of the beliefs of someone who both believes p and knows *not-p* include every proposition whatsoever. So if someone who knew every truth managed, in addition, to believe a falsehood, he or she would be liable to end up believing *every* proposition. It is hard to believe that this is possible. Nevertheless, these considerations show that at most the extra clause of (D1′) is redundant, not that it is mistaken.

3. Incorrigibility and Essential Omniscience

Some of our beliefs are certain, whereas others are not. In describing a belief as certain I mean to ascribe a high epistemic status to it, not merely to indicate that it is firmly held. No doubt there are several concepts of high epistemic status; one interesting one involves immunity from error. Thus, for example, I believe that there is a tree outside my window, and I am right, but it is easy to imagine circumstances in which I believe that proposition although it is false. I could be hallucinating or dreaming or deceived by a clever replica.

---

entirely clear, however, that Plantinga is proposing a definition here. In *Logic and the Nature of God* (Grand Rapids, Mich.: Eerdmans, 1983), p. 26, Stephen Davis explicitly endorses (D1′), as does Joseph Runzo in "Omniscience and Freedom for Evil," *International Journal for Philosophy of Religion* 12 (1981):132.

So I can be mistaken about that proposition. But, at least if Descartes was right, I cannot be similarly mistaken about such propositions as that I exist or that I seem to see a tree outside my window.

We may follow Alvin Plantinga in describing those beliefs about which we cannot be mistaken as *incorrigible*, characterized as follows:

> (2) p is incorrigible for S if and only if (i) it is not possible that S believe p and p be false, and (ii) it is not possible that S believe $\sim p$ and p be true.[8]

It is plausible to think that every proposition is incorrigible for God. His beliefs do not divide into those about which he can be mistaken and those about which he cannot, for he can never be mistaken. If we want a term for this property, we could say that God is an *incorrible believer*, where

> (3) S is an incorrigible believer if and only if every proposition is incorrigible for S.

Our definition of omniscience, (D1), does not obviously capture this feature of God's knowledge. It is unclear, however, whether it ought to; perhaps it is possible to be omnscient without being an incorrigible believer.

There is a related property, however, that does require such global incorrigibility—the property of being *essentially omniscient*. God is not only omniscient but essentially so. That is, it is not possible that he exist without being omniscient; God is omniscient in every possible world in which he exists. Now if God is omniscient in every world in which he exists, there is no world in which he believes a falsehood. Accordingly, there is no world in which for some proposition p he either believes p when p is false or believes $\sim p$ when p is true. Thus, if God is essentially omniscient, he is an incorrigible believer.[9]

8. Alvin Plantinga, "Reason and Belief in God," in *Faith and Rationality*, ed. A. Plantinga and N. Wolterstorff (Notre Dame: University of Notre Dame Press, 1983), p. 58.

9. This argument assumes either that (1) is true or that the definition of omniscience has been amended along the lines of (D2). Note, incidentally, that someone

So we need not settle the question of whether omniscience involves global incorrigibility; God's essential omniscience insures
that every proposition is incorrigible for him.

4. De Dicto et De Re

A more difficult problem for the attempt to define omnscience
arises from the phenomenon of *de re* belief. For examples of *de re*
belief one looks naturally to the work of W. V. Quine. Quine
distinguishes the *de re*

(4) (*Ex*)(Ralph believes that *x* is a spy)

from the *de dicto*

(5) Ralph believes that (*Ex*)(*x* is a spy),

and notes: "Both may perhaps be ambiguously phrased as 'Ralph
believes that someone is a spy', but they may be unambiguously
phrased respectively as 'There is someone whom Ralph believes to
be a spy' and 'Ralph believes there are spies'. The difference is vast;
indeed, if Ralph is like most of us [(5)] is true and [(4)] is false."[10]
The distinction, moreover, is not limited to quantified propositions.
If Ralph suspects the fat man in the doorway, then perhaps

(6) The fat man in the doorway is such that Ralph believes that
      he is a spy.

And if

(7) The fat man in the doorway = the provost of the Univer-
      sity,

---

could be an incorrigible believer without being omniscient, since being an incorrigible believer does not require having any beliefs at all. Even if our definition of an
incorrigible believer were modified to require having at least some beliefs, it would
not require having *every* true belief.
   10. Willard Van Orman Quine, "Quantifiers and Propositional Attitudes," in his
The Ways of Paradox (New York: Random House, 1966), p. 184.

then

    (8) The provost of the University is such that Ralph believes
        that he is a spy.

This could be the case even if Ralph does not recognize the fat man
to be the provost, in which case it could be false that

    (9) Ralph believes that the provost of the University is a spy.

So far our examples have been of belief, but we can easily imagine
that Ralph *knows* these things. Then the following would describe
Ralph's knowledge:

    (10) The fat man in the doorway is such that Ralph knows that
         he is a spy

and

    (11) The provost of the University is such that Ralph knows
         that he is a spy

but not

    (12) Ralph knows that the provost of the University is a spy.

In (11) we have an example of *de re* knowledge in which the corresponding *de dicto* knowledge, (12), is lacking. An interesting question is whether it is possible to have complete *de dicto* knowledge and
yet lack some *de re* knowledge. The answer depends on whether *de
re* knowledge is a special case of *de dicto* knowledge. Before we
investigate this possibility, let us note that if *de re* knowledge is not
reducible to *de dicto* knowledge, a being could know all true propositions and yet, by lacking some *de re* knowledge, fall short of perfect
knowledge. In this case our definition of omniscience would have to
be reformulated, perhaps as

    (D2) A being x is omniscient $=$df For every proposition p, if p is
         true then x knows p, and for every individual y and prop-
         erty G, if y has G then y is such that x knows y to have G.[11]

How could *de re* belief reduce to *de dicto*? It might seem that what gives Ralph his *de re* belief with respect to the provost is the *de dicto* belief reported by

> (13) Ralph believes that the fat man in the doorway is a spy,

coupled with the truth that

> (7) The fat man in the doorway = the provost of the University.

Let us say that an *individual concept* is a property that it is possible that something have and not possible that more than one thing have at a time,[12] and let us follow Roderick Chisholm in introducing a special sense of entailment, "entailment$_c$". A proposition *p* entails$_c$ the property of being *Q* just in case *p* is necessarily such that (i) if it obtains, then something has the property of being *Q*, and (ii) whoever accepts *p* believes that something is *Q*.[13] Then the present suggestion is that

> (14) A person, *S*, believes *de re* with respect to *x* that it is *F* just in case there is an individual concept *C* which is such that *x*

11. *De re* beliefs can be not only with respect to individuals but also with respect to sequences of individuals. For example, Ralph can believe of Joan and Sue that the former is taller than the latter, and he can believe with respect to Joan, Sue, and Mary that the first is standing between the second and the third. Thus, if the definition of omniscience needs to make reference to *de re* knowledge, (D2) will need to be amended. The obvious way is to add the phrases 'or n-ary sequences of individuals' and 'or n-adic relation R' in the appropriate places. The relevance of *de re* knowledge to the concept of omniscience is rarely discussed by recent writers. An exception is A. N. Prior, who, in "The Formalities of Omniscience," *Philosophy* 37 (1962):114–129, rpt. in his *Papers on Time and Tense* (Oxford: Oxford University Press, 1968), lists several examples of *de re* knowledge "which a believer in God's omniscience would wish to maintain." Prior, in effect, treats (D1) as a schema, and he takes as an "instantiation" of it the universal closure of the result of replacing '*p*' with any open sentence.

12. This idea derives from Roderick M. Chisholm, *Person and Object* (La Salle, Ill.: Open Court, 1976), p. 28.

13. Ibid.

> has C and S believes a proposition entailing$_c$ the conjunc-
> tion of C and F.[14]

In our imagined situation Ralph achieves a *de re* belief with respect to the provost that he is a spy in virtue of the belief of Ralph's that (13) reports. This is a belief in a proposition, that the fat man in the doorway is spy, which entails$_c$ the conjunction of an individual concept of the provost (*being the fat man in the doorway*) and the property of being a spy.

  This concept of *de re* belief is "latitudinarian";[15] it makes it relatively easy to acquire a *de re* belief. Suppose that Ralph, who has a low opinion of politicians, learns that his city has a mayor. Then Ralph may form the belief that the mayor is crass. On the latitudinarian account, this *de dicto* belief suffices to give Ralph a *de re* belief with respect to the mayor. Since Ralph may meet the mayor without discovering that he is the mayor, Ralph may also believe with respect to the man he meets (that is, the mayor) that he is not crass. There seem to be at least three options here. The first is to insist that the latitudinarian account is the correct one. It may be defended by noting that when Ralph comes to believe that the mayor is crass, someone could correctly say to the mayor, "Ralph believes that *you* are crass."[16] The second is to make the account of *de re* belief more stringent. Chisholm has adopted this strategy.[17] The third is to recognize various *degrees* of *de re* belief. Here the notion of degrees of belief should not be thought of, as it often is, as a measure of the *strength* of the belief or of the believer's commitment to the proposition. Rather, it should be taken as a measure of the epistemic intimacy the believer has with the object of the belief. In general, a

  14. A proposition entails$_c$ the conjunction of C and F just in case it entails$_c$ that something has both C and F, not merely that C is exemplified and F is exemplified. The proposal in the text is equivalent to the way Roderick Chisholm in *The First Person* (Minneapolis: University of Minnesota Press, 1981), p. 14, characterizes the somewhat more complicated view he had defended in chap. 1 of *Person and Object*. According to (14) all *de re* belief is by way of concepts. Thus, even my *de re* belief with respect to a currently perceived object will involve some such concept as *the (salient) object I am perceiving*.

  15. See Roderick M. Chisholm, "Knowledge and Belief: 'De Dicto' and 'De Re,'" *Philosophical Studies* 29 (1976):1–20.

  16. See Ernest Sosa, "Propositional Attitudes *De Dicto* and *De Re*," *Journal of Philosophy* (1970):883–896.

  17. See, for example, Chisholm, "Knowledge and Belief," p. 13.

person has a *de re* belief with respect to an object by bearing a relation of acquaintance to the object.[18] A minimal relation of acquaintance with an object is that required to believe a proposition entailing$_c$ an individual concept of the object. A somewhat stronger relation is involved in coming to *know* a proposition entailing$_c$ with respect to an individual concept of the object that it is exemplified.[19] Present perception might yield an even stronger relation of acquaintance (in this case the relevant individual concept might be *the thing that I am looking at*). Thus, it might be that relative to one relation of acquaintance Ralph believes of the mayor that he is crass, whereas relative to another relation of acquaintance Ralph believes of the mayor that he is not crass. Alternatively, a stronger *de re* belief might be thought to *defeat* a weaker, contrary one. That is, it might be held that Ralph's belief that the man he is perceiving is not crass defeats Ralph's *de re* belief that the mayor is crass. In other words, a weak relation of acquaintance yields *de re* belief unless it is overridden by a stronger relation of acquaintance that supports a contrary belief. This approach does not succeed, however, in banishing all "near-contrary" *de re* belief,[20] since Ralph may be related by equally strong relations of acquaintance, or even the same relation of acquaintance, to an object in a way that produces contrary beliefs. Thus, Ralph might perceive the two ends of the same train extending from opposite ends of a tunnel and believe of the train on his left that it is a freight train and of the train on his right that is is not a freight train. In such a case Ralph would believe of the same train both that it is a freight train and that it is not.

Fortunately, we do not have to settle the issue of how best to understand *de re* belief in order to make some progress on the concept of omniscience, for the approaches we have considered all share the feature that *de re* belief is a species of *de dicto* belief. If this is correct, then if God believes all true propositions, he will have all of the true *de re* beliefs, and if he knows all true propositions, then he will have all the *de re* knowledge there is.

18. I take the term, though not with exactly his sense, from David Lewis, "Attitudes *De Dicto* and *De Se*," *Philosophical Review* 88 (1979):513–543. Cf. David Kaplan's concept of a *vivid name*, which requires a causal connection with the object of *de re* belief, in "Quantifying In," *Synthèse* 29 (1968):178–214.

19. Chisholm proposes this relation in "Knowledge and Belief," p. 13.

20. The term is from Quine, "Quantifiers and Propositional Attitudes," p. 189.

5. *De Re et De Se*

In Elias Canetti's *Auto da Fé*, the central character, Professor Peter Kien,

> heard someone shouting at someone else. "Can you tell me where Mut Strasse is?" There was no reply. Kien was surprised: so there were other silent people besides himself to be found in the busy streets. Without looking up he listened for more. How would the questioner behave in the face of this silence? "Excuse me please, could you perhaps tell me where Mut Strasse is?" So; he grew more polite; he had no better luck. The other man still made no reply. . . . "Here, are you deaf?" shouted the first man. . . . Kien hoped for a fight. If the second man appeared after all to be a mere vulgarian, Kien would be confirmed in his own estimation of himself as the sole and only person of character walking in this street. . . .
>
> Then Kien felt a nasty jolt. . . . His glance was directed at his briefcase, but it fell instead on a small fat man who was bawling up at him. "You lout! You lout! You lout!" The other man, the silent one, the man of character, who controlled his tongue even in anger, was Kien himself.[21]

Halfway through this incident Kien believed with respect to the one being addressed that he was controlling his tongue while being addressed in anger. Since Kien was the one being addressed, Kien believed of Kien that he was controlling his tongue while being addressed in anger. So Kien had a *de re* belief with respect to himself that he was controlling his tongue while being addressed in anger. But Kien did not believe that he himself was controlling his tongue while being addressed in anger, for he did not believe that he himself was being addressed. The belief that Kien lacked may be called belief *de se*. Examples like this one suggest that belief *de se* is not the same as belief *de re*, and since Kien could have had *de re* knowledge with respect to himself without realizing that it was with respect to himself, knowledge *de se* is not the same as knowledge *de re*. Is belief or knowledge *de se* then a special case of belief or knowledge *de dicto*? Was Kien lacking belief in a *proposition*?

Before we attempt to answer this question, we should note that if the answer is no, if belief *de se* is not reducible to belief *de dicto*, then

21. Elias Canetti, *Auto da Fé* (London: Pan Books, 1978), p. 14.

our definition of omniscience will have to be modified; otherwise a being could know all true propositions and yet lack some crucial information. A natural revision of our definition so as to avoid this possibility is

(D3) A being x is omniscient $=$df (i) For every proposition p, if p is true then x knows p, and (ii) for every individual y and property G, if y has G then y is such that x knows y to have G, and (iii) for every property G, if x has G then x knows that he himself or she herself has G.

How could *de se* belief reduce to *de dicto* belief? It does not seem promising to attempt to formulate a principle analogous to (14) that appeals to individual concepts, for one can believe a proposition entailing an individual concept without the concept being one's own, and one can believe a proposition entailing one's own individual concept, as Kien did, without realizing that it was one's own. But is there something *like* an individual concept that we grasp when we have beliefs about ourselves *as ourselves*? Frege seems to have thought so. He wrote: "Now everyone is presented to himself in a particular and primitive way, in which he is presented to no-one else. So when Dr. Lauben thinks that he has been wounded, he will probably take as a basis this primitive way in which he is presented to himself. And only Dr. Lauben himself can grasp thoughts determined in this way."[22] This suggestion has been developed, using Frege's notions of sense and reference, by Chisholm, who writes: "Each person who uses the first person pronoun uses it to refer to himself in such a way that, in that use, its *Bedeutung* or reference is himself and its *Sinn* or intention is his own individual essence. A corollary would be that, whereas each person knows directly and immediately certain propositions [entailing] his own individual essence, no one knows any proposition [entailing] the individual essence of anyone else."[23] An *individual essence* is a property that it is possible for something to have essentially and not possible for any

<hr>

22. Gottlob Frege, "The Thought," trans. A. M. and Marcelle Quinton, in *Philosophical Logic*, ed. P. F. Strawson (Oxford: Oxford University Press, 1967), p. 26.
23. Chisholm, *Person and Object*, p. 36. Chisholm has since abandoned this view; see *The First Person*.

other thing to have at all.[24] An individual essence of Socrates, for example, is a property such that there is no possible world in which Socrates lacks that property and there is no possible world in which someone other than Socrates has that property.

There are two parts to the Chisholm-Frege proposal. The first is that what a person believes when he or she has a *de se* belief is a special "first-person proposition" that involves or entails$_c$ that person's own individual essence. The second is that no one can grasp the individual essence of another, and so no one can believe or know another's first-person propositions.[25]

We need to make two preliminary points. The first is that nothing prevents an individual from having more than one individual essence. This point has been made by Plantinga. He claims that for every property *P* and possible world *W*, there is a corresponding, "world-indexed" property, *being-P-in-W*. A thing has this latter property just in case in *W* it is true that it has *P*. Since such truths about possible worlds do not vary from world to world, *being-P-in-W* is essential to whatever has it, even if it has *P* contingently or not at all. Plantinga continues:

> But now take any property *Q* that Socrates alone has—*being the shortest Greek philosopher*, perhaps, or *being born at P, t*, where '*P*' names the place and '*t*' the time at which he was born: the world-indexed property *having Q in α* [where 'α' rigidly designates the actual world] will be an essence of Socrates. First, it is one he has necessarily, for Socrates has all his world-indexed properties necessarily; secondly, it is such that in no possible world is there an object

---

24. This is equivalent to the reformulation of Chisholm's definition proposed by Plantinga and accepted by Chisholm. See Alvin Plantinga, "*De Essentia*," *Grazer Philosophische Studien* 7/8 (1979):101–121, and, in the same issue, Roderick Chisholm, "Objects and Persons: Revision and Replies," p. 317.

25. The notion of grasping an essence is somewhat mysterious; it suggests a mental feat of a sort that practically no one discerns by introspection. Our main concern here, however, is whether someone can have the first-person proposition of another as an object of belief. Thus, we may, if we like, follow a suggestion of Plantinga's. He first appeals to Chisholm's special sense of entailment (indicated by a subscript) and then suggests that a person grasps a property just in case he or she knows some proposition entailing$_c$ it ("*De Essentia*," p. 105). We can weaken this proposal, I think, to hold that a person grasps a property just in case the person *believes* a proposition entailing$_c$ it. It will thus follow that if no one grasps another's essence, no one grasps another's first-person propositions.

distinct from him that has it; it therefore follows that this property is an essence of Socrates. So for any property *P* uniquely exemplified by Socrates, there is an essence of Socrates: *having P in W*. But clearly there are many pairs of properties of this sort such that a person could believe that the one but not the other was exemplified. One might believe, for example, that the property *being the shortest Greek philosopher in* α is exemplified, but fail to believe that the same holds for *being born at P, t in* α; hence these are distinct properties. Accordingly, Socrates has several distinct essences.[26]

No doubt Socrates is not unique in this respect. So if things have multiple essences, which is the one entailed$_c$ by a person's first-person propositions? Or does it suffice for a first-person proposition to entail *some* essence of that person? Let us postpone answering these questions for a moment and turn, instead, to another one.

What reason is there to think that no one ever grasps another's essence? Chisholm considers the possibility that we grasp the essences of others through the use of such demonstrative expressions as 'that man' or 'that person.' He says that on this view "these demonstrative expressions are like the word 'I' in that they may be used to intend certain individual essences or haecceities. This seems to have been the view of St. Thomas and Duns Scotus. According to this way of looking at the matter, if I pick you out as being *that* person or *that* thing, then I pick you out *per se*. For I pick you out as being something that has uniquely a certain property—the property of being that person or that thing. And this property, like the property of being identical with me, will be an individual essence or haecceity."[27] But Chisholm goes on to reject this view. He says: "But if I individuate something *per se* as being *that thing* and if tomorrow I individuate something *per se* as being *that thing*, I may well have picked out two different things; whereas if today I individuate something *per se* as being identical with me and if tomorrow I individuate something *per se* as being identical with me, then I will have picked out one and the same thing."[28] Chisholm's argument here seems to be that since the phrase 'that person' can be used on different occasions to pick out different persons, it must not express

26. Plantinga, "*De Essentia*," pp. 103–104.
27. Chisholm, *Person and Object*, p. 34.
28. Ibid.

a property that can be had by at most one person; so this phrase does not express an essence. But as Plantinga notes in discussing this argument,[29] there is no reason to assume that the phrase 'that person' expresses the same property on every occasion of use. If the word 'I' is typically used to express an essence of the person it designates—which will differ for different persons—why cannot 'that person' express different essences when it is used to pick out different persons? But since we do grasp such propositions as that expressed by 'That person has long hair' on a given occasion of use, there would seem to be no reason to think that we do not grasp essences of others.

Now, however, a problem looms for the account of *de se* belief in terms of first-person propositions, if these are just any propositions entailing$_c$ a person's essence. For if such phrases as 'that person' express essences, then such sentences as 'That person needs a haircut' express first-person propositions. But I could come to believe one of these propositions by looking in a mirror not realizing that I was looking at myself. That is, I could believe that that person needs a haircut without believing *de se* that I need a haircut; so the proposed reduction of *de se* belief to *de dicto* does not succeed.

A natural modification to the proposal avoids this objection. It is to hold that among a person's many essences one is special and that first-person propositions are propositions that entail$_c$ this special essence. Which of a person's essences is special? The answer must be that it is the one expressed by that person's use of the word 'I.' In my case, this is the property of *being me*. Let us call it my *haecceity*,[30] and from now on let us reserve the term 'first-person proposition' for propositions entailing$_c$ a special essence or haecceity: my first-person propositions are those which entail my haecceity.[31] Now a

29. Plantinga, "*De Essentia,*" p. 106.

30. Others have used this term, but I am not sure that my usage corresponds exactly to theirs. See Robert Merrihew Adams, "Primitive Thisness and Primitive Identity," *Journal of Philosophy* 76 (1979):5–26, who distinguishes between haecceities and essences.

31. In stating this account of first-person propositions I have followed Chisholm's lead in speaking of propositions which *entail$_c$* a haecceity, but this is an inessential part of the theory; it is really just a device for speaking of a constituent of a proposition without having literally to say that propositions have parts. But clearly propositions do, in some sense, have parts and structure; for the sentences that express them have parts and structure, and a difference in a part or the structure of a

haecceity must be an essence different from any expressed by such demonstratives as 'that person,' 'you,' or 'he,' since I could use any of these phrases to refer to myself without realizing that I was referring to myself; hence, I could believe a proposition entailing an essence expressed by one of these phrases, on a given occasion of use, without having a *de se* belief.

As we have seen, the second part of the Frege-Chisholm proposal—what Chisholm calls a "corollary"—is that first-person propositions are private, that no one can grasp or believe the first-person propositions of another. The fact that I can express one of my first-person propositions by using a sentence beginning with the word 'I' but cannot express a first-person proposition of mine using such words as 'he' or 'that person' suggests that only I can express my first-person propositions, and so, presumably, only I can grasp or believe them. But I think we can see that this is not an essential requirement of the reduction of *de se* belief to *de dicto*; it is not a corollary of it. What is crucial to the reduction is that it should provide as an object of my *de se* belief something that I cannot believe without believing something about myself; it is immaterial whether someone else can believe it, as long as whoever else believes it does not end up with a belief about himself or herself. Thus, we can say that

(15) A person, S, believes *de se* that he himself or she herself is F just in case there is a haecceity E such that S has E and S believes a proposition entailing_c the conjunction of E and F.

Alternatively, if we are willing to speak of propositions as having haecceities and other properties as constitutents, we could say that a first-person proposition, for a given person, is a proposition that has that person's haecceity as a constituent. In this case, we can replace (15) by

(16) A person, S, believes *de se* that he himself or she herself is F just in case there is a haecceity E such that S has E and S

---

sentence may make a difference in the proposition expressed. Accordingly, we could dispense with the circumlocution of *entailing_c a property* and speak instead of first-person propositions as propositions that have a haecceity as a consitutent.

believes a proposition having E as a constituent and which attributes *being F* to whomever has E.

It may well be that none of us does believe anyone else's first-person propositions, but neither (15) nor (16) has as a corollary that such belief is impossible. An interesting question, then, is whether God believes the first-person propositions of others. According to (15) and (16), if I believe that I am standing, I believe a certain first-person proposition. If it is true, does God believe it, too? If I know that I am standing, I know a certain first-person proposition. If I know it, does God know it, too? I can see no reason to think not. Believing this proposition gives *me* a *de se* belief, but it does not give God one, since the haecceity entailed by this proposition is mine and not his.

According to a familar puzzle, God knows everything anyone else knows, but, to use an example due to Norman Kretzmann, what Jones knows when he knows that he is in the hospital is something that no one other than Jones can know. Thus, if omniscience requires knowing everything that anyone knows, God cannot be omniscient without being identical to Jones. More generally, this objection holds that divine omniscience is incompatible with the existence of other persons who have self-knowledge. But it is part of traditional theism that God has created other persons, and it is evident that they have self-knowledge. Hence, on this objection, divine omniscience is incompatible with another tenet of traditional theism.[32]

32. Norman Kretzmann, "Omniscience and Immutability," *Journal of Philosophy* 63 (1966): 409–421. In Kretzmann's presentation and Castañeda's subsequent discussion, this puzzle is taken as showing (or purporting to show) the incompatibility of divine omniscience with theism, "the doctrine of a personal God distinct from other persons" (p. 420). But if theism is the doctrine that there is a God who is "a person without a body (i.e., a spirit), present everywhere, the creator and sustainer of the universe, a free agent, able to do everything (i.e., omnipotent), knowing all things, perfectly good, a source of moral obligation, immutable, eternal, a necessary being, holy, and worthy of worship," then this puzzle purports to show not the incompatibility of divine omniscience with theism but rather the incompatibility of theism with the existence of persons distinct from God who have self-knowledge. (This definition of theism is from Richard Swinburne, *The Coherence of Theism* [Oxford: Oxford University Press, 1977], p. 2.) Hector-Neri Castañeda's discussion is "Omniscience and Indexical Reference," *Journal of Philosophy* 64 (1967):203–210. Kretzmann's objection has recently been endorsed by Patrick Grim in "Against Omniscience: The Case from Essential Indexicals," *Noûs* 19 (1985):151–180.

Adopting (15) (or (16)) yields a simple resolution of this puzzle. When Jones knows that he is in the hospital, his knowledge is not the *de dicto* knowledge that Jones is in the hospital, and it is not merely knowledge *de re* with respect to himself that he is in the hospital. Rather, Jones knows a first-person proposition entailing$_c$ the conjunction of his haecceity and *being in the hospital*. But this proposition is not inaccessible to everyone but Jones; instead, God knows it, too. So cases like this do not show that divine omniscience is incompatible with the existence of other persons who have self-knowledge.

Let us turn now to a consideration of some objections to the view of *de se* belief just presented.

6. Some Objections

In recent years several philosophers have proposed alternative accounts of *de se* belief. One such theory is that all belief is the self-attribution of properties. This view takes as primitive that which we have been trying to explain, and then it seeks to define belief *de dicto* and belief *de re* in terms of this primitive.[33] Defenders of these new views have attempted to support their theories by arguing against the haecceitist account. We should consider some of these objections.

Chisholm, who, as we have seen, has defended the haecceitist account of *de se* belief, now says, "This view is plausible only if it is plausible to suppose there are 'I'-propositions. And. . .the most plausible version of the thesis that there are 'I'-propositions presupposes that there are individual essences and that each person can readily grasp his own; but we are now sceptical about these presuppositions."[34] Chisholm's skepticism is directed against the claim that we can grasp our own individual essences. He writes,

It seems doubtful that I can ever be said . . . to grasp my own individual essence or haecceity. If I were to grasp it, shouldn't I also be able to single out its various marks? Perhaps I can single out *some* of the marks of my individual essence—if I have one. Thus it may include various universal essential properties (for example, being red or non-red, or being a musician if a violinist). And perhaps I can

33. See Chisholm, *The First Person,* and Lewis, "Attitudes *De Dicto* and *De Se.*"
34. Chisholm, *The First Person,* p. 22.

single out certain non-universal essential properties (for example, being an individual thing and being a person). But if I can grasp my individual essence, then I ought to be able to single out in it those features that are unique to it. If *being identical with me* is my individual essence and *being identical with you* is yours, then, presumably, each analyses into personhood and something else as well—one something in my case and another in yours—but I haven't the faintest idea what this something else might be.[35]

Chisholm seems to think that grasping a property is some sort of introspectible mental feat, but it is not clear that the haecceitist account of *de se* belief requires that we actually be able to perform such feats. It is sufficient that we be able to *believe* propositions entailing$_c$ one's own haecceity (or having one's haecceity as constituent). Moreover, although *being identical with me* entails *being a person*, it is not at all clear that it *analyzes* into the conjunction of *being a person* and some other property. Thus, my haecceity might be a simple, unanalyzable property, in which case I need not be able to single out its various constituents in order to grasp it. On the other hand, suppose that my haecceity is analyzable into *being a person* and something else. Then, I suppose, *being yellow* would be analyzable into *being a color* and something else. But what else? What "mark" can we point to that only this something else possesses? Our inability to point to such a mark does not show that we do not grasp the property of *being yellow*; accordingly, it would seem, an analogous inability in the case of the property of *being identical with me* gives us no reason to reject individual essences.

Other objections to the haecceitist account have been given by David Lewis. He writes,

Consider the case of the two gods. They inhabit a certain possible world, and they know exactly which world it is. Therefore they know every proposition that is true at their world. Insofar as knowledge is a propositional attitude, they are omniscient. Still I can imagine them to suffer ignorance: neither one knows which of the two he is. They are not exactly alike. One lives on top of the tallest mountain and throws down manna; the other lives on top of the coldest mountain and throws down thunderbolts. Neither one knows whether he

35. Ibid., p. 16. This passage also occurs in Chisholm's "Objects and Persons: Revisions and Replies," p. 322.

lives on the tallest mountain or on the coldest mountain; nor whether he throws manna or thunderbolts.[36]

Lewis claims, then, that although there is no difference in the propositions that they believe, these gods suffer from a certain ignorance. Hence, knowledge of propositions is not all there is to knowledge. Lewis goes on to claim that even on an haecceitist account of propositions (though perhaps not exactly the account we have been discussing), his gods would fall short of complete knowledge.

> What about the proposition [the god on the tallest mountain] would express if he said, "I am on the tallest mountain"? Doesn't he know it? Of course he does—he knows all the propositions that hold at W, and this is one of them. Doesn't he therefore know that he is on the tallest mountain?
> No. That doesn't follow. Since he is the god on the tallest mountain, his sentence expresses a certain proposition, one true at W but not V [a world in which the gods have traded places], one he knows to be true. Had he been the god on the coldest mountain—as he might be, for all he knows—his sentence would express a different proposition, one true at V but not W, one that he knows to be false. If he doesn't know which he is, he doesn't know which proposition his sentence expresses and he doesn't know whether his sentence expresses a truth. He knows the proposition that he would in fact express by "I am on the tallest mountain," but that doesn't mean that he knows whether he is on the tallest mountain.[37]

It is tempting to take this example as showing the impossibility of there being more than one omniscient being—a conclusion that would no doubt be welcomed by most theists—but that would be the wrong moral to draw.

Instead, we should examine Lewis's contention that the god's complete *de dicto* knowledge does not give him knowledge *de se*. Lewis concedes that the god knows the proposition expressed by the god's utterance of "I am on the tallest mountain." According to the haecceitist's account, (i) that proposition is one entailing$_c$ the conjunction of the god's special individual essence and the property of being on the tallest mountain, and (ii) if the god believes it, he

36. Lewis, "Attitudes *De Dicto* and *De Re*,", pp. 520–521.
37. Ibid., pp. 523–524.

believes himself to be on the tallest mountain. But Lewis denies (ii). Why? Because he thinks that the god could believe this proposition without knowing that his sentence expressed it, and apparently Lewis thinks that in such a case the god would not know that he was on the tallest mountain. But how could it be that "he doesn't know which proposition his sentence expresses"? Call the god's utterance of the sentence 'S' and the proposition it expressed 'p.' Then since the god knows all true propositions, he knows that S expresses p, which, after all, is propositional knowledge. Perhaps, however, Lewis means that the god does not know that S is *his* utterance. Two things may be said in reply. First, it is hard to see why this additional knowledge is required for knowledge *de se*. Suppose I am experiencing a temporary problem with both my vocal cords and my hearing. I try to say, "I am trying to speak." I succeed in uttering the sentence and I hear it, but the hearing problem prevents me from recognizing the utterance as my own. My utterance (call it 'S'') expressed a certain first-proposition, q. Now I may know that I am trying to speak, even though I do not know that S' is *my* utterance or that S' expresses q. So the additional knowledge that Lewis seems to require is not necessary for knowledge *de se*. But second, it is, at least according to (15), knowledge that Lewis's god has. For there is a first-person proposition entailing the conjunction of the god's haecceity and the property of *having S as an utterance* that, by hypothesis, the god knows. So according to (15) the god knows that S is his utterance. Thus, Lewis's argument that *de se* knowledge is not reducible to *de dicto* knowledge seems to depend on holding that (15) does not succeed in effecting such a reduction. We seem to have, then, not an objection to (15) but its rejection.

Lewis appeals to another example that he thinks poses a problem for the view that all belief is propositional: John Perry's case of the mad Heimson who thinks he is Hume.[38] Lewis says that this example raises two problems. The first is that if what Heimson believes is a first-person proposition, it is an *impossible* proposition. Lewis says,

> The proposition that Heimson is Hume . . . is the empty proposi-
> tion, hence unfit to be believed. (Admittedly, we who are not hyper-

38. See John Perry, "Frege on Demonstratives," *Philosophical Review* 86 (1977):474–497.

rational do seemingly believe the empty proposition in some of its
guises, as when we get our sums wrong; but Heimson's mistake
seems nothing like that.) Yet Heimson does believe that he is Hume.
How can that be? I reply that the property of being Hume is a perfectly possible property. Hume actually had it. Heimson couldn't
possibly have this property . . . ; but that doesn't stop him from self-
ascribing it, and that is what he does. The empty proposition doesn't
enter into it.[39]

What exactly is so implausible about the view that Heimson believes
an impossible proposition? Even if Heimson has not made a logical
mistake, there are other ways of believing necessary falsehoods.
Perhaps I am essentially material if material and also essentially
immaterial if immaterial. Then whether I am material or immaterial, I can believe an impossible proposition by believing the
wrong one. Moreover, there seems to be no clear advantage to
Lewis's proposal, according to which Heimson self-ascribes a property that it is *impossible for him to have.*

Lewis derives another objection from this example: "The second
problem arises when we ask why Heimson is wrong. He believes he
is Hume. Hume believed that too. Hume was right. If Hume believed he was Hume by believing a proposition, that proposition
was true. Heimson believes just what Hume did. . . . Any proposition true for Hume is likewise true for Heimson. So Heimson, like
Hume, believes he is Hume by believing a true proposition. So he's
right. But he's not right. He's wrong, because he believes he's
Hume and he isn't."[40] So if Hume and Heimson believe the same
thing, the object of their belief is not a proposition, since the same
proposition cannot be true for Hume but false for Heimson. Now
according to the haecceitist account Hume and Heimson believe
different though related things; they each believe their own first-
person proposition. But Lewis gives two reasons for thinking that
Hume and Heimson believe the same thing. The first is that there is
a univocal predicate, 'believes he is Hume,' which occurs, for example, in "Not everyone believes he is Hume" and which applies to
both Hume and Heimson. But of course this predicate could be true
of both Hume and Heimson in virtue of their each believing a first-

39. Lewis, "Attitudes *De Dicto* and *De Re*," pp. 524–525.
40. Ibid., p. 525.

person proposition entailing$_c$ the conjunction of his own individual essence and the property of being Hume.

Lewis's other reason for holding that Hume and Heimson believe the same thing is that "Heimson may have got his head into perfect match with Hume's in every way that is at all relevant to what he believes"; but if they do not believe the same thing, what they believe depends on more than the "state of their heads." Lewis adds: "The main purpose of assigning objects of attitudes is . . . to characterize states of the head; to specify their causal roles with respect to behavior, stimuli, and one another. If the assignment of objects depends partly on something besides the state of the head, it will not serve this purpose. The states it characterizes will not be the occupants of the causal roles."[41] It is not at all clear that the main purpose of assigning objects to attitudes is to describe objects that play a certain functional or causal role. Perhaps the fact of the matter is simply that people have beliefs, and a purpose of assigning objects to this attitude is just to describe these beliefs. Of course a person's beliefs do fit into a complex including other attitudes as well as behavior. But do the beliefs themselves have to play the causal role Lewis envisages? Perhaps instead there is a *class* of propositions—first-person Hume beliefs—that all play the same causal role. Perhaps, then, a "state of the head" determines whether a person has one of the beliefs in this class but something else—who the person is—that determines which one of these beliefs the person has. So it does not seem that this example poses a serious problem for the attempt to explain knowledge *de se* in terms of knowledge *de dicto*.

These objections to the attempt to reduce *de se* belief to *de dicto* are, then, unpersuasive. I shall tentatively assume that omniscience may be understood, as in (D1), as knowledge of all true propositions.

We continue our discussion of omniscience in the next three chapters. First, we shall examine the contention that omniscience includes foreknowledge and that divine foreknowledge is incompatible with human free action. Next we shall look at whether omniscience includes "middle knowledge," or knowledge of what various agents would freely do in alternative circumstances. Finally, in connection with our discussion of eternity, we shall consider the charge that omniscience is incompatible with immutability.

41. Ibid., pp. 525–526.

3

Foreknowledge, Free Will, and the Necessity of the Past

1. Foreknowledge and Free Will

Omniscience involves knowledge of all true propositions. Within the class of true propositions, however, are those which detail the future free actions of human beings. Thus, if God is omniscient, he knows what people will do; omniscience, therefore, includes *foreknowledge*. But to many it has seemed that if God knows ahead of time that a person will perform a certain action, then that person does not perform the action freely. Divine foreknowledge has seemed, in other words, to be incompatible with future free action.

A well-known presentation of this problem is given by Augustine in his *De libero arbitrio*.

> Surely this is the question that troubles and perplexes you: how can the following two propositions, that [1] God has foreknowledge of all future events, and that [2] we do not sin by necessity but by free will, be made consistent with each other? "If God foreknows that man will sin," you say, "it is necessary that man sin." If man must sin, his sin is not the result of the will's choice, but is instead a fixed and inevitable necessity. You fear now that this reasoning results either in the blasphemous denial of God's foreknowledge or, if we deny this, the admission that we sin by necessity, not by will.[1]

---

1. Augustine, *De libero arbitrio*, bk. III, chap. 3. I quote *On Free Choice of the Will*, trans. Anna Benjamin and L. H. Hackett (Indianapolis: Bobbs-Merrill, 1964), p. 90.

Augustine asks, then, how it can be shown that (where S is any person)

(1) God knows that S will sin

is consistent with

(2) S will sin freely.

The question is made difficult by the fact that there seems to be a persuasive argument for the conclusion that if (1) is true then (2) is false, in which case it is not possible that (1) and (2) both be true. That argument, Augustine suggests, is

(3) If God foreknows that S will sin, then it is necessary that S will sin.

(4) If it is necessary that S will sin, then S will not sin freely.

Therefore,

(5) If God foreknows that S will sin, then S will not sin freely.

It is a matter of dispute among scholars exactly what Augustine's response to this problem is.[2] Moreover, in different passages Augustine seems to say somewhat different things on the subject.[3] Both William Rowe and Jasper Hopkins take Augustine to reject premiss (4), and perhaps that is right.[4] I think, however, that in *De libero arbitrio* Augustine's most explicit remarks are directed against

2. It is even a matter of dispute as to what the argument is. An influential interpretation has been given by William Rowe in "Augustine on Foreknowledge and Free Will," *Review of Metaphysics* 18 (1964): 356–363. Rowe's treatment has come in for criticism by Jasper Hopkins in "Augustine on Foreknowledge and Free Will," *International Journal for Philosophy of Religion* 8 (1977):111–126.

3. See Augustine, *De civitate Dei*, V, 9–10.

4. It is difficult to reconcile this interpretation, however, with Hopkins's further claim ("Augustine on Foreknowledge," p. 120) that Augustine also argues that we do not will by necessity, without importing a distinction from the considerably later passage in *De civitate Dei*. There Augustine distinguishes between two kinds of necessity, and what he says can plausibly be applied to the argument in my text as the claim that in one sense of 'necessary' one premiss is false and in the other sense the other premiss is false.

the conclusion of the argument; that he rejects (5) is clearer than whether it is premiss (3) or (4) that he denies.

Much of the preceding discussion in *De libero arbitrio* was devoted to establishing that sin "is a turning away from immutable goods and a turning toward changeable goods,"[5] that is, a turning away from God, who is the highest good. Moreover, this turning is a turning of the will and is hence voluntary.[6] Thus, when Augustine considers the claim that divine foreknowledge of someone's sin is incompatible with that person's sinning freely, it is natural that he would apply his thesis that sinning involves a voluntary act of will. This he does in the following passage:

> So it follows that we do not deny that God has foreknowledge of all things to be, and yet that we will what we will. For when he has foreknowledge of our will, it is going to be the will that he has foreknown. Therefore, the will is going to be a will because God has foreknowledge of it. Nor can it be a will if it is not in our power. Therefore, God also has knowledge of our power over it. So the power is not taken away from me by His foreknowledge; but because of His foreknowledge, the power to will will more certainly be present in me, since God, whose foreknowledge does not err, has foreseen that I shall have the power.[7]

Augustine thus appears to argue as follows: to sin is, by definition, to will wrongly, and to will is, by definition, to do something within one's power or freely. Thus, rather than being inconsistent with (2), (1) *entails* (2); on the assumption that (1) is true, it follows, given the nature of sin and of the will, that (2) is true.

A similar line of thought has recently been presented by Brian Davies. In replying to an analogous argument he writes: "For the simple fact is that if God knows at time 1 that P will freely do X at time 2 then what God knows is that P will freely do X. In other

---

5. II, 19.

6. II, 20.

7. III, 3; *On Free Choice of the Will*, p. 93. Compare a similar passage in *De civitate Dei*: "It does not follow, therefore, that there is no power in our will because God foreknew what was to be the choice in our will. For, He who had this foreknowledge had some foreknowledge. Furthermore, if He who foresaw what was to be in our will foresaw, not nothing, but something, it follows that there is a power in our will, even though he foresaw it" (V, 10). *The City of God*, ed. Vernon Bourke, (Garden City, N.Y.: Image Books, 1958), p. 110.

words, if God knows at time 1 that P will freely do X at time 2 then God's knowledge at time 1 is dependent on P freely doing X at time 2. . . . For if P were not free at time 2, then God could not know at time 1 that P would be free at time 2."[8] So Davies, too, appears to argue that since God knows that *P* will freely do *X* entails that *P* will freely do *X*, it follows that such foreknowledge is compatible with *P* freely doing *X*.

Unfortunately this line of reasoning is unsuccessful. It follows from the fact that (1) entails (2) that (1) and (2) are consistent only on the additional assumption that (1) itself is possible, but that is exactly what is in question. An analogy might make this clearer. It is not possible that anyone see someone who is invisible. It does not, therefore, constitute a good reply to this claim to point out that if

(1*) I see the invisible man,

the man I see must be as I see him, and consequently to conclude that (1) entails

(2*) The invisible man is invisible.

Pointing out that (1*) entails (2*) shows neither that (1*) and (2*) are consistent nor that being seen is consistent with being invisible. For even if (1*) does entail (2*), it also entails

(2**) The invisible man is visible,

in which case (1*) is impossible (and hence not consistent with any proposition).

So perhaps (1) entails not only (2) but also the denial of (2). If so, (1) is impossible; but the considerations Augustine raises in the quoted passage do not address the question of whether it is.

Rather than present the issue in terms of sinning, which according to Augustine is by definition free, it would be better to state it by reference to an arbitrary action, leaving it open whether the action is free. Thus, we could ask whether

(1') God knows that *S* will do *A*

8. Brian Davies, *An Introduction to the Philosophy of Religion* (Oxford: Oxford University Press, 1982), pp. 88–89.

is consistent with

> (2') S will do A freely.

And, as before, there is a readily available argument for the conclusion that it is not:

> (3') If God foreknows that S will do A, then it is necessary that S will do A.
>
> (4') If it is necessary that S will do A, then S will not do A freely.

Therefore,

> (5') If God foreknows that S will do A, then S will not do A freely.

A version of this argument was endorsed by Boethius in *The Consolation of Philosophy*. His response was to hold that God is "outside of time" and that everything that ever happens is present to him all at once. Strictly speaking, then, God does not have foreknowledge.[9] But if this argument succeeds in showing the incompatibility of divine foreknowledge and human free action, then an exactly parallel argument would seem to show the incompatibility of divine *present* knowledge and human free action.[10] Accordingly, we should look for another response to the argument.

We need not look far. Aquinas noted that "if each thing is known by God as seen by Him in the present, what is known by God will then have to be. Thus, it is necessary that Socrates be seated from the fact that he is seen seated. But this is not absolutely necessary or, as some say, with the *necessity of the consequent*; it is necessary conditionally, or with the *necessity of the consequence*. For this is a necessary

---

9. Boethuis, *The Consolation of Philosophy*, bk. V. C. S. Lewis accepted this argument and, like Boethius, he responded by adopting the doctrine of divine eternity. See his *Mere Christianity* (New York: Macmillan, 1958), p. 133.

10. Just as what is foreknown must be true, so what is known in the present must be true. So replacing (3') by

> (3") If God has present knowledge that S does A at t then it is necessary that S does A at t

and making a minor modification in (2') yields an argument for the conclusion that divine present knowledge is incompatible with human free action.

conditional proposition: *if he is seen sitting, he is sitting.*"[11] We can apply Aquinas's distinction as follows. (3') is ambiguous. It may be taken as affirming the necessity of the consequent, that is, as

(3'a) If God foreknows that S will do A, then the proposition that S will do A is a necessary truth.

Or (3') may express the necessity of the consequence, in which case it is better put as

(3'b) It is necessary that if God foreknows that S will do A, then S will do A.

While (3'b) is true, the argument so taken is invalid. Using (3'a), the argument is valid, but there is no reason to think (3'a) is true. In either case, then, the argument is defective.[12]

We turn next to an argument that is not so easily dismissed.

2. Foreknowledge and Accidental Necessity

A considerably more difficult argument for the conclusion that divine foreknowledge is inconsistent with human free action is suggested in one of the objections Aquinas cites on the negative side of the question of whether God's knowledge extends to future contingents.

Further, every conditional proposition, of which the antecedent is absolutely necessary, must have an absolutely necessary consequent. For the antecedent is to the consequent as principles are to the conclusion: and from necessary principles only a necessary conclusion can follow, as is proved in *Poster.* i [Aristotle's *Posteriori Analytics*, I, 6]. But this is a true conditional proposition, *If God knew that this thing will be, it will be*, for the knowledge of God is only of true things.

11. Aquinas, *S.C.G.*, I, 67, 10. Cf. *S.T.* Ia, 14, 13, *ad* 3.

12. This is the resolution Rowe recommends. It has also been defended by Anthony Kenny in "Divine Foreknowledge and Human Freedom," in *Aquinas: A Collection of Critical Essays*, ed. Kenny (Garden City, N.Y.: Anchor Books, 1969), pp. 255–270, and by Alvin Plantinga in *God, Freedom, and Evil* (1974; rpt. Grand Rapids, Mich.: Eerdmans, 1977), p. 67, and "On Ockham's Way Out," *Faith and Philosophy* 3 (1986):236–237.

Now, the antecedent of this conditional proposition is absolutely necessary, because it is eternal, and because it is signified as past. Therefore the consequent is also absolutely necessary; and so the knowledge of God is not of contingent things.[13]

The argument I am interested in is *suggested* by this passage, but extracting it requires the development of three themes that are either implicit or stated only briefly. The first is that true propositions about the past ("signified as past") are in some sense necessary. The species of necessity Aquinas has in mind is clearly not logical or metaphysical necessity; rather, it is a necessity that attaches to a proposition in virtue of its being a truth about the past.[14] William of Ockham described the kind of necessity in question as necessity *per accidens* or accidental necessity: "Many propositions about the past are of this sort. They are necessary *per accidens* because it was contingent that they would be necessary, and they were not always necessary."[15] The basic idea seems to be that even if a proposition *p*, for example, *Carter is, was, or will be elected President in 1976*, has always been true, it was formerly open for it to be false in a way that is now closed. Prior to the election of November 1976, things could have happened that would have made this proposition false. That is no longer the case; ever since Carter won the election, *p* has been in some way fixed or unalterable and, therefore, accidentally necessary.

Ockham might be read as suggesting that if a proposition is accidentally necessary then there was an earlier time at which it was not accidentally necessary. (Alternatively, the passage might be asserting only that this is often the case.) It is not clear to me that it is part of the concept of accidental necessity that accidentally necessary propositions *acquire* their necessity. (If past time is infinite but only contingently so, then it would seem that *There was a preceding moment* was always accidentally necessary.) What is clear, however, is

13. Aquinas, *S.T.*, Ia, 14, 13, obj. 2.

14. It is thus unfortunate that Aquinas uses the term "absolute" necessity, especially since he elsewhere speaks of "absolute" possibility and impossibility where he clearly intends logical or metaphysical possibility (*S.T.*, Ia, 25, 3).

15. William of Ockham, *Ordinatio*, Prologus, q. 6, quoted in his *Predestination, God's Foreknowledge, and Future Contingents*, trans. Marilyn McCord Adams and Norman Kretzmann, 2d ed. (Indianapolis: Hackett, 1983), p. 38, n. 14. According to Adams and Kretzmann the term derives from William of Sherwood.

that logically or metaphysically necessary propositions are not accidentally necessary; accidentally necessary propositions have their "necessity" contingently.[16]

It is important to observe, as several writers have done,[17] that the claim that the past is fixed in a way in which the future is not, is not the claim that the past cannot be changed; for neither the past nor the future can be changed. A person changes the past just in case there is some proposition *p* which is temporally indexed to a past time and which is true until the person performs an action that renders it false. Thus, someone would change the past if he or she did something now which makes *Carter won the election in 1976* false. Not surprisingly, no one is able to do any such thing. Analogously, for a person to change the future there would have to be some true proposition that is temporally indexed to a future time and that becomes false as a result of the person's action. Suppose it is true that a Democrat will win the presidential election in 1992. Then to change this fact about the future, someone would have to do some action *A* which is such that, although it is now true that a Democrat will win the presidential election in 1992, as a result of doing *A*, it becomes false that a Democrat will win the presidential election in 1992. But clearly this is impossible. If anyone succeeds in making it false that a Democrat wins in 1992, then it will have been false all along that a Democrat wins in 1992.

So the apparent fixity of the past, which contrasts with the openness of the future, does not consist in the fact that it is possible to change the future but not the past. Then how is it to be explained? What exactly is accidental necessity? These are questions we shall need to examine in the course of investigating the argument from the necessity of the past, but first let us continue our attempt to specify the argument.

The second element in the passage from Aquinas requiring elaboration is the principle of inference employed. What Aquinas says is that "every conditional proposition, of which the antecedent is absolutely necessary, must have an absolutely necessary consequent."

16. Cf. Alfred Freddoso, "Accidental Necessity and Power over the Past," *Pacific Philosophical Quarterly* 63 (1982):57.

17. See, for example, Plantinga, "On Ockham's Way Out," p. 244, and Kenny, "Divine Foreknowledge and Human Freedom."

But this is not quite right. A *false* conditional proposition could have an accidentally necessary antecedent without having an accidentally necessary consequent.[18] Aquinas's example is the proposition *If God knew that this thing will be, it will be.* In this case the antecedent *entails* the consequent; that suggests the following principle:

(6) If p is accidentally necessary and p entails q, then q is accidentally necessary.

According to (6), accidental necessity is closed under entailment, and that is just what the argument requires.

The final feature requiring explanation is the relevance of facts about accidental necessity and divine foreknowledge to human free action. The objection Aquinas explicitly considers concludes that God's knowledge is not of contingent things. What exactly is the relation between noncontingency and human freedom? Presumably, the relevant assumption here is that whatever is accidentally necessary is not within anyone's power to render false. Thus, if it is accidentally necessary that a person perform a certain action, then, in particular, it is not within the power of that person to refrain from performing the action; and if it is not within the power of a person to refrain from performing an action, that action is not freely done.

By appealing to these three features we can construct an argument for the thesis that God's foreknowledge of a particular human action is inconsistent with that action's being free. Consider some putative free action that will be performed, and suppose that God has in the past had foreknowledge that it would be performed. Perhaps, to use an example that has become standard in the literature on this topic,

(7) Eighty years ago God foreknew that Jones will mow his lawn tomorrow.

Now (7) is apparently a proposition about the past; accordingly,

(8) It is accidentally necessary that eighty years ago God foreknew that Jones will mow his lawn tomorrow.

18. So could a true *material* conditional.

But (7) entails

> (9) Jones will mow his lawn tomorrow;

hence by (6), the principle that accidental necessity is closed under entailment, and (8) it follows that

> (10) It is accidentally necessary that Jones will mow his lawn tomorrow.

Finally, if what is accidentally necessary is fixed or not within anyone's power to prevent, it follows that

> (11) It is not within Jones's power to refrain from mowing his lawn tomorrow.[19]

19. For a historical example of someone who defends a version of this argument, see Jonathan Edwards, *Freedom of the Will* (1745), sec. 12. The recent literature on this topic is immense. Much of it addresses an argument Nelson Pike defends for the conclusion that God's being *essentially* omniscient is incompatible with human free action. Pike's argument is presented in "Divine Omniscience and Voluntary Action," *Philosophical Review* 74 (1965):27–46, and repeated in his *God and Timelessness* (London: Routledge & Kegan Paul, 1970), pp. 53–86. Early discussion of Pike's piece includes John Turk Saunders, "Of God and Freedom," *Philosophical Review* 75 (1966):219–225; Marilyn McCord Adams, "Is the Existence of God a 'Hard' Fact?" *Philosophical Review* 76 (1967):492–503; and Pike's "Of God and Freedom: A Rejoinder," *Philosophical Review* 75 (1966):369–379.

Pike's argument does not make explicit appeal to the accidental necessity of the past, but Plantinga in "On Ockham's Way Out" shows (pp. 248–249) how the argument depends upon claims about the necessity of the past. I think that Pike's version of the argument has been adequately refuted and thus shall not discuss it directly. See Plantinga, "On Ockham's Way Out" and *God, Freedom, and Evil*, pp. 66–73, and Stephen T. Davis, "Divine Omniscience and Human Freedom," *Religious Studies* 15 (1979):303–316, and *Logic and the Nature of God* (Grand Rapids, Mich.: Eerdmans, 1983):52–67. See also Philip Quinn, "Plantinga on Foreknowledge and Freedom," in *Alvin Plantinga,* ed. J. Tomberlin and P. van Inwagen (Dordrecht: D. Reidel, 1985), pp. 271–287.

For criticism of Saunders as well as of Plantinga's treatment in *God, Freedom and Evil,* see William P. Alston, "Divine Foreknowledge and Alternative Conceptions of Human Freedom," *International Journal for Philosophy of Religion* 18 (1985):19–32. For further discussion of Pike's argument see Joshua Hoffman, "Pike on Possible Worlds, Divine Foreknowledge, and Human Freedom," *Philosophical Review* 88 (1979):433–442, and Hoffman and Gary Rosenkrantz, "Hard and Soft Facts," *Philosophical Review* 93 (1984):419–435. See also the papers by John Fischer, "Freedom and Foreknowledge," *Philosophical Review* 92 (1983):67–79; "Hard-Type Soft

It is customary to note that an argument like this can be generalized; it can be reformulated to apply to any person and any action. But it is instructive, I believe, to note another sort of generalization that is relevant here, namely, the existential generalization that there is a concept of accidental necessity having the features required by the argument. As a first approximation let us put this assumption as follows:

(C) There is a concept of accidental necessity satisfying the following conditions: (i) if God in the past believed a proposition about the future, it is now accidentally necessary that he did, (ii) accidental necessity is closed under entailment, and (iii) if a proposition p is accidentally necessary at a time t, then no one is able at t or later to act in such a way that p is false.[20]

We shall need to modify (C) slightly, but it will be easier to see why after we note how the argument for the incompatibility of fore-

---

Facts," *Philosophical Review* 95 (1986):591–601; "Ockhamism," *Philosophical Review* 94 (1985):81–100; and "Pike's Ockhamism," *Analysis* 46 (1986):57–63. Pike has two recent contributions to the debate: "Divine Foreknowledge, Human Freedom and Possible Worlds," *Philosophical Review* 86 (1977):209–216, which replies to Plantinga's *God, Freedom and Evil*, and "Fischer on Freedom and Foreknowledge," *Philosophical Review* 93 (1984):599–614.

Other relevant literature includes Martin Davies, "Boethius and Others on Divine Foreknowledge," *Pacific Philosophical Quarterly* 64 (1983):313–329; Alfred Freddoso, "Accidental Necessity and Logical Determinism," *Journal of Philosophy* 80 (1983):257–278, and "Accidental Necessity and Power over the Past"; William Hasker, "Foreknowledge and Necessity," *Faith and Philosophy* 2 (1985):121–157; Kenny, "Divine Foreknowledge and Human Freedom," and *The God of the Philosophers* (Oxford: Oxford University Press, 1979), pp. 51–87; George Mavrodes, "Is the Past Unpreventable?" *Faith and Philosophy* 1 (1984):131–146; Bruce Reichenbach, "Hasker on Omniscience," *Faith and Philosophy* 4 (1987):86–92; William Rowe, *Philosophy of Religion* (Encino, Calif.: Dickenson, 1978), pp. 154–169; Richard Swinburne, *The Coherence of Theism* (Oxford: Oxford University Press, 1977), pp. 167–172; Thomas Talbott, "On Divine Foreknowledge and Bringing about the Past," *Philosophy and Phenomenological Research* 46 (1986):455–469; David Widerker and Eddy M. Zemach, "Facts, Freedom and Foreknowledge," *Religious Studies* 23 (1987):19–28; and Linda Zagzebski, "Divine Foreknowledge and Human Free Will," *Religious Studies* 21 (1985):279–298.

20. It is important to note that (C) does not assert merely that there is a concept *of satisfying* conditions (i)–(iii); that would be trivial. Rather, according to (C) there is a concept which *does satisfy* (i)–(iii).

knowledge and free action can be stated in terms of (C). Formulating the argument in this fashion will enable us to make explicit exactly what its key assumptions are.

Consider first the following argument:

Argument A

(12) Necessarily, if (C) then divine foreknowledge of human actions is incompatible with anyone being able to do anything other than what he or she does do.

(13) Necessarily, if no one is ever able to do anything other than what he or she does do, then no one ever acts freely.

Therefore,

(14) Necessarily, if (C) then divine foreknowledge of human actions is incompatible with anyone ever acting freely.

Premiss (12) makes it explicit that the three features specified by condition (C) are sufficient to ensure that if there is a concept of accidental necessity satisfying them, divine foreknowledge of a person's action is incompatible with that person's acting otherwise.[21] And premiss (13) shows how the argument is supposed to bear on *free* action by making explicit the presupposition that acting freely requires the ability to act otherwise.

We may now represent the argument for the incompatiblity of divine foreknowledge and human free action as the argument that results from adding assumption (C) to the premiss set of Argument A and then detaching the consequent of (14). Our discussion of the resulting argument proceeds by examining the three premisses (C), (12), and (13). In the next section we shall see that (12) is plausible provided that we revise (C) slightly; thereafter we shall consider an objection to (13). The task of investigating the proposed revision of (C) will be taken up in Chapter 5.

---

21. Strictly, since (12) speaks of divine foreknowledge of *human* actions, the "anyone" should be interpreted as meaning *any human being*. Of course analogous arguments can be constructed for divine foreknowledge of nonhuman action, but we shall not consider such arguments here.

3. The Assumption Restated

Let us focus first on

> (12) Necessarily, if (C) then divine foreknowledge of human actions is incompatible with anyone being able to do anything other than what he or she does do.

How exactly does this incompatibility follow from (C)? According to (C) there is a certain concept of accidental necessity which satisfies three conditions. The first is that if God in the past believed something about the future it is thereafter accidentally necessary that he did.[22] We can put this more carefully as: (i) for all times t_1 and t_2 such that t_1 is earlier than t_2 and for every proposition p, if at t_1 God believes p, then at t_2 the proposition, *At t_1 God believes p*, is accidentally necessary.

The second condition that (C) specifies is that accidental necessity is closed under entailment. This is not quite right, however, for it conflicts with the claim we noted above that only logically contingent propositions are accidentally necessary. Suppose that *Carter was elected President in 1976* is accidentally necessary. This proposition entails that *either Carter was elected President in 1976 or 2 + 2 = 4*. If accidental necessity is closed under entailment, this disjunction should be accidentally necessary; but it is logically necessary, so it

---

22. According to some treatments of this topic there is an important difference between God's past *belief* and his past *knowledge*. To use some terms to be introduced below, God's past knowledge is sometimes taken to be a "soft" fact about the past and, thus, not accidentally necessary. By contrast, God's past belief, on these accounts, is regarded as a "hard" fact about the past and, thus, accidentally necessary. (See, for example, Fischer, "Freedom and Foreknowledge.") I think that for any proposition p, it is necessary that God knows p if and only if God believes p; so I am not convinced that the distinction between God's knowledge and his belief is crucial here. Nevertheless, we should consider the objection in what is widely regarded as its strongest form, which requires stating it in terms of God's *forebelief*. This can be accomplished by replacing 'foreknowledge' in (12) and (14) with 'forebelief', but I shall not always bother to make this replacement explicit. Note, however, that (C) is stated in terms of God's past *belief* and that if (12) is correct in affirming that the incompatibility of divine foreknowledge and the ability to do otherwise follows from (C), it would be because the incompatibility of divine *forebelief* and the ability to do otherwise follows from (C). Cf. William P. Alston, who in "Does God Have Beliefs?" *Religious Studies* 22 (1986):287–306, tries to sidestep the argument by denying that God has beliefs.

should not be accidentally necessary. The obvious repair is to formulate the second condition as: (ii) for every time t and for all propositions p and q, if p is accidentally necessary, p entails q, and it is (logically) possible that q is false, then q is accidentally necessary.

The final condition that (C) imposes is that if a proposition p is accidentally necessary at a certain time then no one is able at that time or later to act in such a way that p is false. This claim conceals an ambiguity. It might be that a person S is able to act in such a way that p is false just in case S is able to *cause* p to be false. Alternatively, it might be that S is able to act in such a way that p is false is just in case there is an action A that S is able to perform and that is such that if S were to perform A then p would be false.[23]

Let us examine what the consequences of adopting the first interpretation are for premiss (12). According to the example we have been considering, eighty years ago God believed that Jones would mow his lawn tomorrow. By the first condition of (C), that fact is therefore accidentally necessary. But it entails that Jones will mow his lawn tomorrow (call this latter proposition "p", and note that it is contingent); according to the second condition of (C), then, p is accidentally necessary. Now if what the third condition of (C) tells us is that Jones is unable to *cause* p to be false, does it follow that Jones cannot refrain from mowing his lawn tomorrow? It is not clear that it does. Perhaps Jones can go on an all-day bike trip tomorrow, and if he did that action would be sufficient for the falsehood of p even if Jones would not thereby *cause* p to be false.

A different example might help clarify the point. Let q be the proposition that last week Smith correctly believed that Jones would trim his evergreens tomorrow, and suppose that q is true. If Jones cannot *cause* q to be false, does it follow that Jones is unable to refrain from trimming his evergreens tomorrow? Clearly not. Jones can falsify Smith's belief without practicing backward causation. Jones's not triming his evergreens tomorrow would be sufficient for the falsehood of q, and if Jones were not to trim his evergreens tomor-

---

23. This distinction parallels the distinction made in Chapter 2 between strongly actualizing and weakly actualizing a state of affairs. In "Boethius and Others on Divine Foreknowledge," Martin Davies notes the importance of a similar distinction. John Fischer's use of the phrase "being able so to act that p would have been false" suggests that he employs the second interpretation. See his "Freedom and Foreknowledge."

row, Jones can plausibly be said to have made q false. But Jones can be able thus to make q false without having the ability to *cause* it to be false.

Let us return to the case of Jones and his lawn. We assumed for the sake of argument that it is accidentally necessary that Jones will mow his lawn tomorrow. We then asked whether, if the third condition of (C) tells us that Jones is unable to cause p to be false, it follows that Jones is unable to refrain from mowing his lawn tomorrow. The answer seems to be that it does not. Jones might be able to make p false without causing it to be false. On the first interpretation, then, of (C)'s third condition, (12) is dubious. Under this interpretation, it is not clear that divine foreknowledge (or forebelief) is inconsistent with Jones's being able to do anything other than what he does do.

Consider the second interpretation of the third condition of (C), which we may put as follows: (iii) for every time t_1 and proposition p, if p is accidentally necessary at t_1, then there is no person S, action A, and time t_2 at least as late as t_1 such that S can do A at t_2, and if S were to do A at t_2 then p would be false. Where p is, as before, the proposition that Jones will mow his lawn tomorrow, it should be clear that if p is accidentally necessary and (iii) holds for p, then Jones cannot refrain from mowing his lawn tomorrow. For if Jones could refrain from mowing his lawn tomorrow, then Jones could do something such that if he did it p would be false. But if (iii) holds (on the assumption, still, that p is accidentally necessary), there is nothing *anyone* can do—and so not Jones—which is such that if it were done p would be false. But if there is nothing Jones can do according to which p would be false, then Jones cannot do other than what he does do. Thus, with (iii) incorporated into (C), (12) seems to be true: if (C), so understood, is true, then divine foreknowledge (or forebelief) with respect to human actions is incompatible with anyone ever doing anything other than what he or she does do.

In the course of our discussion of (12), which makes a claim about (C), we have come to revise (C). Let us call the revision of (C), "(C*)," and modify (12) accordingly:

(12*) Necessarily, if (C*) then divine foreknowledge of human actions is incompatible with anyone being able to do anything other than what he or she does do.

(C*) is the following:

> (C*) There is a concept of accidental necessity satisfying the
> following conditions: (i) for all times t_1 and t_2 such that t_1 is
> earlier than t_2 and for every proposition p, if at t_1 God
> believes p, then at t_2 the proposition, *At t_1 God believes p*, is
> accidentally necessary, (ii) for every time t and for all prop-
> ositions p and q, if p is accidentally necessary at t, p entails
> q, and it is possible that q is false, then q is accidentally
> necessary at t, and (iii) for every time t_1 and proposition p,
> if p is accidentally necessary at t_1, then there is no person S,
> action A, and time t_2 at least as late as t_1 such that S can do
> A at t_2 and if S were to do A at t_2 then p would be false.

What we have seen is that, given this formulation of (C*), (12)
seems to be true. We turn in the next section to a consideration of
premiss (13).

4. Freedom and the Ability to Do Otherwise

Premiss (13) is the following:

> (13) Necessarily, if no one is ever able to do anything other
> than what he or she does do, then no one ever acts freely.

Until recently (13) would, I believe, have been entirely uncon-
troversial. However, some persuasive examples due to Harry
Frankfurt have convinced some writers that acting freely does not
require the ability to do otherwise than what one does.[24] If that is
correct, premiss (13) is suspect. It is tempting, of course, simply to
accept the Frankfurt-style objections to (13), thereby enabling us to
defuse Argument A and, hence, the argument for the incom-

24. Harry Frankfurt, "Alternative Possibilities and Moral Responsibility," *Journal
of Philosophy* 66 (1969):829–839. Frankfurt's explicit target is not (12) or another
thesis about free action; rather, he attacks the claim that being able to do otherwise is
required for being morally responsible. Thus, rather than attributing objections to
(12) to Frankfurt, I speak of "Frankfurt-style" objections—objections that are inspired by Frankfurt's examples. I have borrowed the term from Peter van Inwagen,
An Essay on Free Will (Oxford: Oxford University Press, 1983), p. 164.

patibility of divine foreknowledge and human free action. It would also spare us the difficult project, to be undertaken in the next chapter, of trying to understand the concept of accidental necessity. Unfortunately, I am not convinced that (13) is false or that Frankfurt-style examples succeed in severing all connection between acting freely and the ability to act otherwise. Accordingly, we should consider those examples and their application to (13).

Frankfurt attacks what he calls the Principle of Alternative Possibilities:

(PAP) A person is morally responsible for an action he has done only if he could have done otherwise.

Rather than presenting Frankfurt's objections to (PAP), I quote a structurally similar one given by Peter van Inwagen:

Suppose there is a man called Gunnar who has decided to shoot his colleague Ridley. Suppose a third man, Cosser, very much desires that Gunnar shoot Ridley. Cosser is naturally delighted with Gunnar's present intention to shoot Ridley, but he realizes that people sometimes change their minds. Accordingly, he devises the following plan: if Gunnar should change his mind about shooting Ridley, Cosser will cause Gunnar to shoot Ridley. We may suppose that Cosser is able directly to manipulate Gunnar's nervous system, and is thus able, in the fullest and strongest sense of the word, to *cause* Gunnar to act according to his wishes. Let us suppose, moreover, that there is nothing Gunnar can do about Cosser's intentions or about the power Cosser has over his acts. It would seem therefore, that Gunnar has no choice about whether he shoots Ridley. If he does not change his mind, he will shoot Ridley. If he does change his mind he will shoot Ridley. . . .

Time passes, we suppose, and Gunnar does not change his mind and does shoot Ridley without having been caused to do so by Cosser. Could he have done otherwise than shoot Ridley? Obviously not: before he shot he had no choice about whether he would shoot Ridley, and so we may now say, after the fact, that he couldn't have done otherwise than shoot him. Is he responsible for having shot Ridley? It would certainly seem so, at least if anyone is ever responsible for anything.[25]

25. Van Inwagen, *An Essay on Free Will*, pp. 162–163.

Does this example refute (PAP)? The answer depends upon exactly how (PAP) is understood. If (PAP) is merely a claim about every *actual* instance of morally responsible action, then a fictitious example does not refute it. Van Inwagen's example makes it plausible to suppose that someone *could* be morally responsible for an action without having been able to do otherwise, but it gives us no reason to think that anyone ever has been in a situation like Gunnar's. On the other hand, (PAP) might be intended to express a stronger claim, a claim about a *conceptual* connection between moral responsibility and the ability to do otherwise. In this case (PAP) should be taken as a claim of necessity, that is, as

> (PAP′) Necessarily, for every person S and action A, S is morally responsible for performing A only if S could have refrained from performing A.[26]

Since Gunnar's situation seems to be *possible*, the example does seem to refute (PAP′). It is not necessary that every case of morally responsible action requires the ability to do otherwise.

Do examples such as this also count against (13)? If it is possible for an agent to be *morally responsible* although he or she could not have done otherwise, is it also possible for an agent to act *freely*, even though he or she could not have done otherwise? In the case of Gunnar, it certainly seems as though he shot Ridley freely, so that his action of shooting Ridley was both free and such that he could not have done otherwise. But (13) does not deny that it can happen that an action is both free and that its agent could not have done otherwise. What (13) says is that, necessarily, if no one is *ever* able to do other than what he or she does so, then no one *ever* acts freely. Thus (13) leaves it open that *some* actions are both free and such that their agents could not have avoided them.

Let us say that if an action is such that its agent could not have done otherwise, then the action is *unavoidable* (for the agent). Our question, then, is whether it is possible that although there are some free actions, *every* free action is unavoidable. If this is possible, then

26. Since Frankfurt notes that (PAP) "has generally seemed so overwhelmingly plausible that some philosophers have even characterized it as an *a priori* truth" ("Alternative Possibilities and Moral Responsibility," p. 829), it does not seem inaccurate to take his target to be (PAP′).

(13) is false. A way of approaching this question is by asking whether Frankfurt-style counterexamples can be constructed for *every* free action. Or is there instead a limited domain for which (PAP') holds?

Van Inwagen claims that there are several near-relatives of (PAP') which are immune to Frankfurt-style counter examples. We shall not examine all of van Inwagen's proposals, but it will be instructive to look at two of them. The first, which he calls the Principle of Possible Actions, is something like

> (PPA) Necessarily, a person is morally responsible for failing to perform a given act only if he could have performed the act.[27]

Van Inwagen tries to construct a Frankfurt-style counterexample to (PPA), but he concludes that the example he considers does not succeed and that the prospects for finding one that does succeed are dim. The example van Inwagen concocts involves a case in which someone looks out of his window and sees a man being beaten and robbed. The witness considers calling the police but elects not to. Unbeknownst to him, however, the telephone is out of order, and so he could not have called the police. If this is to constitute a counterexample to (PPA), it must be a case in which the witness is morally responsible for failing to call the police even though he could not have called them. But as van Inwagen correctly notes, in this case the witness is *not* morally responsible for failing to call the police (although he may be morally responsible for failing *to try* to call the police). Van Inwagen concludes, "Perhaps there are Frankfurt-style counter-examples to PPA. But I don't see how to construct one. I conclude that Frankfurt's style of argument cannot be used to refute PPA."[28]

I think, however, that it is not difficult to frame a Frankfurt-style counterexample to (PPA); a variation on the case of Gunnar and Ridley will do. Suppose that Gunnar considers shooting Ridley but decides to refrain from so doing. Presumably, the way to refrain from shooting Ridley to do something else instead. Suppose, also, that Cosser wants no harm to come to Ridley and so he resolves to

27. Van Inwagen, *An Essay on Free Will*, p. 165. Van Inwagen's actual principle is (PPA) with "necessarily" omitted.
28. Ibid., p. 166.

cause Gunnar to do something other than shoot Ridley (that is, to refrain from shooting Ridley) if Gunnar were to try to shoot Ridley. As before, Gunnar is unable to do anything to thwart Cosser's plan. Given that it is Gunnar himself who decides not to shoot Ridley, Gunnar is morally responsible for refraining from shooting Ridley. But since Cosser was waiting in the wings, prepared to ensure that Gunnar did something other than shoot Ridley, Gunnar could not have done otherwise than refrain from shooting Ridley. Thus, (PPA) is subject to a Frankfurt-style counterexample.[29]

Van Inwagen proposes another variant of (PAP), also allegedly immune to Frankfurt-style counterexamples, which he states in terms of *event particulars*. It is not easy to say what event particulars are; but if there are such things, they are, presumably, datable, nonrepeatable occurrences.[30] Van Inwagen's proposal, this time labeled a principle of possible prevention, is

(PPP1) Necessarily, a person is morally responsible for a certain event particular only if he could have prevented it.[31]

Before considering potential Frankfurt-style counterexamples to (PPP1), van Inwagen introduces a criterion of individuation for event particulars. According to van Inwagen, we need a "counterfactual" criterion of identity for events because "we want to know how to tell of some given event whether *it*, that very same event, would nevertheless have happened if things had been different in certain specified ways."[32] The criterion van Inwagen gives is

(15) x is the same particular event as y if and only if x and y have the same causes.

In summarizing van Inwagen's view, John Fischer describes (15) as "the *essentialist principle*, since it asserts the essentiality of the causal

---

29. More cautiously, (PPA) is subject to a Frankfurt-style counterexample *if (PAP) is.*

30. Van Inwagen refers to Donald Davidson's "On Events and Event Descriptions," in *Fact and Existence*, ed. Joseph Margolis (Oxford: Basil Blackwell, 1969), pp. 74–84, and "The Individuation of Events," in *Essays in Honor of Carl G. Hempel*, ed. Nicholas Rescher (Dordrecht: D. Reidel, 1969), pp. 216–234.

31. I have again added "necessarily."

32. Van Inwagen, *An Essay on Free Will*, p. 168.

genesis of an event."[33] The claim that a cause of an event is essential to it is exactly the consequence van Inwagen hopes to ensure by (15); however, (15) does not have this consequence. To see this point, compare a principle that van Inwagen himself gives as an example:

(16) x is the same person as y if and only if x and y have the same siblings.

Even if (16) is necessarily and not merely contingently true, it does not entail that a person has the same siblings in every world in which he or she exists; it does not entail that a person has his or her siblings essentially. As van Inwagen puts it, (16) "does not help us if we are interested in counter-factual questions about persons." Analogously, if (15) is a necessary truth, it entails that if x and y are the same event, then in every world in which x occurs, y has the same causes as x; but (16) does not entail that if x occurs in a world then it has the same causes in every world in which it occurs.

Rather than try to find a criterion of identity that has the consequence that event particulars have their causes essentially, I think it is simpler just to state the desired condition itself.[34] Even this task is not a simple matter, for van Inwagen has a proposal that seems not quite right. Immediately after stating (15), he adds, "that is to say, if x is the product of certain causes, then, necessarily, an event y is the product of *those* causes if and only if y is x."[35] That is, van Inwagen appears to endorse

(17) For every event x and cause C, if C causes x then, necessarily, for every event y, C causes y if and only if $x = y$.

However, (17) does not capture the idea that events have their causes essentially; it says, instead, that causes have their effects essentially. What van Inwagen needs, it seems to me, is

---

33. John Fischer, "Responsibility and Control," *Journal of Philosophy* 79 (1982):29.
34. For a discussion of the function of identity conditions and the difficulties associated with settling essentialist claims about events, see Edward Wierenga and Richard Feldman, "Identity Conditions and Events," *Canadian Journal of Philosophy* 11 (1981):77–93.
35. Van Inwagen, *An Essay on Free Will*, p. 169.

(18) Necessarily, for all events e and f, if f causes e, then, necessarily, if e occurs then f causes e.[36]

But is there any reason to think that (18) is correct? Van Inwagen
says merely, "I do do not know how to justify my intuition that this
criterion is correct. . . . I can only suggest that since substances
(such as human beings and tables) should be individuated by their
causal origins, and since we are talking about events that, like substances, are particulars, the present proposal is plausible."[37] I do not
find the thesis that substances have their origins essentially, that, for
example, each of us derives essentially from some particular sperm
and ovum, especially plausible, despite the Kripkean origin of the
thesis.[38] The thesis that events have their causes essentially is even
less compelling. It has the consequence that if I had used my other
hand to turn my computer on, then that event which is my computer's being on would not have occurred. According to van Inwagen,
if a "historian writes, 'Even if the murder of Caesar had not resulted
in civil war, it would nevertheless have led to widespread blood-
shed', he does not convict himself of conceptual confusion. But he is
certainly presupposing that the very event we call 'the murder of
Caesar' might have had different effects."[39] We should be similarly
charitable to the historian who says, "Even if the murder of Caesar
had been caused by a desire for power rather than by hatred of his
dictatorship, it would still have been approved by many Romans,"
and who thus seems to presuppose, without conceptual confusion,
that the same event could have had different causes.[40] So (18) seems
to have little to recommend it. This is crucial for van Inwagen's

36. Van Inwagen does affirm something close to (13). He says: "No event could
have had causes other than its actual causes" (p. 170). But this statement leaves it
open, as (13) does not, that an event that is caused could have been uncaused, and an
event that is overdetermined could have been caused by just one of its actual causes.
On neither of these two possibilities do events have their causes essentially.

37. Van Inwagen, *An Essay on Free Will*, p. 169.

38. See Saul Kripke, "Naming and Necessity," in *Semantics of Natural Language*,
ed. Donald Davidson and Gilbert Harman (Dordrecht: D. Reidel, 1972), pp. 312–
314.

39. Van Inwagen, *An Essay on Free Will*, p. 168.

40. See Suetonius, *The Twelve Caesars*, I, 80, who lists alternative locations where
the murder of Caesar might have occurred had it not occurred in the Pompeian
Assembly Hall.

defense of (PPP1), however, since he requires (18) in order to dismiss Frankfurt-style counterexamples to (PPP1).

Van Inwagen considers the following attempt at a Frankfurt-style counter-example to (PPP1):

> Gunnar shoots and kills Ridley (intentionally), thereby bringing about Ridley's death, a certain event. But there is some factor, F, which (i) played no causal role in Ridley's death, and (ii) would have caused Ridley's death if Gunnar had not shot him—or, since factor F might have caused Ridley's death by *causing* Gunnar to shoot him, perhaps we should say, "if Gunnar had decided not to shoot him"— and (iii) is such that Gunnar could not have prevented it from causing Ridley's death except by killing, or by deciding to kill, Ridley himself. So it would seem that Gunnar is responsible for Ridley's death, though he could not have prevented Ridley's death.[41]

But van Inwagen rejects this counterexample by appealing to (18). He writes:

> It is easy to see that this story is simply inconsistent. What is in fact denoted by 'Ridley's death' is not, according to the story, caused by factor F. Therefore, if Gunnar had not shot Ridley, and, as a result, factor F had caused Ridley to die, then there would have been an event other than the event in fact denoted by 'Ridley's death' which had factor F as (one of) its cause(s). But then this event would have been an event other than the event in fact denoted by 'Ridley's death'; the event in fact denoted by 'Ridley's death' would not have happened at all. But if this story is inconsistent, it is not a counterexample to PPP1.[42]

But just as, as far as I can tell, the computer's being on could have been caused by my pressing the switch with my left hand instead of my pressing it with my right hand; and just as the murder of Caesar might have been caused by fewer stab wounds; so there seems no compelling reason to think that the very event which is Ridley's death could not have been caused by factor F instead. It looks as though there is a successful Frankfurt-style counter example to (PPP1).[43]

41. Van Inwagen, *An Essay on Free Will*, p. 170.

42. Ibid.

43. More cautiously, there are successful Frankfurt-style counterexamples to (PPP1) if there are to (PAP).

Van Inwagen's strategy of trying to find a variant of (PAP) which is immune to Frankfurt-style counterexamples seems to me to be a good one. We have seen, however, that the particular variants he endorses do not have this feature.[44] Perhaps we should look in a different direction. Let us see whether there is a *restricted class* of actions for which (PAP) holds.

A familiar idea in the theory of action is that for many actions there is a complex chain of events that trace back to some more basic action of the agent. Thus, if I raise my arm, I also contract certain muscles. The contraction of those muscles is caused by electrical impulses traveling along nerves from the brain. And those electrical impulses are caused by some events that occur within my brain. It is tempting to think that at the start of this chain is something that *I* do to get things going. If it is not I who initiates the chain, then it is not I who raises my arm, or at least I do not raise it of my own free will. A traditional answer to the question "What is that initial action?" is that the initial action is an act of will. This view need not presuppose that there is a special faculty, the Will, that does a person's willing. On the contrary, willing is something a *person* does. Moreover, such initial actions need not be only acts of willing; they might also include, for example, acts of deciding or intending.[45]

Let us examine how Frankfurt-style counterexamples fit into this picture of human action. In van Inwagen's most explicit example, the supposition is made that "Cosser is able directly to manipulate Gunnar's nervous system, and is thus able, in the fullest and strongest sense of the word, to *cause* Gunnar to act according to his [Cosser's] wishes."[46] Now it might be held that this example is a *possible* scenario provided that Cosser's neural manipulation is not supposed to cause Gunnar to will to shoot Ridley but that, bypassing Gunnar's act of will, Cosser's manipulation is what initiates the chain of events culminating in Gunnar's shooting Ridley. In other words, it

---

44. Van Inwagen offers one more proposal, which I shall not not discuss, but I believe that he is unsuccessful in defending it against counterexamples.

45. Cf. a recent statement by William P. Alston: "The core concept of human action is not *movement of one's own body*, but rather *bringing about a change in the world—directly or indirectly—by an act of will, decision, or intention.*" Alston, "Functionalism and Theological Language," *American Philosophical Quarterly* 22 (1985): 225.

46. Van Inwagen, *An Essay on Free Will*, pp. 162–163.

might be thought that one's act of will cannot, by its very nature, be caused by anyone else; if so, Frankfurt-style counterexamples are possible cases only if the potential intervention involved does not require someone's being able to cause another's act of will. In Frankfurt's original presentation of the objection, he offers a formula for constructing counterexamples (where Black and Jones₄ play the roles of Cosser and Gunnar, respectively),

> Let Black pronounce a terrible threat, and in this way force Jones₄ to perform the desired action and prevent him from performing a forbidden one. Let Black gives Jones₄ a potion, or put him under hypnosis, and in some such way as these generate in Jones₄ an irresistible inner compulsion to perform the act Black wants performed and to avoid others. Or let Black manipulate the minute processes of Jones₄'s brain and nervous system in some more direct way, so that causal forces running in and out of his synapses and along the poor man's nerves determine that he chooses to act in the one way and not in any other. Given any conditions under which it will be maintained that Jones₄ cannot do otherwise, in other words, let Black [be in a position to] bring it about that those conditions prevail.[47]

According to the proposal we are now considering, this general strategy does not yield a successful counterexample in cases in which it attributes to Black the ability to cause Jones₄'s acts of will.

It is clear what the defender of this proposal will suggest in place of (PAP), namely,

(PAPW) Necessarily, for every person S and act of will A, S is morally responsible for performing A only if S could have refrained from performing A.

According to this view, moreover, it is necessary that an agent's act is free only if it is an act of the agent's will or it is an action of the agent which is caused by an act of the agent's will. Thus, my willing to raise my hand is a free action, and since it causes my raising my hand, the latter is a free action, too. But if this is right, then if (PAPW) is true, so is (13). For if no one is ever able to do anything other than what he or she does do, then no one ever engages in an

---

47. Frankfurt, "Alternative Possibilities and Moral Responsibility," pp. 835–836.

act of will; and if no one ever engages in an act of will, no one ever performs a free action.

I find this defense of (13) attractive but not entirely successful. The reason is that it is not obvious that no one can cause another's act of will. In fact, a strand in the Christian tradition assumes that God can cause someone to will something. Of course, if God does cause someone else's act of will, it would not be a *free* act of will, just as any act that God causes (other than his own) is not a free act. But that does not mean that God *cannot* cause acts of will in others.

One source of the idea that God can cause others' acts of will is Psalm 51:10, where the psalmist prays, "Create a pure heart in me, O God, and give me a new and steadfast spirit."[48] This theme is repeated in Augustine's famous prayer, "Give me chastity and continence, but not yet,"[49] which, but for its final retraction, requests God to change his will, to ensure that Augustine no longer wills that which is unchaste or incontinent.[50] As Eleonore Stump suggests in connection with this passage, "it is a fact well-attested in religious literature that people who find it next to impossible to will what (they believe) they ought to will may nonetheless find it in themselves to will that God alters their wills."[51] Presumably such people do not will for something impossible.[52] But if God can change someone's will, then, with God in the role of Ridley, it is easy to construct a Frankfurt-style counterexample to (PAPW).

If God is the cause of a person's act of will, then the person is not

48. Compare a versification of this line, "Gracious God my heart renew / Make my spirit right and true," which appears to ask God to make the petitioner do what is right.

49. Augustine, *Confessions,* bk. VIII, chap. 7.

50. A similar sentiment, without the retraction, is expressed by John Donne: "Batter my heart, three-personed God; for You / As yet but knock, breathe, shine, and seek to mend; / That I may rise and stand, o'erthrow me, and bend / Your force, to break, blow, burn, and make me new. / . . . for I, / Except you enthrall me, never shall be free, / Nor ever chaste, except You ravish me." I owe this reference to Eleonore Stump.

51. Eleonore Stump, "Evil," lecture presented at the 1986 Summer Institute in Philosophy of Religion, Bellingham, Washington.

52. Compare Aquinas: "The will . . . can be moved by two things. First, by its object . . . ; secondly, by that agent which moves the will inwardly to will, and this is none other than either the will itself or God." *S.T.,* Ia–IIae, 80, 1. Cf. Ia–IIae, 9, 6, and Ia–IIae, 109, 2, *ad* 1.

the cause. That fact can be used to construct one final variant of (PAP).

(PAPC)   Necessarily, for every person S and act of will A such that
         S causes A, S is morally responsible for performing A only
         if S could have refrained from causing A.

It seems to me that (PAPC) is immune to Frankfurt-style counterexamples. Clearly it is not subject to any that we have considered thus far, for in each of those cases the agent could have refrained from causing his act of will. But if (PAPC) is true, it can be used to defend (13).

We noted above that if God causes a person's act of will, the act is not a free one. Presumably the only way in which an act of will is free is if the agent himself or herself causes it. And if an agent freely causes his or her own act of will, then even if another agent lurks in the area prepared to cause it if the agent does not, the first agent must have the ability to refrain from causing the act. In addition, any act of an agent is free only if it is an act of will caused by the agent or if it is caused by such an act. But then if (PAPC) is true, so is (13). For if no one is ever able to do anything other than what he or she does do, then no one ever causes an act of will, and if no one ever causes an act of will, then no one ever performs a free action.[53]

This defense of (13) seems to me to be correct; thus, I am unable to reject (13). But this defense of (13) appeals to the doctrine of agent causation, a doctrine that is surely controversial. I will not mind, therefore, if anyone is unpersuaded by my defense of (13). My goal, after all, is to find a reason to reject the argument for the incompatibility of divine foreknowledge and human free action that has (13) as one of its premises, and anyone who is justified in rejecting (13) will be justified in rejecting that argument. But I am also interested in discovering the truth about this argument, and it does not seem to me that the truth about the argument is that premiss (13) is false. I must look elsewhere for a flaw in the argument.

53. The view presented in this paragraph is similar to the view William Rowe attributes to Thomas Reid. See Rowe's 1987 presidential address to the Central Division of the American Philosophical Association, "Two Concepts of Freedom," *Proceedings and Addresses of the American Philosophical Association* 61 (1987):43–64.

4

Accidental Necessity

1. Foreknowledge and Fatalism

It is time to turn our attention to (C*), the remaining premiss of the argument for the incompatibility of divine foreknowledge and human free action. After our detour through the thicket of issues involved with the ability to do otherwise, we begin by considering again what that argument is. It is:

Argument B

(C*) There is a concept of accidental necessity satisfying the following conditions: (i) for all times t_1 and t_2 such that t_1 is earlier than t_2 and for every proposition p, if at t_1 God believes p, then at t_2 the proposition, *At t_1 God believes p*, is accidentally necessary, (ii) for every time t and for all propositions p and q, if p is accidentally necessary at t, p entails q, and it is possible that q is false, then q is accidentally necessary at t, and (iii) for every time t_1 and proposition p, if p is accidentally necessary at t_1, then there is no person S, action A, and time t_2 at least as late as t_1 such that S can do A at t_2 and if S were to do A at t_2 then p would be false.

(12*) Necessarily, if (C*) then divine foreknowledge of human actions is incompatible with anyone being able to do anything other than what he or she does do.

(13) Necessarily, if no one is ever able to do anything other than what he or she does do, then no one ever acts freely.

Therefore,

(14*) Necessarily, if (C*) then divine foreknowledge of human actions is incompatible with anyone ever acting freely. (12*) (13)

Therefore,

(19) Divine foreknowledge of human actions is incompatible with anyone ever acting freely. (C*) (14*)

In Section 3 of the last chapter we concluded that (12*) is correct, and in Section 4 of that chapter I argued against an attempt to discredit (13) and conceded that it seems true. That leaves us with (C*). Is (C*) true? There is no satisfactory way to investigate this question short of a detailed examination of concrete proposals as to exactly what the concept of accidental necessity amounts to. Accordingly, I devote several sections of this chapter to that project. First, however, I note that a simple and straightforward way of defending (C*) does not succeed.

We began to consider the topic of accidental necessity in Section 2 of the previous chapter, where we noted that Aquinas held that it applied to propositions "signified as past," and we also saw that it is connected to the idea that the past is somehow "fixed." Perhaps, then, *every* proposition about the past is accidentally necessary, in which case (C*) may be seen as an instance of a more general principle:

(F) There is a concept of accidental necessity satisfying the following conditions: (i) for all times t_1 and t_2 such that t_1 is earlier than t_2 and for every proposition p, if at t_1 p is true, then at t_2 p is accidentally necessary, (ii) for every time t and for all propositions p and q, if p is accidentally necessary, p entails q, and it is possible that q is false, then q is accidentally necessary, and (iii) for every time t_1 and proposition p, if p is accidentally necessary at t_1, then there is no person S, action A, and time t_2 at least as late as t_1 such that

S can do A at t_2 and if S were to do A at t_2 then p would be
false.

(F) differs from (C*) only in the first feature it attributes to accidental necessity. According to (F), *every* proposition true in the past is
subsequently accidentally necessary. The first condition specified by
(C*), then, is the special case in which the proposition true in the
past is a proposition reporting what God believed at some past time.

Fatalism, as Peter van Inwagen defines it, is the doctrine that it is a
conceptual truth that no one is able to act otherwise than he or she
does.[1] And a "fatalistic argument in a narrow sense" is, according to
van Inwagen, an argument for fatalism that depends upon the notions of time and truth.[2] It is easy to see that (F) lends itself to a
fatalistic argument. Consider the following variant of the argument
we used in Section 2 of the last chapter. Let us assume that

> (20) It was true eighty years ago that Jones will mow his lawn
>   tomorrow.

Now (20) is about the past, so by clause (i) of (F),

> (21) It is accidentally necessary that it was true eighty years ago
>   that Jones will mow his lawn tomorrow.

Since (20) entails

> (9) Jones will mow his lawn tomorrow

(and (9) is contingent), it follows from (21) and clause (ii) of (F) that

> (10) It is accidentally necessary that Jones will mow his lawn
>   tomorrow.

Finally, it follows from (10) and clause (iii) of (F) that

> (12) It is not within Jones's power to refrain from mowing his
>   lawn tomorrow.

1. Peter van Inwagen, *An Essay on Free Will* (Oxford: Oxford University Press,
1983), p. 23.
2. Ibid.

So from (F) and the past truth of (9), it follows that Jones is unable to refrain from mowing his lawn, and since this argument can be generalized, it follows from (F) and the past truth about any future action that it will be performed, that no one can do other than what he or she will do. That is, (F) provides an argument for fatalism. I think that is sufficient reason for rejecting (F), and if (C*) is supposed to be supported by being an instance of (F), that is slim support indeed. Of course, some philosophers have accepted fatalism, and examining their arguments in favor of it is a worthwhile philosophical activity.[3] But we may legitimately decline to engage in it here. We are also entitled to reject any argument for the incompatibility of divine foreknowledge and human free action which entails fatalism independently of premises about divine omniscience.

A natural way of attempting to preserve the insight that the past is fixed is to modify (F) and hold that not all propositions apparently about the past are accidentally necessary. This idea may be developed in several ways. One way is to concede that (20) is true and about the past, but to hold that it is one of a collection of exceptions to the claim that all true propositions about the past are accidentally necessary. Another is to hold that although (20) is *apparently* about the past, it is not *really* or *strictly* about the past. The second approach seems to have been taken by Ockham. He wrote:

> Some propositions are about the present as regards both their wording and their subject matter (*secundum vocem et secundum rem*). Where such [propositions] are concerned, it is universally true that every true proposition about the present [has corresponding to it] a necessary one about the past—e.g., 'Socrates is seated,' 'Socrates is walking,' 'Socrates is just,' and the like.
>
> Other propositions are about the present as regards their wording only and are equivalently about the future, since their truth depends on the truth of propositions about the future. Where such [propositions] are concerned, the rule that every true proposition about the present has [corresponding to it] a necessary one about the past is not true.[4]

3. See ibid., chap. 2.
4. William Ockham, *Predestination, God's Foreknowledge, and Future Contingents*, trans. Marilyn McCord Adams and Norman Kretzmann, 2d ed. (Indianapolis: Hackett, 1983), pp. 46–47.

Presumably Ockham would make a similar distinction with respect to propositions apparently about the past; he would say, that is, that some propositions are about the past "as regards their wording only and are equivalently about the future." Included in this category is (20), since its truth depends upon the truth of a proposition about the future, namely (9). Following recent tradition, we can put this point by saying that (20) expresses a "soft" fact about the past as opposed to a "hard" fact about the past.[5]

Claiming that (F) holds only for propositions expressing hard facts about the past avoids fatalism; since (20) is not a hard fact about the past, it is a mistake to take (F) to apply to it. This is a sensible position to take, but it leaves the defense of (C*) incomplete. It now cannot plausibly be claimed that (C*) is a simple instance of (F). Given that (F) must be restricted to hard facts about the past, (C*) is an instance of (F) only if propositions reporting God's past beliefs are hard facts about the past, and that remains to be established. A thorough investigation of this issue requires that we examine the attempt to delineate hard and soft facts about the past.

2. Accidental Necessity

Ockhamists agree that hard facts about the past are accidentally necessary, but they hold that God's past beliefs about future actions are typically soft facts about the past and, thus, not accidentally necessary. Morever, even those who hold that claims about the necessity of the past can be used to show that divine foreknowledge of human action is incompatible with human free action recognize the distinction between hard and soft facts about the past; otherwise they would be led into fatalism.[6] Ironically, however, it is the compatibilists who have expended the most effort in trying make this distinction precise,[7] despite the fact that it is the incompatibilist

5. Nelson Pike, "Of God and Freedom: A Rejoinder," *Philosophical Review* 75 (1966):369–379.

6. See ibid. and Pike's subsequent essays. See also the papers by Fischer and Hasker cited in chap. 3, n. 19.

7. See the papers by Adams, Freddoso, Hoffman and Rosenkrantz, Plantinga, and Zemach and Widerker cited in chap. 3, n. 19. Incompatibilist exceptions to this claim include Hasker, who has a detailed account of the distinction (though based on the work of Freddoso), and, to a certain extent, Fisher, some of whose remarks can be developed into an account.

objector, after all, who affirms (C*); supporting (C*) would seem to require explaining and defending the relevant concept of accidental necessity. None of the accounts of accidental necessity with which I am familiar is, I believe, completely successful; the important point for our present purposes, however, is that, lacking such an account, we seem to have no reason to accept (C*). And if we have no reason to accept (C*), Argument B is a failure. Let us turn to a consideration of the attempt to demarcate hard and soft facts about the past.

There are two basic approaches to this problem. The first tries to find certain formal features of propositions which identifiy those propositions whose truth value does not depend in any way on what happens in the future. Contingently true propositions with those formal features are then alleged to be accidentally necessary. The second approach tries to identify accidentally necessary propositions by reference to the actual or possible abilities of agents to falsify them. The formal approach is dominant in recent literature,[8] and it offers the hope of uncovering a metaphysically deep reason for the asymmetry of our abilities with respect to the future and the past; however, it seems to require a treatment of great complexity. The ability approach seems more direct—whether a proposition is accidentally necessary depends simply on whether anyone is able, now or later and within certain constraints, to do something according to which it is false—but this very directness seems to threaten the polemical usefulness of the account. Someone who objects that the proposition that God believed in the past that Jones will mow his lawn tomorrow is now accidentally necessary is not likely to be persuaded by the reply that there is something Jones can do according to which this proposition is false and is thus not accidentally necessary. Still, problems with the formal approach often make the direct, ability approach seem more attractive. Nevertheless, we begin with the dominant tradition and examine some formal attempts to delineate accidental necessity.

An ingenious treatment has been proposed by Alfred Freddoso.[9]

---

8. Formalists include Adams, Freddoso, Hasker, Zemach and Widerker, and, presumably, Fischer. The ability approach is developed by Plantinga in "On Ockham's Way Out." (For full references see chap. 3, n. 19.)

9. Alfred Freddoso, "Accidental Necessity and Logical Determinism," *Journal of Philosophy* 80 (1983):257–278.

He begins with the idea that there are "immediate" propositions that, for any possible world and any time, determine what is true in that world at that time in a way independent of what is true in that world at any other time. For any world and time, the set of such immediate propositions true at that time Freddoso calls the *submoment* of the time. Then two worlds share the same history at a time *t* just in case they share the same submoments (in the same order) prior to *t*. And a proposition is accidentally necessary in a world at a time just in case it is contingent and true from then on in every world sharing the same history up to that time.[10]

Clearly the success of this strategy depends upon whether immediate propositions can be adequately characterized. Freddoso's treatment consists in developing a model theory for a language *L*. *L* contains lower-case letters, intended to represent propositions, truth-functional connectives, a modal operator, and tense operators (read, "It will be the case that . . ." and "It was the case that . . ."). We need not examine all of the details here; it is sufficient for our purposes that we take note of three restrictions Freddoso places on the interpretation of *L*. First, the proposition-letters ("atomic consitutents") "represent only propositions that may be expressed in English by grammatically present-tense sentences."[11] Other tenses are to represented by the application of the tense-operators. Second, "no proposition is represented by an atomic constituent of *L* if it is, intuitively, most properly represented in *L* by a formula which involves operations on *L*'s atomic constitutents."[12] This condition is intended to require that a proposition such as

(22) David correctly believes that Katie will at some time be in Rome

is not represented by an atomic proposition-letter but rather by a compound sentence such as "*p* and it will be the case that *q*." Finally, "no atomic constituent of *L* represents a proposition whose proper philosophical analysis contains quantifiers, unless those quantifiers fall within the scope of a propositional attitude."[13] This condition is

10. Ibid., p. 266.
11. Ibid., p. 269.
12. Ibid., pp. 269–270.
13. Ibid., pp. 270–271.

intended to insure that the atomic sentences of L represent neither an explicitly quantified proposition such as

(23) All manatees are ugly

nor a proposition such as

(24) Katie is omniscient,

which, presumably, is to be analyzed as, for every proposition p, if p is true then Katie knows p.

Freddoso proceeds by defining the property of temporal indifference for formulas of L:

(25) A is *temporally indifferent* iff either (a) A or its negation is not logically possible or (b) A, as well as its negation, is such that it (i) is true at some (w, t) where t is the first moment of w, and (ii) is true at some (w, t) where t is the last moment in w, and (iii) is true at some (w, t) where t is an intermediate moment in w.[14]

So the way for the truth value of a proposition at a given time to be independent of what happens at other times, if it is not necessary or impossible, is for it to be possible that the proposition is true at the first moment of time, possible for it to be true at the last moment of time, and possible for it to be true at an intermediate moment of time.[15]

14. Ibid., p. 272. Freddoso adds that a proposition is temporally indifferent just in case it is expressed by a temporally indifferent sentence of L. (Freddoso holds that propositions may change their truth value over time.)

15. It is important to realize that (20) does not require that temporally indifferent propositions be such that it is possible that they be true for only an instant. Zemach and Widerker appear to interpret Freddoso in this way, and they then object that propositions that Freddoso takes to be temporally indifferent are not ("Facts, Freedom and Foreknowledge," p. 24). Freddoso holds that *Socrates is drinking hemlock* is temporally indifferent. Adapting the criticism of Zemach and Widerker to this example, we may agree that it is not possible for this proposition to be true only for an instant. An instantaneous state of Socrates with hemlock in his throat would be Socrates' drinking hemlock only if it were preceded or followed by appropriate other states; otherwise it would be indistinguishable from states that would occur if Socrates were gargling with hemlock or if he were regurgitating hemlock. So if Socrates is drinking hemlock, there are either preceding moments or there are

Freddoso assumes that any temporally indifferent atomic sentence of L is immediate, but he denies that compound sentences expressing such temporally indifferent propositions as

(26) David is standing or Katie will at some time be in Rome

are immediate. So he extends the notion of immediacy to compound sentences in the following way. He takes S to be the set of temporally indifferent atomic sentences and $V(S)$ any valuation that assigns a classical truth-value to each of the members of S at a given (w, t). Then

> (27) A is *immediate* iff both (a) for any (w, t), if A is true at (w, t), then A is true at every (w^*, t^*) such that $V(S)$ at $(w^*, t^*) = V(S)$ at (w, t); and (b) if A is false at (w, t), then A is false at every (w^*, t^*) such that $V(S)$ at $(w^*, t^*) = V(S)$ at (w, t).[16]

Thus, the truth-value of immediate sentences depends only on the truth-values of their temporally indifferent atomic constituents. In particular, (26) turns out not to be immediate because its truth-value does not depend only on the truth-value of its sole atomic constituent, 'David is standing.'

With this definition of immediacy, the remaining steps of Freddoso's strategy are easy to carry out. A *submoment* for a pair (w, t) is the set of immediate formulas true at (w, t). Two worlds *share the same history at a time* just in case the same submoments are true in each at all prior times. And a proposition is accidentally necessary at (w, t) just in case it is contingently true in w at t and true at every later time in every world that shares the same history with w at t.[17]

This account seems to have the results Freddoso wants. Freddoso argues, for example, that "the past-tense proposition that Socrates

---

succeeding moments. It is not clear, however, that there would have to be *both* preceding and following moments (since there could be both a first moment of drinking and a last), but this latter claim is what is required to sustain the objection that *Socrates is drinking hemlock* is not temporally indifferent.

16. Freddoso, "Accidental Necessity and Logical Determinism," p. 273.

17. Ibid., pp. 274–276.

drank hemlock is now necessary *per accidens*, since the immediate proposition that Socrates is drinking hemlock is a member of some submoment which has already obtained."[18] Since this submoment has already occurred, it has already occurred in every world sharing a history with this world. Hence, the proposition that Socrates drank hemlock is now true in every such world and is, accordingly, accidentally necessary. And if it is now true that Jones will mow his lawn at t, some time tomorrow, say, there is an immediate proposition that Jones mows his lawn at t which has not yet been true and which, accordingly, is not a member of any submoment that has already occurred. So presumably there is a possible world that shares a history with this world until now but in which it is not true that Jones mows his lawn at t. Consequently, the proposition that Jones will mow his lawn at t is not true in every world sharing a history with the actual world until now, and so it is not accidentally necessary.

From the point of view of the theistic compatibilist, Freddoso's account has, moreover, the proper results with respect to (C*). The first feature that (C*) attributes to accidental necessity is that for all times t_1 and t_2 such that t_1 is earlier than t_2 and for every proposition p, if at t_1 God believes p, then at t_2 the proposition, *At t_1 God believes p*, is accidentally necessary. But on Freddoso's account, accidental necessity does not satisfy this condition. To see this, suppose that God believes that Jones will mow his lawn at t, as before, some time tomorrow. The proposition that

(28) God believes that Jones will mow his lawn at t

is not an immediate proposition; hence, it is not included in any submoments and, in particular, not in any submoments that have obtained before now. Accordingly, it need not be true in every world sharing a history with the actual world. The reason (28) is not an immediate proposition is that, given that God is essentially omniscient, it is not possible that (28) be true at a last moment of time; thus, it does not satisfy (25), the definition of temporal indifference. Nor does the truth-value of (28) at a given time depend only on the

18. Ibid., p. 276.

atomic propositions true then; accordingly, it does not satisfy (27), the definition of immediacy.[19]

Whether Freddoso's account is a completely adequate treatment of accidental necessity depends in part on whether he has successfully identified the class of immediate propositions. I believe, however, that (25), the definition of temporal indifference, is flawed. If it is, then so is (27), the definition of immediacy, which depends on (25). According to (25), for a contingent proposition to be temporally indifferent, it must be possible for it to be true at the first moment of time and it must be possible for it to be true at the last moment of time. But these conditions can be satisfied only if it is possible for there to *be* a first moment of time and possible for there to *be* a last moment of time. If this is not possible, there are no contingent temporally indifferent propositions; in that case submoments contain only necessary truths, every world shares a history with every other, and, since the only propositions true in every possible world are necessary truths, no propositions are accidentally necessary.

I do not find it at all obvious that it is possible for there to be first and last moments of time.[20] Here is one reason against that assumption. Some theists have affirmed that God is everlasting.[21] Perhaps

19. Freddoso himself does not give this argument. His explicit focus is on logical determinism rather than on theological determinism. He does suggest, however, that *God believes p* is equivalent to *God correctly believes p* and, thus, best represented by '*p* and God believes *p*,' in which case it is not represented by an atomic sentence of *L* (ibid., p. 270, n. 10). (Freddoso does not say whether the occurrence of 'God believes *p*' in his recommended translation is itself best represented by '*p* and God believes *p*,' and so on.) I shall continue to make use of the assumption that God is essentially omniscient. It is, I believe, a widespread, if not universal, commitment of classical theism; and it would be at best a minor victory for the incompatibilist objector to show only that inessential foreknowledge is incompatible with human free action, for then the theist could easily avoid the objection merely by holding God to be essentially omniscient. It is worth noting, moreover, that at least one incompatibilist objector, Nelson Pike, claims that the incompatibility obtains *only* on the assumption that God is essentially omniscient. See his "Divine Omniscience and Voluntary Action."

20. Cf. Plantinga, who takes it to be a "plausible (but widely disputed) assumption that necessarily, for any time *t* there is a time *t** eighty years prior to *t*." "On Ockham's Way Out," p. 249.

21. See, for example, Nicholas Wolterstorff, "God Everlasting," in *God and the Good: Essays in Honor of Henry Stob*, ed. C. J. Orlebeke and L. B. Smedes (Grand

they have meant that for every time *t* there is an earlier time at which God exists and there is a later time at which God exists (and there is no time at which God does not exist).[22] This view seems to be possible, in which case it is possible that time have no first or last moment. Of course, all (25) requires, in order for there to be contingent immediate propositions, is that it also be possible that time does have a first moment and possible that it has a last. I suppose some would supplement the claim that God is everlasting with the claims that God is essentially everlasting and necessarily existent. Such claims would be inconsistent, according to (25), with there being contingent immediate propositions. I do not wish to make my case against (25) depend upon these claims, however. All I have claimed thus far is that it is not obviously possible that time have first and last moments. Suppose, however, that this is possible. Then another problem looms for (25).

If it is possible that there be a first and a last moment of time, then there is a possible world in which there is a first moment and there is a last.[23] Consider some such world, *W*, a world in which time begins, some things happen, and then time ends. For the sake of the example, suppose that among the things that happen is that Jones mows his lawn at some intermediate time t_n. Consider, then, the proposition that

(29) *W* is actual.

Rapids, Mich.: Eerdmans, 1975), pp. 181–203; reprinted in *Contemporary Philosophy of Religion*, ed. Steven Cahn and David Shatz (New York: Oxford University Press, 1982), pp. 77–98. Other sources for this view are cited below in Chapter 6.

22. Philip Quinn has suggested (in correspondence) that God is everlasting just in case he exists at every time. On this interpretation, God can be everlasting even if there are first and last moments of time. This view also allows, however, that God can be everlasting even if there is no time at all. Quinn welcomes this consequence because it permits God's being essentially everlasting and necessarily existent to be compatible with there being no time. However, Quinn's account of *being everlasting* seems to allow that, if there are no times, God can be both everlasting and eternal (see Chapter 6); but these are usually taken to be contraries.

23. Freddoso is committed only to its being possible that there is a first moment and also to its being possible that there be a last moment. I assume that if these are both possible then it is possible that there is a first moment *and* a last moment. It seems to me bizarre to affirm that time could have a beginining and to affirm that it could have an end, but to claim that if it had one it could not have the other.

(29) is expressible by a present-tense English sentence. Moreover, given the limitations on the expressive capability of L, (29) does not seem more properly represented by operations on L's atomic constituents. Finally, it does not seem that the proper philosophical analysis of (29) requires quantifiers—indeed, it is plausible to think that (29) is not susceptible of analysis. Thus, (29) does not violate the three stipulations Freddoso places on the interpretation of L; accordingly, (29) seems to be represented by an atomic constituent of L. As we have seen, Freddoso holds that temporally indifferent atomic constituents of L are immediate. It remains to be shown, then, that (29) (or the sentence-letter representing it in L) is temporally indifferent. But that is easy to see. To be temporally indifferent (29) needs only to satisfy the conditions that it (i) is true at some (w, t) where t is the first moment of w, and (ii) is true at some (w, t) where t is the last moment in w, and (iii) is true at some (w, t) where t is an intermediate moment in w. But (29) is true at the first, the last, and every intermediate time in W, so clearly it satisfies these conditions. Hence, (29) is temporally indifferent, and since it is atomic, it is also immediate.

Note again that (29) is true at (W, t_1), where t_1 is the first moment of W. Thus, at every subsequent time in W, (29) is included in a past submoment. Consequently, (29) is true at every time in every world sharing a past history up to any time with W.[24] Also, since (29) is a contingent proposition—indeed, true in W and false in all other worlds—it satisfies, at every time in W, Freddoso's definition of accidental necessity. So in W, (29) is always accidentally necessary.

Now (29) entails every proposition that is true in W. By assumption,

(30) Jones mows his lawn at t_n

is true in W. So (29) entails (30). Call the submoment obtaining at (W, t_1) (where t_1 is the first moment of W) "A." We saw above that (29) is included in A. Since (29) entails (30), every world that has A for a submoment is a world in which (30) is ever thereafter true.

24. Given that (29) is included in every past submoment of W, the *only* world ever sharing a past history with W is W itself.

Accordingly, in W, (30) is at all times accidentally necessary.[25] More generally, in W every contingently true proposition is always accidentally necessary. So if it is possible for time to have a first and last moment, in any world in which it does, every contingently true proposition turns out, on Freddoso's account, to be accidentally necessary. That is surely an unwelcome consequence.

A final feature of Freddoso's account of accidental necessity is that it provides no reason for our thinking that it satisfies the third condition of (C*). This might be taken merely to show that (C*) is far from being established, but many would take it as showing instead that Freddoso's account does not succeed in capturing the notion of accidental necessity. The third condition of (C*) is that for every time t_1 and proposition p, if p is accidentally necessary at t_1, then there is no person S, action A, and time t_2 at least as late as t_1 such that S can do A at t_2 and if S were to do A at t_2 then p would be false. How could Freddoso's account of accidental necessity fail to satisfy this condition? If *Socrates drank hemlock* is now accidentally necessary, is there really some action A which someone now or later could do such that if A were done this proposition would have been false? Incredible as it may seem, for all anyone knows, there is such an action. Perhaps this point will be clearer if we appeal to an example Alvin Plantinga employs in this connection. He suggests that

> perhaps you will be confronted with a decision of great importance—so important that one of the alternatives is such that if you were to choose *it*, then the course of human history would have been quite different from what in fact it is. Furthermore, it is possible that if God had foreseen that you would choose *that* alternative, he would have acted very differently. Perhaps he would have created different persons; perhaps, indeed, he would not have created [Socrates]. So it is possible that there is an action such that it is within your power to perform and such that if you were to perform it, then God would not have created [Socrates].[26]

---

25. Freddoso may try to block this inference by claiming that (30) is a "tensed" proposition and therefore true *only* at t_n. Cf. "Accidental Necessity and Logical Determinism," p. 258. In that case we may restate the argument with (30) prefixed with "It was, is now, or will be the case that. . . ."

26. Plantinga, "On Ockham's Way Out," p. 257.

But if this is the case, then you have it within your power to do something such that if you were to do it then *Socrates drank hemlock* would have been false. It seems unlikely, of course, that many of us face such momentous decisions, but if even one person is or will be in this situation, then the third condition of (C*) is not satisfied on Freddoso's account. And I think we have no reason to believe that *no one* is or will be in such a situation. Accordingly, there is no reason to think that Freddoso's account of accidental necessity satisfies the third condition of (C*)

3. Another Formal Approach

Eddy Zemach and David Widerker try to distinguish hard and soft facts about the past in a way that does not require immediate propositions (about whose existence they are skeptical.)[27] Zemach and Widerker appeal instead to classes of propositions that are restricted in a certain way to the past. Their approach involves introducing two sets of primitive locutions and then defining several other concepts in terms of them. First, they use 'TRUE$_W$' to denote, for a given world W, the set of all propositions true in W. Second, they use 'ANH$_t$' to represent, for any time t, the proposition that there are no times after t.

Next Zemach and Widerker introduce 'PAST$_{(t, W)}$' to stand for the set of propositions p such that p is a member of TRUE$_W$ and the conjunction of p and ANH$_t$ is possible. Finally, 'C$_{(W, t)}$' denotes the set of worlds W^* such that W^* shares the same ontology with W and PAST$_{(t, W^*)}$ = PAST$_{(t, W)}$.[28] C$_{(W, t)}$ is thus the set of worlds that, to use Freddoso's term, "share the same history with" W up to t.

---

27. Zemach and Widerker, "Facts, Freedom and Foreknowledge," pp. 19–28.

28. I do not understand the restriction that W and W^* share the same ontology. I take it this means that the same things exist in both W and W^*. Suppose, for the sake of example only, that I will father another child; presumably that child, then, is included in the ontology of the actual world. No doubt, however, it is within my power to refrain from fathering another child. So there are worlds like this one up to the present in which I do not have any more children. Those worlds (or at least some of them—maybe in some that child is fathered by someone else) do not share the same ontology with this world. In fact, it appears that no world in which that child does not exist shares the same ontology with this world. So the existence of that child is future necessary, and that despite the fact that it is within my power to prevent his or her conception. The obvious repair is to require only that W and W^*

Zemach and Widerker then offer the following definitions.[29]

(FC) A proposition p is *future contingent* in W at t iff there is a world W^* in $C_{(W,\,t)}$ such that the truth value of p in W^* differs from its truth value in W.

(FN) A proposition p is *future necessary* in W at t iff there is no world W^* in $C_{(W,\,t)}$ such that the truth value of p in W^* differs from its truth value in W.

(SF) A proposition p expresses a *soft fact* about the past in W at t iff (i) p is of the form ϕt_i, (ii) p is true in W, (iii) t_i is earlier than t, and (iv) p is future contingent at t.

(HF) A proposition p expresses a *hard fact* about the past in W at t iff (i) p is of the form ϕt_i, (ii) p is true in W, (iii) t_i is earlier than t, and (iv) p is future necessary at t.

Suppose again that

(28) God believes that Jones will mow his lawn at t,

where t is some time tomorrow. Now (28) is not, according to (HF), a hard fact about the past, simply because it is not of the form ϕt_i. We should therefore consider instead something like

(31) In 1980 God believes that Jones will mow his lawn at t,

which we may assume to be true. Given the assumption that God is essentially omniscient, (31) does not now satisfy (HF), either. For (31) to be true, given God's essential omniscience, there must be the time t tomorrow, later than now, at which Jones mows his lawn. So (31) is not a member of $\text{PAST}_{(\text{now, the actual world})}$, because it is not possible that (31) is true but there are no times after the present. But then (31) is not included in every world that shares the same history with the actual world up to now. Thus, (31) does not satisfy (HF).

So if a proposition is accidentally necessary just in case it is a hard

share the same ontology up to t, but then it is hard to see what this adds to the remaining condition that $\text{PAST}_{(t,\,W^*)} = \text{PAST}_{(t,\,W)}$.

29. Ibid., p. 22. I have supplied the needed index 'at t' to the fourth clauses of (SF) and (HF), and I have made several minor and inessential changes in these definitions.

fact about the past, Zemach and Widerker's account turns out not to help the defender of (C*), since on this theory accidental necessity does not satisfy the first condition specified by (C*): God's past beliefs are not accidentally necessary.

It is tempting to take this result just as further evidence that accidental necessity does not satisfy all the conditions specified by (C*), but as in the case of Freddoso's definition, there is also some reason to be skeptical about whether this account adequately captures the idea of accidental necessity. In fact, two of the drawbacks of Freddoso's account are shared by this one. First, if any proposition is a member of $PAST_{(t, w)}$, for some world and time, then it is possible that there is a last moment of time. It is not obvious, however, that this is possible. If it is not, then all worlds with the same ontology share the same past, so the only propositions that are hard facts about the past will be propositions specifying what exists. On the other hand, if it is possible for there to be a last moment of time, then by the argument of the previous section, in any world in which there is a last moment of time all contingent truths of the form ϕt_i are accidentally necessary. Second, it is not at all clear that Zemach and Widerker's account of accidental necessity satisfies the third condition of (C*). We have been given no reason to think that just because a proposition is future necessary—despite that imposing title—no one can act in such a way that the proposition would have been false.

Even if Zemach and Widerker's proposal can avoid these difficulties, it has other flaws.[30] For one thing, the restriction of hard facts to propositions of the form ϕt_i means that being a hard fact about the past is not closed under entailment or under conjunction. Thus, if t is the time at which Socrates drank hemlock,

(32) Socrates drank hemlock at t

is now a hard fact about the past. But since the following propositions are not of the right form, neither

(33) There is a time t' such that Socrates drank hemlock at t'

---

30. In order to give various examples of hard facts, I assume, for the remainder of this section, that it is possible for there to be a last moment of time.

nor

> (34) It was, is, or will be the case that Socrates exists

is a hard fact, despite being entailed by (32). And if t^* is the time at which Plato was born, then

> (35) Plato was born at t^*

is now a hard fact. But the conjunction of (32) and (35) is not of the form ϕt_i, so it does not qualify as a hard fact.[31]

Finally, if it is true now (in 1989), for example, that

> (36) It is not the case that a Republican will be elected president in 1992,

then (36) is now (in 1989) future necessary. For (36) is consistent with ANH_{1989}, that is, it is consistent with the claim that there are no times after the present. Accordingly, if (36) is true, it is included in every world sharing the same past with the actual world up to now and, thus, is future necessary.[32]

Zemach and Widerker try to avoid this objection by claiming that, "given the truth of [ANH_{1989}], '199[2]' fails of reference, and therefore [(36)] is truth-valueless." Apparently they hold that if (36) lacks a truth-value, then so does

> (37) It is possible that (36) and ANH_{1989},

or, at least, that (37) is not true; for if (37) is not true, then (36) is not future necessary. Note that even if this reply were correct, it would

31. Zemach and Widerker give examples of propositions like the conjunction of (32) and (35) which they regard as hard facts, so perhaps the interpretation of the canonical form (ϕt_i) can be modified accordingly. But, where t is the time Socrates drank hemlock and t^* is the time Plato was born, the proposition that *At t, t^* was past* is a hard fact and together with (32) and (35) entails *Plato was born before Socrates drank hemlock*, but Zemach and Widerker explicitly deny that propositions of this form (lacking temporal indices) are hard facts.

32. If we modify (36) to obtain a proposition of canonical form, say

> (36*) In 1957 it was true that it is not the case that a Republican will be elected president in 1992,

we have an example of a proposition that meets Zemach and Widerker's definition of a hard fact about the past but that should not.

not block related objections, for example, that on Zemach and Widerker's account

> (38) It is not the case that a Republican is elected president twelve years after Reagan was first elected president

is future necessary if true. But Zemach and Widerker's response to (36) is not correct. Perhaps it is true that if ANH_{1989} were true, then '1992' would lack a referent. That fact, however, does not discredit (37). Surely

> (39) It is possible that there are no people and it is not the case that Socrates drank hemlock,

despite the fact that if there were no people then 'Socrates' would lack a referent. The point is that there is such a proposition as *It is not the case that Socrates drank hemlock*, and there would have been such a proposition even if Socrates did not exist.[33] Similarly, there is such a proposition as (36), and there would be such a proposition even if there were no year 1992. Accordingly, Zemach and Widerker do not succeed in defending their account against this objection.

4. A Final Formal Approach

John Fischer makes some claims that suggest another formal approach to the distinction between hard and soft facts. He writes,

> Consider the fact that Caesar dies 2009 years prior to Saunders' writing his paper. What lies behind our view that this fact is not a hard fact about 44 B.C.? We might say that it is a soft fact about 44 B.C. because one and the same physical process would have counted as Caesar's dying 2009 years before Saunders' writing his paper, if Saunders wrote his paper in 1965, and would *not* have counted as Caesar's dying 2009 years prior to Saunders' writing his paper, if Saunders hadn't written his paper in 1965. This captures the "future dependence" of soft facts; a soft fact is a fact *in virtue* of events which occur in the future.

33. See Alvin Plantinga, "On Existentialism," *Philosophical Studies* 44 (1983):1–20, and "Replies to My Colleagues," in *Alvin Plantinga,* ed. James Tomberlin and Peter van Inwagen (Dordrecht: D. Reidel, 1985), pp. 314–327.

Similarly, suppose that Smith knew at T_1 that Jones would do X at T_2. Smith's knowledge is a soft fact about T_1 because one and the same state of Smith's mind (at T_1) would count as knowledge if Jones did X at T_2 and would not count as knowledge if Jones didn't do X at T_2. Exactly the same sort of future dependence explains why both facts—the fact about Caesar's death and the facts about Smith's knowledge—are soft facts.

Thus, an incompatibilist might insist on the following sort of constraint on an account of the hard fact/soft fact distinction: the only way in which God's belief at T_1 about Jones at T_2 could be a soft fact about the past relative to T_2 would be if one and the same state of mind of the person who was God at T_1 would count as one belief if Jones did X at T_2, but a different belief (or not a belief at all) if Jones did not do X at T_2. But it is implausible to suppose that one and the same state of mind of the person who was God at T_1 would count as different beliefs given different behavior by Jones at T_2.[34]

Despite the somewhat tentative character of Fischer's presentation ("an incompatibilist might insist on the following sort of constraint"), it is clear, I believe, that Fischer does intend to endorse a proposal contained in this passage, for he later asserts that "the constraint I have proposed captures the incompatibilist's notion of the fixity of the past."[35] Thus, we should attempt to evaluate Fischer's proposal. That requires, in the first place, determining what the proposal is.

Unfortunately, Fischer does not make explicit what principle he thinks these examples illustrate. I have a suggestion, but it is complicated, and I cannot be confident that Fischer means to endorse it. In the first example, that of Caesar's dying occurring 2009 years before Saunders's writing his paper, Fischer refers to a certain physical process. That is not a promising approach to the treatment of God's past belief, which is certainly not a physical process. In the second example, that of Smith's knowing at t_1 that Jones will mow his lawn at t_2, however, Fischer speaks instead of a mental state. Perhaps the concept of a concrete event encompasses both particular

34. John Fischer, "Freedom and Foreknowledge," *Philosophical Review* 92 (1983):76–77. Fischer realizes (p. 71) that only 2008 years separate Caesar's death in 44 B.C. and Saunders's writing his paper in 1965. I follow Fischer in the fiction that it is 2009 years.

35. Ibid., p. 78.

physical processes and particular mental states. Interpreting Fischer's proposal in terms of concrete events would allow us to understand Fischer's talk of "counting as" as talk of event tokens *instantiating* event types or states of affairs. Developing this idea, we can try to explicate Fischer's principle as:

> (40) A proposition p is a soft fact about a time t iff p is true at t and there is a concrete event e, a contingent proposition q, a state of affairs S, and a time t' such that (i) e occurred at t, (ii) t is in the past, (iii) e is an instance of S, (iv) the conjunction of p and e occurs at t entails q, (v) q is wholly about t', (vi) t' is in the future, (vii) necessarily, p is true iff S obtains, and (viii) if q were false then e would still have occurred but it would not have been an instance of S.[36]

To see how (40) applies to the first example we may observe that p is the proposition that Caesar dies 2009 years before Saunders's writing his paper, S is the state of affairs of Caesar's dying 2009 years before Saunders's writing his paper, e is the concrete event of Caesar's death, q is the proposition that Saunders writes his paper in 1965, and t and t' are 44 B.C. and 1965, respectively. Under this interpretation, conditions (i) through (viii) of (40) seem to be satisfied and thus, according to (40), the proposition that Caesar dies 2009 years before Saunders's writing his paper is a soft fact about 44 B.C.

Since (40) is designed to accommodate the claim that Smith's knowing at t_1 that Jones will mow his lawn at t_2 is a soft fact about t_1, it is clear that Fischer holds that cases of past knowledge (and, no doubt, past correct belief) about the future can be soft facts about the past. In the case of Smith's knowing at t_1 that Jones will mow his lawn at t_2 there is, on Fischer's account, a particular mental event of Smith's, m, say, having these features: m is Smith's believing that Jones will mow his lawn at t_2; in virtue of the truth about Jones and the justifaction Smith has, m is an instance of Smith's knowing at t_1 that Jones will mow his lawn at t_2; but if it were false that Jones mows his lawn at t_2, then m would still have occurred, but it would

---

36. Fischer does not use the expression 'is wholly about t.' I do not see how to formulate the principle without some such device for insuring that q be about the future. In addition, Fischer's remarks suggest that he would add an additional clause: (ix) if q were true then e would occur and it would be an instance of S. Since (ix) appears to be entailed by the assumption that p is true together with conditions (i), (iii), and (iv), I do not formally add it to (34).

not have been an instance of Smith's knowing at t_1 that Jones will mow his lawn at t_2. Given these claims, it is easy to see that if the proposition that Smith knows at t_1 that Jones will mow his lawn at t_2 is true, it satisfies (40).

But Fischer claims that God's past beliefs about future free action do not satisfy (40). Suppose that, like Smith,

(41) God believes at t_1 that Jones will mow his lawn at t_2.

Then, according to Fischer, there must be a mental event of God's, m^*, which occurs at t_1 and which is an instance of God's believing at t_1 that Jones will mow his lawn at t_2. Fisher denies, however,

(42) If Jones were not to mow his lawn at t_2 then m^* would occur but would not be an instance of God's believing at t_1 that Jones will mow his lawn at t_2.

He claims, as we have seen, that "it is implausible that one and the same state of mind of the person who was God at T_1 would count as different beliefs given different behavior by Jones at T_2." Even if this contention is correct, it does not follow, however, that (41) fails to satisfy (40); the most that follows is that *God's believing at t_1 that Jones will mow his lawn at t_2* is not a specification for S in (40) in virtue of which (41) is a soft fact. That leaves it open that the right-hand side of (40) is satisfied with some other choice of instances for its existential quantifiers. Still, this is certainly the expected way for (41) to satisfy (40), if it does; so we should consider whether Fischer's denial of (42) is justified.

It seems to me that in order to deny (42), Fischer assumes that if m^* is an instance of *God's believing at t_1 that Jones will mow his lawn at t_2*, it is so essentially. Why, if Jones does not mow his lawn at t_2, would it be false that m^* occurs but is not an instance of *God's believing at t_1 that Jones will mow his lawn at t_2*? That m^* is essentially an instance of this state of affairs would be a decisive and effective reason. However, concrete events, if there are such things, are so poorly understood that it seems impossible to tell what nontrivial essential properties they have.[37] Why could not m^* be the state of God's believing every truth? In that case, if Jones mows his lawn at

---

37. See Edward Wierenga and Richard Feldman, "Identity Conditions and Events," *Canadian Journal of Philosophy* 11 (1981):77–93.

t_2 then $m*$ is an instance of *God's believing at t_1 that Jones will mow his lawn at t_2*, but if Jones were not to mow his lawn at t_2 then $m*$ would be an instance of *God's believing at t_1 that Jones will not mow his lawn at t_2*. Given the obscurity of what is essential to concrete events, Fischer's case against (42) is inconclusive. In that case, however, it is not clear that (41) is not a soft fact about t_1. So it is not clear that the first condition of (C*) is satisfied.

Finally, Fischer's account shares a defect with the formal proposals of Freddoso and of Zemach and Widerker. It is not clear that on Fischer's account no one has it within his or her power so to act according to which a proposition that is a hard fact about the past would have been false instead.[38] Accordingly, there is no reason to think that Fischer's proposal satisfies the third condtion of (C*), either.

5. Accidental Necessity and Ability

There are at least two morals to be drawn from the discussion of the last three sections. The first is that leading attempts to define accidental necessity by reference to formal features of propositions, or of concrete events and the states of affairs they exemplify, seem not to capture adequately the idea of accidental necessity. The second is that, even if the first moral is mistaken, these accounts provide no reason to think that accidental necessity satisfies the three conditions specified by (C*). Let us turn, then, to an alternative approach that attempts to define accidental necessity by reference to the powers or abilities of agents.

Plantinga provides a proposal of this sort. To understand it, we need first to look at two concepts on which it depends. The first is that of an action one can *directly* perform, that is, "perform without having to perform some other action in order to perform it."[39] Plantinga tentatively endorses Chisholm's claim that undertakings or endeavorings are the only actions you and I can perform directly.[40] Second, an "action A is basic for a person S if and only if there is an action $A*$ that meets two conditions: first, S can directly

---

38. See the discussion at the end of Section 2 above.
39. Plantinga, "On Ockham's Way Out," p. 260.
40. Roderick Chisholm, *Person and Object* (La Salle, Ill.: Open Court, 1976), p. 85.

perform $A*$, and secondly, S's being in normal conditions and his directly performing $A*$ is causally sufficient for his performing A."[41] Plantinga adds that by normal conditions he means to include "the absence of pathological conditions as well as the absence of such external hindrances as being locked in a steamer trunk or having my hands tied behind my back."[42] Thus, raising my hand is a basic action for me since I can undertake to raise my arm and my doing so in normal circumstances is causally sufficient for my raising my arm.

Next, Plantinga offers the following:

> (43) p is accidentally necessary at t if and only if p is true at t and it is not possible both that p is true at t and that there exists an agent S and an action A such that (1) A is basic for S, (2) S has the power at t or later to perform A, and (3) necessarily, if S were to perform A at t or later, then p would have been false.[43]

Now (43) is supposed to have the consequence that God's past foreknowledge and forebelief need not be accidentally necessary. Suppose that

> (44) Eighty years ago God foreknew that Jones will not mow his lawn tomorrow

is true. In this case Plantinga apparently believes that there is something Jones can do directly tomorrow, namely, endeavor to mow his lawn, which is such that his doing it in normal circumstances is causally sufficient for his mowing his lawn. Hence, there is a basic action, mowing his lawn, that will be within Jones's power tomorrow and that is such that, necessarily, if Jones were to do it, (44) would have been false. Hence, (44) is not now accidentally neces-

---

41. Ibid.

42. This exclusion of pathological conditions suggests that walking, for example, is a basic action for someone who is paralyzed, despite the fact that such a person is unable to walk. Thus, on Plantinga's account, an action can be basic for a person and yet the person is unable to perform it.

43. Ibid., p. 261. Plantinga goes on to defend a revision of (43) designed to accommodate joint ventures freely undertaken; we need not consider that complication.

sary. So according to (43), accidental necessity does not satisfy the first condition of (C*).[44] This is a consequence Plantinga welcomes, but (43) has other, less desirable features.

The first is minor and easy to repair. It is that (43) allows logically or metaphysically necessary propositions to count as accidentally necessary. This result is easily avoided by modifying (43) to require not merely that accidentally necessary propositions be true but that they be contingently true.

Two other problems are more difficult to resolve. The first is that certain troublesome disjunctive propositions count as accidentally necessary when they should not. Suppose it is true, for example, that

(45) Either Socrates did not drink hemlock or Jones will not mow his lawn at t,

where t is some time tomorrow. Since Socrates did drink hemlock, the truth of (45) depends upon its future-oriented right disjunct. Accordingly, (45) should not now be taken to be accidentally necessary. However, according to (43), (45) is accidentally necessary. No one has the power to perform a basic action that entails that (45) is false. In particular, although Jones has the power to mow his lawn at t, his doing so does not entail that (45) is false, since there are worlds in which he mows his lawn at t but in which Socrates did not drink hemlock.[45]

Second, accidental necessity is not, according to (43), closed under conjunction. That is, (43) allows that a pair of propositions are each accidentally necessary although their conjunction is not. But if

44. On the assumption that God is essentially omniscient, an exactly analogous argument is available to show that God's past forebelief need not now be accidentally necessary. Notice, however, that in both cases this result depends upon its being possible that mowing his lawn is a basic action for Jones. Perhaps the term "normal conditions" is broad enough to include the existence of grass and the proper functioning of Jones's mower. If so, then if Jones is in normal conditions and endeavors to mow his lawn, he succeeds; so mowing his lawn would be a basic action.

45. Plantinga is aware of this objection. He replies by claiming that he is not giving an "analysis of our preanalytic notion of accidental necessity" but only stating a condition that propositions strictly about the past satisfy whereas those about the future often do not (ibid., p. 269, n. 30). I consider below a proposal Plantinga makes to deal with this objection.

accidental necessity is not closed under conjunction, then it seems hard to justify the claim that accidental necessity is a "well-behaved" modality.[46] To see that (43) does not require conjunctive closure, suppose that

(46) Everything Smith believed yesterday is true

and

(47) Yesterday Smith believed that Jones will not mow his lawn at t (some time tomorrow)

are both true. Clearly (47) ought to satisfy (43) and it does (given that Smith is not essentially omniscient); no one can now or later perform a basic act the performing of which entails that (47) is false. But (46) satisfies (43), as well, and for a similar reason. No one can now or later perform a basic act the performing of which entails that (46) is false. Perhaps the act of mowing his lawn at t will be basic and within Jones's power tomorrow. But Jones's performing that act does not *entail* that (46) is false; for there are worlds in which Jones performs it and in which Smith had different, but nevertheless all true, beliefs yesterday. So according to (43), (46) and (47) are both accidentally necessary. Their conjunction is not, however, since there is a basic action for Jones, namely, Jones's mowing his lawn at t, which is such that, necessarily, if Jones were to mow his lawn at t, at least one of (46) and (47) would be false.

In response to the first of these objections Plantinga somewhat tentatively offers the following proposal. First, he says that a proposition "p is *past* accidentally necessary if and only if p is a proposition about the past (not necessarily strictly about the past) and p is accidentally necessary in the sense of [(43)]," and he defines P as a conjunction of the past accidentally necessary propositions. Then he proposes

(43*) p is accidentally necessary *simpliciter* if and only if p is true and it is not possible that both (a) P but no proposition properly entailing P is past accidentally necessary, and (b) there is a past accidentally necessary proposition q, an

46. See Freddoso, "Accidental Necessity and Logical Determinism," p. 258.

agent $S[,]$ and an action A such that (1) A is basic for S, (2) S can perform A at t or later, and (3) necessarily, if q is true and S were to perform A, then p would have been false.[47]

There are two technical flaws in this definition. First, the variable 't' is unbound. Second, P is defined as a conjunction of propositions that *are* (in fact) past accidentally necessary, but what is past accidentally necessary is different at different times. Both of these defects can be avoided by reformulating the principle. First, let 'P_t' denote, for a given time t, the set of all propositions that are past accidentally necessary at t. Then consider

(43**) p is accidentally necessary *simpliciter* at t if and only if p is (contingently) true at t and P_t is such that it is not possible that both (a) for every proposition r, r is past accidentally necessary at t if and only if r is a member of P_t, and (b) there is a past accidentally necessary proposition q, an agent S, and an action A such that (1) A is basic for S, (2) S can perform A at t or later, and (3) necessarily, if q is true and S were to perform A, then p would have been false.

(43**) appears to avoid the first of our two objections. Suppose, as before, that

(45) Either Socrates did not drink hemlock or Jones will not mow his lawn at t

is true. It does not follow from (43**) that (45) is accidentally necessary. That is because there is a past accidentally proposition q, namely, *Socrates drank hemlock*, an agent, Jones, and an action, mowing his lawn at t, which are such that the action is basic for Jones, he can perform it at t, and necessarily, if q is true and Jones were to mow his lawn at t, then (45) would have been false. Moreover, this is compatible with that which is past accidentally necessary being as it is at t. So (43**) is not satisfied in this case.

Our second objection alleged that Plantinga's account of acciden-

47. Plantinga, "On Ockham's Way Out," p. 268. p properly entails q just in case p entails q but q does not entail p. Thus clause (a) says that P is past accidentally necessary and entails every past accidentally necessary proposition.

tal necessity did not require that accidental necessity be closed under conjunction. (43**) seems to avoid this objection, too. Consider once again

(46) Everything Smith believed yesterday is true

and

(47) Yesterday Smith believed that Jones will not mow his lawn at t (some time tomorrow),

and suppose that they are true. Then (47) is accidentally necessary and, as it should, satisfies (43**). But (46) does not satisfy (43**), and so the objection is blocked. There is a past accidentally necessary proposition, namely (47), which is such that, necessarily, if (47) is true and Jones were to mow his lawn at t, then (46) would be false. With the help of this example, then, it can be shown that (46) does not satisfy (43**), and thus, this case provides no reason to think that (43**) does not impose conjunctive closure.

Whether (43**) is completely adequate remains, I think, to be seen. But it is clear that it provides no support for (C*), for, like (43), it does not entail that God's past foreknowledge or forebelief is accidentally necessary.

We have now surveyed four attempts to define accidental necessity. None of them gives us any reason to think that (C*) is true. We are therefore entitled to conclude that the prospects for establishing (C*) are dim indeed. Accordingly, the argument for the incompatibility of divine foreknowledge and human free action based on the accidental necessity of the past must be judged to be a failure. We shall briefly consider in the final section of this chapter an alternative response to this argument.

6. Incompatibilism and Divine Timelessness

We began our discussion of the argument from the accidental necessity of the past for the incompatibility of divine foreknowledge and human free action by considering the statement of the argument given by Aquinas. We should not conclude our discussion of that argument without looking, at least briefly, at Aquinas's response to the argument. ("Argument B" stated at the beginning of this chapter.)

Aquinas distinguishes knowing a thing "in itself," which is knowing it "in so far as it is already in act, and in this sense it is not considered as future, but as present," from knowing it "in its cause," which is to know that causally sufficient conditions obtain that will bring it about, and this is to know a thing as future.[48] Aquinas attributes both kinds of knowledge to God, but he holds that there are unique features to God's knowledge.

> Now God knows all contingent things not only as they are in their causes, but also as each one of them is actually in itself. And although contingent things become actual successively, nevertheless God knows contingent things not successively, as they are in their own being, as we do, but simultaneously. The reason is because His knowledge is measured by eternity, as is also His being; and eternity, being simultaneously whole, comprises all time, as was said above. Hence, all things that are in time are present to God from eternity, not only because He has the essences of things present within Him, as some say, but because His glance is carried from eternity over all things as they are in their presentiality. Hence, it is manifest that contingent things are infallibly known by God, inasmuch as they are subject to divine sight in their presentiality; and yet they are future contingent things in relation to their own causes.[49]

Aquinas thus endorses the doctrine of divine eternity, a topic we shall discuss in detail in Chapter 6. For now, I anticipate some of that discussion and note that part of what is involved in claiming that God is eternal is that he is timeless, where, I suggest,

> (48) x is timeless if and only if there is no property P and time t such that x has P at t.

In particular then, if God is timeless, he does not have his knowledge at any moments of time.[50]

The view, then, that God is timeless does not require denying (C*) or any of the other premises of Argument B. The response that

48. Aquinas, S.T., Ia, 14, 13.
49. Ibid.
50. We shall also discuss in Chapter 6 the question of what the objects of such timeless knowledge are.

God is timeless may thus concede that divine foreknowledge (literally understood) is incompatible with human free action. Instead, the view that God is timeless denies that God has foreknowledge; if God is timeless, there are no times t and t^* (where t is earlier than t^*) and no epistemic or doxastic property as *knowing that Jones will mow his lawn at* t^* or *believing that Jones will mow his lawn at* t^* such that God has that epistemic or doxastic property at t. Thus God does not know ahead of time that Jones will mow his lawn. Of course, there remains on this view a nonliteral sense in which God has foreknowledge: from God's point of view, Jones's mowing his lawn at t is eternally present.

This response to Argument B is not, by itself, completely satisfactory. It is now open to the objector to claim that

(49) Eighty years ago it was true that God has (timelessly) present knowledge that Jones mows his lawn at t

is true and about the past. Hence, the objection continues, (49) is accidentally necessary, and since it entails that Jones mows his lawn at t, the latter is accidentally necessary, too.[51]

Thus, it seems to me, there is no substitute for a critical examination of the concept of accidental necessity. If that examination reveals, as I think it does, that propositions expressing God's past foreknowledge are not accidentally necessary (or that if they are, it is nevertheless possible to do something according to which they would have been false), then the doctrine of divine timelessness is not required in order to reconcile divine foreknowledge and human free action. On the other hand, if propositions expressing God's past foreknowledge are accidentally necessary and if there is therefore nothing that anyone can do according to which they would have been false, then merely interpreting these propositions as claims about God's "present" knowledge does not, as the example of (49) makes clear, succeed in reconciling divine foreknowledge (understood now as "timeless present knowledge") and human free action.

51. See Plantinga, "On Ockham's Way Out," p. 239. Cf. Linda Zagzebski, "Divine Foreknowledge and Human Free Will," *Religious Studies* 21 (1985):282.

5

Omniscience, Free Will, and Middle Knowledge

1. Middle Knowledge

Omniscience, if the account presented in Chapter 2 is correct, includes knowledge of every true proposition.[1] Since there are true propositions referring to the future as well as to the present and the past, omniscience extends, as we saw in Chapter 3, to the future and the past. And since there are true propositions not only about what *is* the case but also about what *could be* the case, omniscience extends beyond the actual to the merely possible. Thus not only does God know that there *are* no unicorns, but he knows that it is *possible* that there are unicorns; and not only does God know that there are the human beings he has created, but he knows that he could have created other human beings instead.[2]

The sixteenth-century Jesuits Francesco Suarez and Luis de Molina recognized a category of knowledge which they took to be

---

1. Presumably, if that account is not correct, the only exceptions to the claim that omniscience requires knowledge of all true propositions are first-person propositions of others and perhaps temporally indexical propositions. Since the propositions known in knowledge of possibilities and in middle knowledge are not in this category, the existence of exceptions of this sort would not affect the points being made in the text.

2. The second example is from Luis de Molina, 'De scientia Dei,' quoted by Anthony Kenny, *The God of the Philosophers* (Oxford: Oxford University Press, 1979), p. 62.

intermediate between knowledge of what is merely possible and what is actual. They held that God knows not only what could happen and what will happen but also what *would have happened* if things had been different in various respects. In particular, they held that God knows what free creatures would have done had they been in various alternative circumstances, and they called such knowledge "middle knowledge."[3] Knowledge of what is possible is knowledge of necessary truths and hence was taken to be knowledge of truths that "followed from" God's nature. Knowledge of what is actual is "free knowledge" because it is dependent upon what God wills to be actual. Middle knowledge was supposed to be intermediate between these two because, like the former, its objects are thought to be independent of God's will but, like the latter, its objects are contingent rather than necessary truths.[4]

The objects of middle knowledge are counterfactual conditionals the consequents of which specify what an agent would freely do in the circumstances described by the antecedents of the conditionals. Molina produced scriptural examples of such propositions.[5] One was from the Wisdom of Solomon 4:11. There the untimely death of a virtuous man is explained: "He was snatched away before his mind could be perverted by wickedness or his soul deceived by falsehood." Molina apparently took this statement as affirming that God knew that if the man had lived longer, his mind would have been perverted by wickedness; perhaps, unless wickedness posed an imminent threat, it is somewhat more plausible to take the text as affirming that if the man had lived a usual lifespan, his mind would have been perverted by wickedness. Another example was found in

3. Luis de Molina, *Liberi arbitrii cum gratiae donis, divinis praescientia, praedestinatione et reprobatione concordia,* ed. John Rabeneck (Ona and Madrid, 1953); Francesco Suarez, *De gratia* and *De scientia Dei futurorum contingentium,* in his *Opera omnia* (Paris, 1856–1878), vols. 7 and 11, respectively. Part 4 of Molina's *Concordia* is available in English as *On Divine Foreknowledge,* trans. Alfred Freddoso (Ithaca, N.Y.: Cornell University Press, 1988). See also Robert M. Adams, "Middle Knowledge and the Problem of Evil," *American Philosophical Quarterly* 14 (1977): 109–117, and Kenny, *The God of the Philosophers,* pp. 61–65.

4. See Adams, "Middle Knowledge," p. 109; Freddoso, "Introduction," ms. p. 61. I question below whether all objects of divine middle knowledge are independent of God's will.

5. The following examples are presented and discussed by Kenny, *The God of the Philosophers,* pp. 63–64.

Matthew 11: 20–21, according to which Jesus "spoke of the towns
in which most of his miracles had been performed, and denounced
them for their impenitence. 'Alas for you, Chorazin!' he said; 'alas
for you, Bethsaida! If the miracles that were performed in you had
been performed in Tyre and Sidon, they would have repented long
ago in sackcloth and ashes.'"

A third example will be presented more fully, not only because of
its use in the sixteenth century but also because of its prominence in
recent discussion of these topics. According to I Samuel 23, David
escaped from King Saul after consulting the ephod, an instrument of
divination. Beginning at verse 7, the text is as follows:

> Saul was told that David had entered Keilah, and he said, "God has
> put him into my hands; for he has walked into a trap by entering a
> walled town with gates and bars." He called out the levy to march on
> Keilah and besiege David and his men. When David learnt how Saul
> planned his undoing, he told Abiathar the priest to bring the ephod,
> and then he prayed, "Oh Lord God of Israel, I thy servant have heard
> news that Saul intends to come to Keilah and destroy the city because
> of me. Will the citizens of Keilah surrender me to him? Will Saul
> come as I have heard? O Lord God of Israel, I pray thee, tell thy
> servant." The Lord answered, "He will come." Then David asked,
> "Will the citizens of Keilah surrender me and my men to Saul?", and
> the Lord answered, "They will." Then David left Keilah at once with
> his men, who numbered about six hundred, and moved about from
> place to place. When the news reached Saul that David had escaped
> from Keilah, he made no further move.[6]

This passage suggests that God knew

> (1) If David were to remain in Keilah, Saul would (freely)
> besiege the city.

and

> (2) If David were to remain in Keilah and Saul besieged the
> city, the men of Keilah would (freely) surrender David to
> Saul.

Certainly the story makes it seem that (1) and (2) are *true*, especially
in the case of (1), inasmuch as the text details Saul's intentions and

6. I Sam. 23:7–13.

his ability to raise an army. But if such propositions as (1) and (2) are true and omniscience requires knowledge of all truths,[7] then God's knowledge includes middle knowledge.[8]

Let us follow recent practice in describing such propositions as (1) and (2) as *counterfactuals of freedom*.[9] In the next two sections we review two topics in which God's knowledge of counterfactuals of freedom figures prominently: God's actualizing the world and the problem of evil. In the balance of this chapter we consider recent objections to the view that God has such middle knowledge.

2. Creation, Actualization, and Providence

In the beginning God created heaven and earth; according to Christian theology, that is not all that he does. For, in addition to creating the universe and all it contains, God continuously *conserves* his creation. Moreover, what happens in the course of the history of the universe is thought to be part of God's plan, so that much of what occurs is intended by God. A crucially important doctrine of Christianity is that God's plan for the world includes the redemption of the people he has created. Thus God desires that people turn to him, put their trust in him, and be remade in the image of his son Jesus Christ. Accordingly, many events in a person's life are intended by God to contribute to those ends. Hence, there is a good deal more to God's involvement in the world than his creation of it; indeed,

7. This is also subject to the qualification described in note 1 above.

8. Adams quotes Suarez in this regard: "The whole controversy comes back to this, that we should see whether those conditionals have a determinate truth." "Middle Knowledge," p. 110. Note that it is open to someone to maintain that although such propositions as (1) and (2) are true it is not possible for anyone to know them. Such a person could then understand omniscience as involving knowledge of all *knowable* truths (truths that are possibly known). I know of no one who has taken this approach, however, and so I concentrate on the question of whether propositions such as (1) and (2) are true. Cf. Alvin Plantinga, "Self-Profile," in *Alvin Plantinga*, ed. James Tomberlin and Peter van Inwagen, (Dordrecht: D. Reidel, 1985), p. 96, n. 13.

9. Robert Adams attributes his use of the term to David Vriend; see Adams, "Plantinga on the Problem of Evil," in Tomberlin and van Inwagen, *Alvin Plantinga*, p. 254. William Hasker attributes his use of the term to Plantinga's *The Nature of Necessity* (Oxford: Oxford University Press, 1974), but although counterfactuals of freedom are discussed in that work, they are not so-called. See Hasker's "A Refutation of Middle Knowledge," *Noûs* 20 (1986):546. Plantinga does use the term in his "Self-Profile" and "Replies to My Colleagues" in *Alvin Plantinga*, pp. 3–97 and 313–396, respectively.

many, if not all, of the contingent states of affairs that obtain do so, either directly or indirectly, as a result of God's activity.

We can put this last point somewhat more precisely if we employ some concepts used in our discussion of omnipotence in Chapter 1. Recall that an agent *strongly actualizes* a state of affairs if the agent causes that state of affairs to obtain. But if I arrange for a certain state of affairs to obtain by contriving to have you bring it about, then I do not strongly actualize it, since I cannot cause your free action. Nevertheless, I can be said to bring it about in a weaker sense, or to *weakly actualize it.* More formally, an agent (strictly) weakly actualizes a state of affairs S just in case there is a state of affairs T such that (i) the agent strongly actualizes T, (ii) the agent's strongly actualizing T counterfactually implies S, and (iii) the agent does not strongly actualize T.

Returning to the view being developed one paragraph back, we can now ask what God actualizes. Clearly God does not strongly actualize every state of affairs that obtains; one reason is that God does not strongly actualize necessary states of affairs.[10] And God does not even strongly actualize every *contingent* state of affairs, for there are agents other than God who act freely and, as we also saw in Chapter 1, God cannot strongly actualize such an agent's freely performing a given action. So what God strongly actualizes is a (proper) part of all that is the case. Some of the rest of what is the case is strongly actualized by agents God has created. So which among the multitude of possible worlds is actual depends both on what God does and on what his free creatures do.[11] Thus only part of what obtains is brought about directly by God.

10. This is not to deny that necessary states of affairs depend in some other way upon God, perhaps, as Plantinga has suggested, as being necessarily thought by God to obtain. Cf. "How To Be an Anti-Realist," *Proceedings and Addresses of the American Philosophical Association* 56 (1982):47–70.

11. Leibniz recognized this point, though he couched it in terms of his notion of an individual concept. He wrote, "Since the individual concept of each person contains once and for all everything that will ever happen to him, one sees in it the *a priori* proofs or reasons for the truth of each event, or why one event has occurred rather than another. But these truths, though certain, are nevertheless contingent, *being based on the free will of God and of creatures* [emphasis added]." The quotation is from Leibniz's summary of the *Discourse* in a letter to the landgrave Ernst von Hessen-Rheinfels, 1–11 February 1686, in *The Leibniz-Arnaud Correspondence*, ed. and trans. H. T. Mason (Manchester: Manchester University Press, 1967), p. 5.

What, if anything is brought about *indirectly* by God? If God strongly actualizes some states of affairs, does he weakly actualize others? Before we answer these questions we should note that if what happens in the universe is really part of God's *plan*, then it seems both that God had alternatives from which to choose and that he knew how to ensure that the alternative he chose would come about. How could this be? One view is suggested by Leibniz, who pictures God prior to creation as surveying countless possible worlds as alternatives to the actual world and, thus, as considering an "infinite number of other Adams." God chose, however, to have this world be actual. Leibniz says, "God, forseeing and regulating everything from all eternity, chose in the first place the whole successive connexion of the universe, and in consequence not just an Adam but a particular Adam whom he foresaw as doing particular things and having particular children without this divine providence regulated from all time running counter to his freedom."[12] But how could God ensure that he got the world he chose? The answer seems to be that God knew what would happen if he were to strongly actualize those states of affairs which constitute his direct contribution to the world. This would seem to involve knowledge of at least two sorts of counterfactual conditionals. The first are counterfactuals of freedom describing what various individuals would do in various circumstances, including the circumstances of having been created. Leibniz recognized this sort of counterfactual: "Lying or wickedness springs from the Devil's own nature, . . . from his will, because it was written in the book of eternal verities, which contains the things possible before any decree of God, that this creature would freely turn toward evil if it were created. It is the same with Adam and Eve; they sinned freely, albeit the Devil tempted them."[13] But for what takes place to be within God's providence, it would seem, as I have suggested, that he must also know what would happen if *he* were to strongly actualize his complete share of the world. We can put this more precisely as follows. For any world

12. Leibniz, letter to the landgrave, 12 April 1686, *The Leibniz-Arnaud Correspondence*, p. 19. The phrase "infinite number of other Adams" is also from a letter to the landgrave (p. 16). I do not mean to endorse Leibniz's apparent acceptance in these passages of the "theory of world-bound individuals."

13. Leibniz, *Theodicy*, pt. 3, para. 276; trans. E. M. Huggard, ed. Diogenes Allen (Indianapolis: Bobbs-Merrill, 1966), pp. 133–134.

W, let '$T(W)$' designate the largest state of affairs God strongly actualizes in W. That is, for any state of affairs S God strongly actualizes in W, $T(W)$ includes S.[14] Now if W is a world in which, say, Adam freely eats the forbidden fruit, then $T(W)$ does not include Adam's freely eating the forbidden fruit, since God cannot *cause* Adam freely to eat the fruit. Accordingly, it is possible that God strongly actualize $T(W)$ and that Adam not eat the forbidden fruit. Hence, there is a possible world W' distinct from W which includes both $T(W)$ and Adam's not eating the forbidden fruit. Now if God wanted to W to be actual rather that W', how could he arrange it? It would seem that God could only ensure that W is actual if it is true that

> (3) If God were to strongly actualize $T(W)$ then W would be actual.

And God could knowingly bring about W, it would seem, only if he knew that (3) was true.

We are now in a position to answer the question of what God weakly actualizes. If such "counterfactuals of world-actualization" as (3) are true, God weakly actualizes an entire possible world.[15] For if God strongly actualizes $T(W)$ and if (3) is true, that is, if God's strongly actualizing $T(W)$ counterfactually implies W, then it follows that God weakly actualizes W.

Anthony Kenny has several objections to this way of conceiving of God's relation to the world, some of which we consider below. For now, let us consider Kenny's contention in the following passage:

> To actualize a possible world, on the face of it, is to turn a non-actual world into an actual one: but a moment's reflection shows this to be a self-contradictory feat which not even omnipotence could achieve. No doubt the Molinist will reply that he does not mean that God turns a non-actual world into an actual one, but that he has from all eternity made actual a world which but for his decision would not have been actual; and that continuously he is making actual particular states of affairs which before his actualization were non-actual states

14. Cf. Plantinga, *The Nature of Necessity*, p. 181.
15. Perhaps this is what Leibniz meant when he said in the passage quoted above that God chose "the whole successive connexion of the universe."

of affairs. But even this formulation presupposes that one and the same individual state of affairs may change from possessing the property of being merely possible to possessing the property of being actual. And this involves the type of identification across possible worlds which is found unintelligible by many critics. Unactual states of affairs can no more be individuated, many philosophers claim, than non-existent persons can: there can be no individuation without actualization.[16]

Kenny is certainly correct that the view we have been considering does not have the implausible consequence that God be able to turn nonactual worlds into actual worlds; rather, as Kenny notes, it requires that God be able to turn a merely possible state of affairs into an actual one, that is, to actualize states of affairs. The heart of Kenny's criticism, then, is that this cannot be done. But why not? Kenny's objection is not entirely clear, but apparently it depends upon the claim that there are no nonactual states of affairs. He claims first that the thesis "that one and the same individual state of affairs may change from possessing the property of being merely possible to possessing the property of being actual . . . involves the type of identification across possible worlds which is found unintelligible by many critics." Kenny does not identify the critics he has in mind here, but several of the leading critics of transworld-identity with whom I am familiar would not object to the claim that a certain state of affairs is actual in one world and merely possible in another.[17] Possible worlds *themselves* are states of affairs that are merely possible in some worlds (each in all but one) and actual in another (each is actual only at itself). Moreover, the claim that a certain state of affairs, say, Reagan's being president, used to be merely possible but later became actual does not obviously require identification across possible worlds; at most it requires identification over time, and it is hard to find anything objectionable about that. Kenny's final remark, that "unactual states of affairs can no more be individuated . . . than non-existent persons can: there can be no individuation

16. Kenny, *The God of the Philosophers,* pp. 70–71.
17. Roderick Chisholm, for example, was an early critic of transworld identity; see his "Identity through Possible Worlds: Some Questions," *Noûs* 1 (1967):1–8. But he has persistently recognized unactual states of affairs; see *Person and Object* (La Salle, Ill.: Open Court, 1976), and *The First Person* (Minneapolis: University of Minnesota Press, 1981).

without actualization," suggests another confusion. Surely there are
no nonexistent persons, so they cannot be individuated. But what
Kenny takes to be analogous to nonexistent persons is not *nonexistent* states of affairs but *nonactual* states of affairs. These, however,
are not the same. There clearly are no nonexistent states of affairs; it
does not follow, however, that all states of affairs obtain or are
actual. Perhaps 'unactual' is ambiguous between *nonexistent* and *nonactual*; then Kenny's statement "Unactual states of affairs cannot be
individuated" would be ambiguous between *Nonexistent states of affairs cannot be individuated* and *Nonactual states of affairs cannot be individuated*. The former is no doubt true; but it is the latter claim that is
required for Kenny's objection, and that claim is unsubstantiated.

It might also be objected that although the view that God can
actualize a world containing free agents by choosing from among
alternatives requires that God have knowledge of what I have called
counterfactuals of world–actualization, it does not require that God
know any counterfactuals of freedom, and, hence, this view does
not require that God have middle knowledge. This objection would
be a mistake, however. For if God is able to actualize a world in this
way and he has knowledge of counterfactuals of world–actualization, then it can be shown that he also has knowledge of counterfactuals of freedom. To see this, suppose that God could have weakly
actualized a world W in which David remained in Keilah and in
which Saul is free to besiege Keilah or not to besiege it. Then there is
a largest state of affairs, $T(W)$, which God strongly actualizes in W
and which is such that God would have known that if he were to
strongly actualize $T(W)$ then W would be actual. In such a case,
then,

(4) God knows that (God strongly actualizes $T(W) > W$ is
    actual),

(where '>' represents the counterfactual connective). From (4), of
course, it follows that

(5) God strongly actualizes $T(W) > W$ is actual.

Now either Saul (freely) besieges Keilah in W or he does not. Suppose that he does. Then W includes *Saul's (freely) besieging Keilah*,
that is,

(6) Necessarily, if *W* is actual then Saul (freely) besieges Keilah.

From (5) and (6) it follows that

(7) God strongly actualizes $T(W)$ > Saul (freely) besieges Keilah.

Given that an omniscient being knows the logical consequences of what he knows, it follows from (4) and (7) that

(8) God knows that (God strongly actualizes $T(W)$ > Saul (freely) besieges Keilah).

Now (7) is a counterfactual of freedom, since its consequent says what Saul would freely do if a certain condition—the condition of God strongly actualizing $T(W)$—held. Accordingly, if (8) is true, God has middle knowledge. On the other hand, perhaps in *W* Saul (freely) refrains from besieging Keilah. In that case, it would follow by an exactly parallel argument that

(9) God knows that (God strongly actualizes $T(W)$ > Saul (freely) refrains from besieging Keilah).

So if God could have weakly actualized a world in which David remained in Keilah and Saul was free with respect to besieging Keilah, then either (8) or (9) is true, and in either case God has middle knowledge. I have assumed that God *could* have actualized a world in which David remained in Keilah and Saul was free with respect to besieging Keilah, but this assumption, though harmless,[18] is dispensable. All that is required is the assumption that there is *some* world God can knowingly actualize in which a person is free with respect to an action, and that is clearly part of the view of world-actualization we have been considering. Thus, I conclude that according to that view, if God has knowledge of counterfactuals of

---

18. Note that it is not claimed that the world is one in which David remains in Keilah *freely*. Perhaps it is logically possible that nothing God could do would induce or persuade David freely to remain, but there is no reason why God could not force him to stay.

world-actualization for worlds in which there is free action, he has middle knowledge.

We have seen in this section that according to a plausible view of how the world is planned by God or governed by his providence, God has middle knowledge.[19] In the next section we briefly survey another area in which God's middle knowledge seems to be involved.

3. Evil and the Free Will Defense

"Is [God] willing to prevent evil, but not able? then he is impotent. Is he able, but not willing? then he is malevolent. Is he both able and willing? Whence then is evil?"[20] If we add to this famous passage from Hume's *Dialogues* the question "Is there evil, but God does not know about it? then he is not omniscient," we have the rudiments of the logical problem of evil, that is, the charge that the propositions

(10) God is omnipotent,

(11) God is omniscient,

(12) God is wholly good,

and

(13) There is evil

are logically inconsistent.[21] Since these propositions are obviously not inconsistent in first-order logic, the person who claims that they

19. For an interesting discussion of providence and its relation to middle knowledge, see Thomas Flint, "Two Accounts of Providence," in *Divine and Human Action,* ed. Thomas Morris (Ithaca: Cornell University Press, 1988).

20. David Hume, *Dialogues concerning Natural Religion,* pt X. Hume attributes these questions to Epicurus, but according to J. C. A. Gaskin, they occur in no extant work of Epicurus. Gaskin, *The Quest for Eternity: An Outline of the Philosophy of Religion* (Harmondsworth: Penguin Books, 1984), p. 185, n. 1.

21. This is not the place to review the voluminous literature on this topic. For a representative and influential defense of the claim that (10)–(13) are inconsistent, see J. L. Mackie, "Evil and Omnipotence," *Mind* 64 (1955):200–212, and *The Miracle of Theism: Arguments for and against the Existence of God* (Oxford: Oxford University Press, 1982), chap. 9.

are inconsistent must presuppose that there is an additional necessary truth connecting the concepts of goodness, omniscience, and omnipotence that can be used to demonstrate their inconsistency.[22] Presumably the objector holds that for any evil there is something God could have done (and which God would have known about) such that if God had done it, the evil would not have occurred. More generally, the objector seems to assume that God could have arranged for a world without evil. In other words, the objector seems to be committed to holding that for any world (or any world including God's existence, or any world including God's existence and free agents but no evil) there is something God could have done (and knew about) such that if he had done it, that world would have been actual. The objector thus seems to be committed to holding that there are true counterfactuals of freedom. As Alvin Plantinga asks, "How can God be reproached for not having created a better world if there is no state of affairs he could have strongly actualized such that, if he had, a world containing moral good but no moral evil, say, would have been actual?"[23]

In recent years the most successful response to the logical problem of evil has been the Free Will Defense, which attempts to show that (10)–(13) are not inconsistent by appealing to the ideas that perhaps God values creatures who freely choose to do what is right, that evil results from the morally wrong actions of free creatures, and that in order to obtain the moral good of creatures freely choosing rightly God had to put up creatures who occasionally go wrong. In Plantinga's important and influential development, the task of the Free Will Defense is to find a proposition r such that it is clear that the

22. Analogously, *Jones is a bachelor* and *Jones is married* are not inconsistent in first-order logic, but in conjunction with the necessary truth, *no bachelor is married,* a contradiction is deducible from them.

23. Cf. Plantinga, "Self-Profile," p. 49. Strictly speaking, Plantinga's claim here is that the objector is committed to the truth of counterfactuals of world-actualization, but if God could have actualized a world with free creatures, then, by the argument at the end of the last section, there would be true counterfactuals of freedom if there are true counterfactuals of world-actualization. Moreover, the simplified version of the objector's position, as I have presented it, is committed only to the truth of counterfactuals of world-actualization. As it is usually developed, however, the objection presumes that God could have created free creatures who never do wrong (cf. Mackie, "Evil and Omnipotence"), and this presumption involves a commitment to the truth of counterfactuals of freedom.

conjunction of r with the conjunction of (10) and (11) and (12) is consistent and entails (13).[24] Plantinga's presentation proceeds in two stages. In the first he argues that there are possible worlds God cannot actualize. The second stage proposes a candidate for r according to which among the worlds God cannot actualize are those containing moral good but no evil.

There is a straightforward argument for the first-stage conclusion that there are worlds God cannot actualize. Let W be a world in which an agent S is in circumstances that include being free with respect to an action A. Suppose that in W, S freely does A. As before, let $T(W)$ be the largest state of affairs God strongly actualizes in W. Since God cannot cause *S's freely doing* A, $T(W)$ does not include *S's freely doing* A. Hence, there is a world W' such that in W', S freely refrains from doing A and such that $T(W') = T(W)$. Now if it is true that

(14) If God were to strongly actualize $T(W)$, S would freely do A,

then God cannot actualize W'; for, in virtue of (14), if God were to try to actualize W' by strongly actualizing $T(W')$, W would result instead.[25] On the other hand, if

(15) If God were to strongly actualize $T(W)$, S would not freely do A

24. This is an application of the principle that if the conjunction of p [e.g., (10) & (11) & (12)] and r is consistent and entails q [e.g., (13)], then p and q are consistent. Note that this principle does not require that r be true or even that it be remotely plausible. See Alvin Plantinga, *The Nature of Necessity* and *God, Freedom, and Evil* (1974; rpt. Grand Rapids, Mich.: Eerdmans, 1978). Of course, merely *finding* or even *exhibiting* a proposition r which satisfies these conditions does not *show* that p and q are consistent, for it may not be apparent that r *does* satisfy these conditions. For example, let p be the conjunction of the axioms of Zermelo-Frankel set theory and let $q = r =$ the denial of the continuum hypothesis. Then r satisfies the above conditions, and p and q are accordingly consistent, but this fact is no substitute for Cohen's proof. For this reason I have in the text inserted the requirement that *it be clear that* r satisfies the relevant conditions.

25. This argument presupposes "Lewis' Lemma," that God can actualize a world W only if his strongly actualizing $T(W)$ counterfactually implies W. For an argument for this assumption, see Plantinga, "Self-Profile," p. 51.

is true, then God cannot actualize W; for, by virtue of (15), if God were to try to actualize W by strongly actualizing $T(W)$, W' (or some other world distinct from W) would result instead. Since either (14) or (15) (suitably interpreted) is true, there is a world God cannot actualize.

This argument, which parallels one given in *The Nature of Necessity*,[26] presupposes that some counterfactuals of freedom are true. Indeed, it makes an even stronger assumption: since it assumes that either (14) or (15) is true, it seems to presuppose that Conditional Excluded Middle holds for counterfactual conditionals, or at least that it holds for counterfactuals of freedom. Conditional Excluded Middle for counterfactuals is the principle that, for any propositions p and q,

(16) $(p > q)$ or $(p > \sim q)$.

Conditional Excluded Middle should be distinguished from the considerably less controversial principle of (ordinary) excluded middle:

(17) $(p > q)$ or $\sim(p > q)$.

If (16) is true, it follows that there are true counterfactuals of freedom; and, of course, if there are true counterfactuals of freedom, God knows them. Hence, if we could appeal to (16), we would have an easy argument for the thesis that God has middle knowledge; however, many philosophers have found (16) objectionable.[27] We shall return to this topic below, but for now let us resume our discussion of the claim that there are worlds (which include God's existence) that God cannot actualize.

Plantinga has two more arguments for this conclusion. Considering them in all of their complexity would take us too far afield. Rather, let us simply note some of their assumptions. The first is found in *The Nature of Necessity*.[28] It dispenses with the assumption

26. Plantinga, *The Nature of Necessity*, pp. 181–182.
27. See David K. Lewis, *Counterfactuals* (Oxford: Basil Blackwell, 1973), pp. 79–82, and Adams, "Middle Knowledge and the Problem of Evil," p. 110.
28. Plantinga, *The Nature of Necessity*, pp. 182–184.

of Conditional Excluded Middle, but it does assume *bivalence*. Bivalence is the principle that for any pair of propositions p and $\sim p$, exactly one is true. In particular, this argument assumes that for a pair of counterfactuals of freedom, $(p > q)$ and $\sim(p > q)$, exactly one is true. This is not as strong an assumption as Conditional Excluded Middle, but it is not quite as innocuous as ordinary excluded middle.[29]

Plantinga's most recent argument for the conclusion that there are worlds God cannot actualize is an especially elegant argument presented in his "Self-Profile."[30] This argument assumes that there are counterfactuals of freedom, but it does not assume Conditional Excluded Middle, and it does not assume that God knows any counterfactuals of freedom or that it is possible that he does. And it does not even assume bivalence.[31] Thus, given this most recent argument, it is not the first stage of the Free Will Defense that requires that God have middle knowledge. Accordingly, we turn to the second stage.

The second stage of the Free Will Defense consists in finding a proposition r whose conjunction with (10)–(12) clearly is consistent and entails (13). To that end Plantinga introduces the concept of *transworld depravity*:

(18) A person P *suffers from transworld depravity* if and only if for every world W such that P is significantly free in W and P

29. Someone who thought that propositions do not have a truth value until they are somehow "fixed" might have the following view. A proposition is true at a time just in case it is true in every possible future of that time. As time goes by, more and more possible futures are excluded, and more and more propositions come to have a truth value. On this view, it could happen that at some time t a proposition p is true in some futures of t and its negation, $\sim p$, is true in other futures of t. In such a case, neither p nor $\sim p$ has a truth value at t; so bivalence would not hold. But it could well be the case that in the futures of t in which p is not true, $\sim p$ is, in which case excluded middle, p or $\sim p$, would hold. For this account I am indebted to Calvin Normore, "Divine Omniscience, Omnipotence, and Future Contingents: An Overview," in *Divine Omnipotence and Omniscience in Medieval Philosophy*, ed. T. Rudavsky (Dordrecht: D. Reidel, 1985), p. 12. Normore cites R. Thomason, "Indeterminist Time and Truth Value Gaps," *Theoria* 36 (1970):264–281.

30. Plantinga, "Self-Profile," pp. 50–52.

31. As Plantinga notes (ibid., p. 52), if no counterfactuals of freedom are true, it follows that God cannot actualize a world with free persons. But this is just what we saw in Section 2 above and, thus, does not introduce a new reason for attributing middle knowledge to God.

does only what is right in W, there is a state of affairs T and an action A such that

(1) God strongly actualizes T in W and T includes every state of affairs God strongly actualizes in W,

(2) A is morally significant for P in W, and

(3) if God had strongly actualized T, P would have gone wrong with respect to A.[32]

Suppose a person P suffers from transworld depravity. Then consider any world W in which P is a free moral agent but never goes wrong. If God were to actualize W, it would be by strongly actualizing some large state of affairs T—what we earlier called '$T(W)$'—which is such that

(19) *God strongly actualizes T counterfactually implies W is actual.*

But if P suffers from transworld depravity, (19) is false. To see this, note that according to the third clause of (18), if God were to strongly actualize T, P would have gone wrong with respect to a morally significant action; hence, if God were to strongly actualize T, the resulting world would *not* be W, a world in which, by hypothesis, P never goes wrong. So if a person suffers from transworld depravity, among the worlds God cannot actualize are those in which that person is a free moral agent and never goes wrong.

It certainly seems possible for someone to suffer from transworld depravity. (Note that anyone that has it, has it accidentally.) Moreover, someone's having it seems to be consistent with God's being omnipotent. God's being limited in this way with respect to which worlds he can *weakly* actualize does not count against his omnipotence, which, if the account presented in Chapter 1 is correct, depends only upon what he can *strongly* actualize. Thus, someone's having transworld depravity would seem to be consistent with (10)–(12), the propositions that God is omnipotent, omniscient, and wholly good. By similar reasoning, everyone's having transworld depravity would seem to be consistent with (10)–(12). Now I shall

32. Plantinga, *The Nature of Necessity*, p. 186. I have corrected a misprint in the definition.

simplify and assume the fiction that there are possible persons and that (18) applies to them as well as to actual persons.[33] Finally, then, by further similar reasoning, every possible person's having transworld depravity is consistent with (10)–(12). But then so is

> (20) Every possible person suffers from transworld depravity and God actualizes a world containing free persons and moral good.

(20) can serve as the proposition r needed for the Free Will Defense. As we have just seen, it is consistent with (10)–(12). But it also entails that there is evil; so its conjunction with (10)–(12) does, too. Hence, (10)–(12) is consistent with (13).

The important point for our purposes is that the Free Will Defense assumes that it is possible that persons suffer from transworld depravity. But in virtue of the third clause of (18), if a person has transworld depravity, certain counterfactuals of freedom are true. The Free Will Defense is therefore committed to holding that (at least some) counterfactuals of freedom are possibly true. If God is essentially omniscient and necessarily existent, it is also committed to the view that it is possible that God have middle knowledge. In contrast, the leading objections to middle knowledge seem to hold that counterfactuals of freedom are necessarily false;[34] accordingly, if those objections are correct, it is not even possible that God have middle knowledge, and the Free Will Defense, at least as Plantinga has developed it, is defective.[35] We should turn, then, to an examination of those objections. First, however, let us specify more precisely what is involved in the doctrine of middle knowledge.

---

33. Plantinga shows how to avoid these assumptions, but I suppress the complications needed to do so. See ibid., pp. 187–189.

34. Except for ones in which the antecedent *entails* the conclusion, for example, *If Saul were (freely) to besiege Keilah then Saul would (freely) besiege Keilah*. In what follows I ignore these analytic counterfactuals of freedom.

35. I have focused on Plantinga's version of the Free Will Defense and shown it presupposes that it is possible that God have middle knowledge. It is worth noting that other versions of the Free Will Defense also seem to have this commitment. For example, Eleonore Stump develops a version of the Free Will Defense which is similar to Plantinga's but which adds the proviso that "a perfectly good entity who was also omniscient and omnipotent must govern the evil resulting from the misuse of . . . significant freedom in such a way that the sufferings of any particular person

4. The Doctrine of Middle Knowledge

Middle knowledge, as we have seen, is knowledge of a counter-factual of freedom, that is, knowledge of a counterfactual conditional the consequent of which specifies what an agent would freely do if the circumstances described by its antecedent obtained. Should we understand the doctrine of divine middle knowledge to be the claim that for every counterfactual of freedom, God knows whether it is true? That is, as

(21) For every counterfactual of freedom, $(p > q)$, either God knows $(p > q)$ or God knows $\sim(p > q)$?

Presumably not, for (21) does not explicitly affirm that God knows any counterfactuals of freedom—perhaps none is true and he knows only their denials. We could instead take the doctrine to be the thesis that

(22) For every counterfactual of freedom, $(p > q)$, either God knows $(p > q)$ or God knows $(p > \sim q)$.

---

are outweighed by the good which the suffering produces *for that person*," and she develops an account of how God can use such suffering to draw a person to him. "The Problem of Evil," *Faith and Philosophy* 4 (1985):411. It is hard to see how God could be justified in permitting evil for the sake of the person who suffers unless he knew what the person would do in response to such suffering. Moreover, there is some hint that Stump explicitly endorses the view that God has middle knowledge, for she cites with approval the story of David at Keilah (I Sam. 23) as an example of a Bible passage in which God is portrayed as able to reveal to people the consequences of their choices.

Another version of the Free Will Defense is given by Richard Swinburne, who agrees with Plantinga's treatment of moral evil but declines to follow Plantinga's suggestion that natural evil may be due to the free action of nonhuman agents. Rather, according to Swinburne, natural evil is justified because it is required for our knowledge of the consequences of our free actions, a knowledge without which we could not exercise significant free choice. *The Existence of God* (Oxford: Oxford University Press, 1979). I am not sure whether Swinburne anywhere endorses the thesis that God has middle knowledge. He notes that "a God knows how much men will suffer and what the effects of their suffering will be" (p. 217), but this explicitly attributes only foreknowledge to God and not middle knowledge. Nevertheless it is hard to see how God could be justified in permitting such evil if, although he knows that it *will* lead to a good result, he does not know whether that result could have been achieved without the evil. So alternative developments of the Free Will Defense also seem to be committed to at least the possibility of divine middle knowledge.

(22) seems to have been accepted by Molina,[36] and it certainly is part of the view attacked by Hasker and Adams.[37] But (22) entails the principle of Conditional Excluded Middle (see (16) above), which, as we have seen, has its detractors.

In thinking about these matters we will find it helpful to make use of the possible worlds accounts of the truth conditions of counterfactual conditionals. Those accounts appeal to a relation of comparative similarity holding among worlds. In the simplest version, a counterfactual, $(p > q)$, is true if and only if either (i) p is impossible or (ii) in the world most similar to the actual world in which p is true, q is true, too.[38] It might be, however, that two worlds in which p is true ("p-worlds") are equally similar to the actual world. In that case, there would be no such thing as the *closest* world in which p is true. Or it could even be the case that there is an infinite series of ever closer p-worlds. (Is there a closest world in which I am over seven feet tall? Perhaps instead there is an infinite series of worlds in which I exceed seven feet, respectively, by one inch, by one-half inch, by one-quarter inch, etc.) To accommodate these possibilities, the theory may be complicated as follows: a counterfactual, $(p > q)$, is true if and only if either (i) there is no world in which p is true or (ii) there is a world in which p is true and q is true and there is no world as close or closer in which p is true and q is false.[39]

If a pair of worlds, W and W', say, in which p is true are equally similar to the actual world (and there is no closer p-world), then there are a pair of conditionals, $(p > q)$ and $(p > {\sim}q)$, neither of which is true. For if W and W' are distinct worlds in which p is true, there must be some other proposition q that is true in one but false in the other. David Lewis thinks the following pair of propositions is an example of this case:

(23) If Verdi and Bizet were compatriots, Bizet would be Italian

---

36. Cf. Normore, "Divine Omniscience, Omnipotence, and Future Contingents," p. 15.

37. Hasker, "A Refutation of Middle Knowledge," p. 547; Adams, "Middle Knowledge and the Problem of Evil," p. 110.

38. See Robert Stalnaker, "A Theory of Conditionals," in *Studies in Logical Theory*, ed. N. Rescher (Oxford: Basil Blackwell, 1968).

39. See Lewis, *Counterfactuals*.

and

> (24) If Verdi and Bizet were compatriots, Bizet would not be Italian.

Lewis's suggestion is that the closest worlds in which Bizet and Verdi are compatriots include worlds where they are both French and worlds in which they are both Italian. If so, neither (23) nor (24) is true.[40] And Robert Adams thinks that

> (1) If David were to remain in Keilah, Saul would (freely) besiege the city.

and

> (25) If David were to remain in Keilah, Saul would not (freely) besiege the city

are another example.[41] These examples are not entirely convincing, however. In the case of the latter, which we shall discuss more fully below, it is tempting to think that (assuming the biblical story is correct) (1) is true and (25) is false. And in the case of the former example, it may be that because of gaps in our knowledge of the actual world, we just do not know whether a world in which Verdi and Bizet are both Italian is more similar to the actual world than any world in which they are both French. Did Bizet's ancesters ever contemplate emigrating to Italy and if so would they still have produced the children they did? Or did Verdi's ancesters harbor a desire to relocate in France? If some such facts as these obtained, they might determine whether the French or the Italian world is more similar to the actual world, but perhaps no one knows enough about the family histories of these composers to tell whether one is more similar than the other to the actual world. Thus, our inability to judge one more similar might reflect our ignorance rather than a fact about the world. Nevertheless, in virtue of the controversial nature of Conditional Excluded Middle, it is worth seeing if the doctrine of divine middle knowledge can be formulated in a way

40. Ibid., pp. 80–82.
41. Adams, "Middle Knowledge and the Problem of Evil," p. 110.

that avoids commitment to it. To that end we should first take note
of the following phenomenon.

Unless all counterfactuals of freedom are false, it can happen that
the truth value of a counterfactual of freedom changes as its antecedent is strenghtened. For example, if (1) was in fact true, it might
nevertheless be that

> (26) If David were to remain in Keilah and all of Saul's infor-
>   mants were to tell him that David had fled to Horesh, Saul
>   would (freely) besiege Keilah

was false. Something similar can happen if there are exceptions to
Conditional Excluded Middle. Suppose that both (23) and (24) are
false. It might nevertheless be that

> (27) If Verdi and Bizet were compatriots and Verdi were not
>   French, Bizet would be Italian

and

> (28) If Verdi and Bizet were compatriots and Verdi were not
>   Italian, Bizet would not be Italian.

are both true.

So let us concede, for the sake of argument, that some counterfactuals of freedom do not obey Conditional Excluded Middle and
consider what follows. Suppose that (1) and (25) are both false after
all. It does not follow that, where W is a world in which David
remains in Keilah, Saul is free with respect to besieging Keilah, and
$T(W)$ is the largest state of affairs God strongly actualizes in W,

> (29) If God were to strongly actualize $T(W)$ and David were to
>   remain in Keilah, then Saul would (freely) besiege the city

is false. It might well be true. But how could it be?

Perhaps it will be easier to see this if we switch examples. Plantinga tells a story in which at a certain time t the director of high-
ways, Lewis B. Smedes, offers Curley Smith, the mayor of Boston,
a bribe of $35,000 to drop his opposition to a proposed freeway

project, and Curley accepts.[42] Presumably, however, according to this tale

> (30) If Smedes had offered a bribe of $10 at t, Curley would have accepted it

is false. Curley, after all, has his pride, and he will not sell himself cheaply. We do not reason, however, that a world W in which Smedes offers $10 at t and Curley accepts is more similar to the actual world than a world W' in which Smedes offers $10 at t and Curley refuses on the grounds that *after t W* is so much more like the actual world than W' is. It is true, of course, that after t in W the freeway is built, just as it is in the actual world, whereas in W' the freeway is not built and the landmarks are preserved. The moral is that in evaluating the comparative similarity of these worlds in a way that is relevant to the truth of (30), we place greater emphasis on similarities that obtain before t than on those which obtain after t.[43]

Now suppose that there are some counterfactuals of freedom in this case for which Conditional Excluded Middle does not hold. Perhaps,

> (31) If Smedes had offered a bribe of $20,000 at t Curley would have accepted it

and

> (32) If Smedes had offered a bribe of $20,000 at t Curley would have refused it

are both false. Perhaps Curley's pride and venality balance each other in such a way that worlds in which he is offered $20,000 and accepts are as similar to the actual world as worlds in which he is offered $20,000 and refuses. Still, there might be ways of strengthening the antecedent of (31), for example, that would turn it into a truth. Let W be a world in which Smedes offers Curley a bribe of $20,000 and in which Curley is free with respect to accepting the

---

42. Plantinga, *The Nature of Necessity*, pp. 173–180.
43. Cf. Lewis, *Counterfactuals*, p. 76.

bribe. Also, as before, let $T(W)$ be the largest state of affairs God strongly actualizes in W. Now consider

> (33) If God had strongly actualized $T(W)$ and Smedes had offered a bribe of \$20,000 at t, Curley would have accepted the bribe.

Since $T(W)$ includes everything God strongly actualizes in W, and that, presumably, includes many states of affairs that obtain after t, when we come to consider the comparative similarity of worlds in which the antecedent of (33) is true, we no longer emphasize only similarities obtaining before t. Suppose $T(W)$ includes the continued existence of the concrete of which the proposed freeway was constructed. Then the relevant comparison will be between worlds in which Curley accepted the bribe and worlds in which the freeway was built despite Curley's opposition.[44] And given Curley's actual power, it would seem that the former worlds are more like the actual world than the latter. In that case, (33) would be true.

Another way of arriving at the conclusion that (33) could be true even if (31) is false is as follows. Suppose that both

> (34) If God were to strongly actualize $T(W)$ then W would be actual

and

> (35) *W includes Curley's accepting the bribe*

are true. Then it follows that

> (36) If God were to strongly actualize $T(W)$ then Curley would accept the bribe.

But by assumption, W is a world in which Smedes offers a bribe of \$20,000 at t. So from (34) and (36) it follows that (33) is true.

---

44. There are also worlds in which Curley rejects the bribe but drops his opposition to the freeway for entirely blameless motives, and also worlds in which Curley rejects the bribe but the freeway is constructed by pranksters and not the Highway Department, but since these worlds are even more remote from reality, they do not need to be considered.

Since strengthening the antecedent can turn a false counterfactual into a true one, it might well be that even if some counterfactuals of freedom do not obey Conditional Excluded Middle, conditionals whose antecedents are so strong as to specify God's entire activity do obey Conditional Excluded Middle. In Section 2 above we called such conditionals as

(37) If God were to strongly actualize $T(W)$ then W would be actual

counterfactuals of world-actualization, and we saw that for any world W, person P, and action A such that P does A in W, (37) entails

(38) If God were to strongly actualize $T(W)$ then P would do A.

In virtue of this entailment, let us extend the term 'counterfactual of world-actualization' to include propositions of the form of (38) as well as those of the form of (37). Then we can state the following doctrine of middle knowledge:

(39) For every counterfactual of world-actualization, $(p > q)$, either God knows $(p > q)$ or God knows $(p > {\sim}q)$.

(39) allows that Conditional Excluded Middle might not hold for every counterfactual of freedom, although it explicitly assumes that it holds for counterfactuals of world-actualization. But it was these counterfactuals which we saw to be relevant to God's creation and providence as well as to be presupposed (as at least possible) by the Free Will Defense. Accordingly, I take (39) as expressing the doctrine of middle knowledge.[45] In the remainder of this chapter we consider objections to this doctrine.

45. Thomas Flint has pointed out that (39) does not adequately characterize the doctrine of middle knowledge that was accepted by the Molinists and rejected by their Thomist opponents. In that dispute two additional points are relevant. First, God's knowledge of his *own* counterfactuals of freedom—counterfactuals specifying what *he* would freely do in various circumstances—is not middle knowledge but free knowledge. Second, and more imporant, the sixteenth-century dispute did not focus on the *truth* of counterfactuals of freedom or of world-actualization but on

5. The No Grounds Objection

Some of the most profoundly difficult challenges to the doctrine of middle knowledge have been presented by Robert M. Adams.[46] In Adams's view, counterfactuals of freedom are all false.[47] On the face of it, this is a counterintuitive claim, since, as Adams notes, it has the consequence that it is false that if I were to ask the butcher to sell me a pound of meat he would.[48] Adams accepts this consequence, however, and holds that what is true instead is that if I were to ask the butcher to sell me a pound of meat it would be probable that he would.

Adams defends his contention that all counterfactuals of freedom are false by claiming that for a counterfactual of freedom to be true, there must be *grounds* for its truth or something that makes it true.[49] Adams then surveys various candidates for this role and rejects them as inadequate. In the case of a proposition such as

> (1) If David were to remain in Keilah, Saul would (freely) besiege the city,

---

their *status*. According to the Molinists, (some) such counterfactuals are both contingent and independent of God's will, and according to the Thomist opponents of Molinism, such counterfactuals are either contingent but dependent upon God's will or independent of God's will but necessary. Neither side, therefore, disputed the truth of the relevant conditionals.

The thesis that I have called the doctrine of middle knowledge, (39), has the following features. First, it seems to be required by an adequate account of divine providence and by the Free Will Defense. Second, it is cautiously formulated so as to avoid explicit commitment to Conditional Excluded Middle. Thus it should be possible to come to some conclusions about it without having to settle the controversial logical question of whether Conditional Excluded Middle is valid. Third, (39) is denied by such contemporary critics of "middle knowledge" as Robert Adams and William Hasker. For these reasons, (39) is worth examining, even if it was not central to the sixteenth-century debate between the Jesuits and the Dominicans.

Finally, it should be clear in the text that I regard counterfactuals of world-actualization as contingent and independent of God's will. Accordingly, I do defend a version of Molinism.

46. See especially Adams, "Middle Knowledge and the Problem of Evil," but also his "Plantinga on the Problem of Evil."

47. Except, of course, analytic ones. Let us continue our practice of ignoring them. In a note added to "Middle Knowledge and the Problem of Evil" as reprinted in his *The Virtue of Faith and Other Essays in Philosophical Theology* (Oxford: Oxford University Press, 1987), Adams makes it explicit that he regards counterfactuals of freedom as false and not merely as lacking in truth value (p. 91).

48. "Middle Knowledge and the Problem of Evil," p. 116.

49. Ibid., pp. 110–111; Adams, "Plantinga on the Problem of Evil," p. 232.

Adams apparently holds that if the antecedent either logically or causally necessitates the consequent, there would be a ground of truth for (1). But Adams correctly rejects both of these alternatives: it is surely possible that David remain in Keilah and Saul not besiege the city, and if David's remaining in Keilah *causes* Saul to besiege the city, Saul would not besiege the city *freely*.

Adams then considers the proposal that "we . . . seek non-necessitating grounds for the truth of (1) . . . in the actual intentions, desires, and character of Saul."[50] He claims, however, that "the basis thus offered for the truth of (1) . . . is inadequate precisely because it is not necessitating. A free agent may act out of character, or change his intentions, or fail to act on them."[51] For simplicity, let us ignore the role of intentions and desires and consider just the truncated proposal that an agent's character grounds his counterfactuals of freedom. We then take Adams's claim to be simply that an agent may act out of character. What we discover will apply, I believe, to the full claim that an agent may act out of character, change his intentions, or fail to act on his intentions. So in the case of (1) Adams concedes that

> (40) It is part of Saul's character to besiege Keilah if David remains there.[52]

But Adams alleges that, in virtue of

> (41) Saul may act out of character (and not besiege Keilah if David remained there),

(40) does not *ground* (1). Now the modal auxiliary in (41) can be interpreted in several ways. Accordingly, (41) may be understood as

> (41a) Saul has (and would have) it within his power to act out of character (and not besiege Keilah if David remained there),

50. Adams, "Middle Knowledge and the Problem of Evil," p. 111.
51. Ibid.
52. This represents a further simplification. It is part of Saul's character to try to beseige Keilah if David remains there. It is not part of his character that he has the power to do it. But since he does, as king, have the power, I shall not bother to separate these two elements.

or in a way that entails

> (41b) It might be that David remains in Keilah and Saul acts out
> of character (and does not besiege the city),

or, finally, as

> (41c) If David were to remain in Keilah then it might be that
> Saul would act out of character (and not besiege the city).

Of these interpretations, (41a) attributes to Saul a certain ability,
(41b) asserts a certain logical possibility, and (41c) is a might-counterfactual.[53] We should therefore investigate whether any of these
interpretations discredit (1) or show that it is not grounded.

It is plausible to think that both (41a) and (41b) are true. Saul
surely had the ability to refrain from besieging Keilah, and he would
not have lost that ability had David remained there. Hence, (41a).
And since if David had remained in Keilah and Saul besieged it,
Saul's besieging would have been *free*, there is a possible world in
which David remains in Keilah and Saul does not beseige it. Thus,
(41b). Note, however, that (41a) and (41b) do not in the least discredit (1). Here is an analogy to (41a). I have it within my power to
give my child a stone (and not some bread) if she were to ask for
bread; but that fact does not by itself show that it is not true that if
she were to ask for bread I would give her bread. The same is true
for (41b). It is logically possible that my child ask for bread and I
give her a stone instead; but that possibility does not show that that
it is not true that if she were to ask for bread I would give her bread.

Of course, it need not be Adams's claim that (41) (or one of its
variants) can be used to show that (1) is false. All he explicitly claims
is that it somehow shows that (40) does not constitute adequate
grounds for (1). But how does it do that? Perhaps as follows: since
(41a) and (41b) both seem to be true, they are clearly each cotenable
with (40). And noticing that they are each cotenable with (40) makes
it easier to see that (40) does not *entail* (1). But does that show that
(40) does not *ground* (1)? Here we face the difficult problem of deter-

---

53. In Lewis's theory the might-counterfactual *if it were the case that p then it might
be the case that q* is defined as *it is not true that if it were the case that p then it would be the
case that not-q*. See *Counterfactuals*, pp. 2, 21, 80–83.

mining exactly what Adams intends by a ground of truth. Perhaps we can avoid settling that issue, however, if we recall that Adams is willing to allow that a causally sufficient condition can ground a proposition. Since a causally sufficient condition for the truth of a proposition need not entail the proposition, it seems clear that Adams does not require that a ground of a proposition entail the proposition. Hence, the fact that (40) does not entail (1) does not seem to show that it does not ground it.

Things are different with (41c). If (41c) is true, then (1) is false; and if (1) is false, (40) does not ground its truth. But, of course, the reason that (1) is false if (41c) is true is simply that (41c) is equivalent to the denial of (1). So (41c) is not an independent reason against (1). Moreover, whatever plausibility (41c) seems to have may well be due to a failure to distinguish it from (41a) and (41b).[54] So I cannot see that Adams has shown that (1) is ungrounded or that there is nothing that makes it true. There remain the questions of whether there is something that makes it true and whether it cannot be true otherwise. We pursue these questions below; first, however, let us consider a puzzle Adams raises for the possible worlds account of counterfactuals of freedom.

6. Acting out of Character

According to Adams, "A world in which David stays in Keilah and Saul besieges the city is perhaps more similar to the actual world in respect of Saul's character than a world in which David stays in Keilah and Saul does not besiege the city." But, Adams warns, "we had better not conclude that therefore the former is more similar to the actual world than the latter for purposes of the possible worlds explanation [of counterfactuals]." But why not? According to Adams, "We have a well-entrenched belief that under many counterfactual conditions many a person *might* have acted out of character, although he probably would not have. If the possible worlds explanation is to be plausible, it must not give such decisiveness to similarities of character and behavior as to be inconsistent with this

---

54. I do not mean to accuse Adams of failing to see these distinctions. I am merely trying to persuade the reader who is sympathetic to (41) not to accept (41c) by confusing it with (41a) or (41b).

belief."[55] Does the possible worlds account of counterfactual conditionals have the consequence that it is never the case that a person
might act out of character? Answering this question requires making the distinctions we made in the case of (41) above, and it also
requires that we have a clearer grasp of the concept of acting out of
character.

Let us tackle the second issue first. A person's character has to do
not only with what that person has in fact done and not only with
what that person will do; it involves a great many dispositions to act
in predictable ways in a wide range of circumstances. Perhaps the
best way to think of a character, then, is as a set of true counterfactuals of freedom. What would it be for a person to act out of character? In a strict sense,

> (42) A person S acts out of character$_S$ just in case there are
> circumstances C and an action A such that (i) S's character
> includes a counterfactual of freedom specifying that in cir-
> cumstances C S would do A, (ii) S is in C, and (iii) S does
> $\sim A$, the complement of A.[56]

The "might" in the claim that a person might act out of character$_S$
could attribute an ability to act in a certain way, it could indicate a
certain logical possibility, or it could signal a might-counterfactual.
It is clear that, given the above definition, no one has the ability to
act out of character$_S$. That would require doing the complement of
some action A in circumstances in which it is true that if one were in
those circumstances one would do A, and no one has the ability to
do that. Indeed, it is not possible for anyone to do that. So on our
first two interpretations of "might," it is not true that someone
might act out of character$_S$.[57] Formulating the third interpretation
requires finding the relevant might-counterfactual. Perhaps this version of the claim that someone might act out of character$_S$ can be put

55. "Middle Knowledge and the Problem of Evil," p. 113.

56. The subscript is used to distinguish this sense of acting out of character from
one to be introduced below. Clause (i) may be replaced by "if S were in C, S would
do A," thus avoiding explicit commitment to "characters."

57. That means that, strictly speaking, (41a) and (41b) are not true, after all. The
essential points of the preceding section remain, however, if (41a), (41b), and (41c)
are reformulated in terms of Saul's besieging Keilah and without reference to acting
out of character.

as follows. There are a person S, circumstances C, and an action A such that it is part of S's character to do A in C and if S were in C it might be that S would do $\sim A$. But that is equivalent to the claim that there are a person S, circumstances C, and an action A such that if S were in C S would do A and it is false that if S were in C S would do A; and that is impossible. Accordingly, our third interpretation of the claim that someone might act out of character$_S$ comes out false, too. So in the strict and philosophical sense of acting out of character$_S$, it is no defect if the possible worlds account of counterfactuals of freedom precludes acting out of character$_S$.

It will no doubt be objected that our strict and philosophical account of acting out of character$_S$ is neither the ordinary concept nor the concept intended by Adams. Perhaps the more familiar concept (the "loose and popular sense") can be understood as follows.

(43) A person S acts out of character$_L$ just in case there are circumstances C and an action A such that (i) S performs A in C, (ii) S has previously been in circumstances similar to C, and (iii) on all (or most) of the previous occasions on which S was in circumstances similar to C (which include having the opportunity to perform an action A' similar to A), S has performed $\sim A'$ (the complement of A').

In the loose and popular sense, then, acting out of character$_L$ involves a departure from previous patterns of behavior.

It is clear that people often have the ability to act in ways that are dissimilar from the ways they have acted previously, and, hence, it is also possible that they so act. Thus, in our first two interpretations of "might," people might act out of character$_L$. It is also clear that the possible worlds account of counterfactuals is not inconsistent with these facts. Even if that theory provides an interpretation according to which a given counterfactual turns out true, for example, that leaves it open that the agent would be able to refrain from performing (and a fortiori that it is possible that the agent refrain from performing) the action specified in the consequent of the conditional were the agent to be in the circumstances specified by the antecedent.

The third interpretation of "might" may seem more troublesome, for it is also true that for many persons, S, there are circumstances C

and an action A such that (i) on all (or most) of the occasions on which S has been in circumstances like C, S has refrained from performing an action like A, and (ii) if S were in C S might perform A.[58] Hence, it is also true in the third interpretation of "might" that a person might act out of character$_L$. The possible worlds account of counterfactuals of freedom is not inconsistent with these facts, however.

But how can this be? Suppose that whenever S has been in circumstances similar to C, S has refrained from doing A (or has done $\sim A$). Then let us ask whether S would do A if S were in C. According to the possible worlds account of counterfactuals,

(44) If S were in C, S would do A

is true just in case there is some world sufficiently similar to the actual world in which S is in C and does A and there is no world as similar in which S is in C but does $\sim A$. But if whenever S has been in C-like circumstances in the past S has refrained from doing an A-like action, how could it fail to be the case that some world in which S is in C and refrains from A is more similar to the actual world than any world in which S is in C but does A? But then it appears that the possible world account makes (44) false, and, accordingly, it is false both that if S were in C S might do A and that S might act out of character$_L$.

We should not be persuaded, however, by this argument that the possible worlds account supplies an interpretation of (44) according to which it is false. The reason is that it is a mistake to think that the only similarities relevant to the comparative similarity of worlds essential to the possible worlds account are those having to do with what S has previously done. An example may make this point clearer. Suppose that whenever I have been offered a piece of chocolate mousse cake I have accepted. Suppose also that I have never been offered more than two pieces in succession. And now suppose that having just consumed two pieces I am offered a third. Should we say that some world in which I accept the third piece is more

---

58. This is not to assert that it is also true that if S were in C S might do $\sim A$. (Note that *If S were in C S might do A* is compatible with *If S were in C S would do A*.) Thus the claim in the text does not depend on denying Conditional Excluded Middle.

similar to the actual world than any world in which I reject it, on the grounds that in the actual world I have always accepted the dessert when offered? What if I am offered a dozen pieces? Other features of the actual world include my (apparently overridable) aversion to excessive caloric intake as well as my body's capacity for ingestion of chocolate and cream. These features might well be relevant to the truth of the counterfactuals in question. In fact, the counterfactuals *themselves* are germane to the relevant comparative similarity among worlds. Suppose that in fact it is true that if I were offered a third piece of chocolate mousse cake, I would decline it. Now consider a world W in which I am offered a third piece and accept it and a world W' in which I am offered a third piece and decline it. W is perhaps more like the actual world with respect to my accepting every piece of cake offered, but W' is more similar to the actual world with respect to sharing the same counterfactuals. It is not obvious that W is closer in overall similarity; perhaps the balance tilts toward W'. If so, however, the possible worlds account does not automatically assign an interpretation that is false to *If I were offered a third piece of chocolate mousse cake I would decline it.*

Let us apply this reasoning to (44). Suppose that whenever S has been in C-like circumstances, S has refrained from doing an A-like action. What if S were in circumstances C? Would S do A? Suppose that W is a world in which S is in C and refrains from A and that W' is a world in which S is in C and does A. Is that enough to make W more similar to the actual world than W'? Perhaps not; for if in addition to including S's history of refraining from A-like actions the actual world includes the true counterfactual that *If S were in C, S would do A*, then although W would be more similar to the actual world with respect to S's past behavior, W' would be more similar to the actual world with respect to which counterfactuals are true. And, as before, it may happen that the overall similarity of W' to the actual world is greater than the overall similarity of W. If so, (44) is true, in which case the possible worlds account of counterfactuals is not committed to counting it as false.

The point that "one measure of similarity between worlds involves the question whether they share their counterfactuals" has been made by Plantinga.[59] He gave an example in which Royal

59. Plantinga, *The Nature of Necessity*, p. 178.

Robbins slipped and regained his balance while climbing El Capitan unroped. Plantinga then considered

> (45) If Robbins had slipped and fallen at Thanksgiving Ledge, he would have been killed,

and noted that a world W' in which Robbins slipped and fell and then nevertheless showed up on Thanksgiving Ledge might seem more similar to the actual world—in virtue of the fact that in the actual world Robbins did not fall—than a world W in which Robbins slips and falls to the valley below. Plantinga then replied that W' does not share its causal laws with the actual world and, given the close connection between causal laws and counterfactuals, does not share its counterfactuals with the actual world, either. Accordingly, W is closer to the actual world than W', and (45) is true, after all.

It is also worth repeating the moral Plantinga draws from this example, since it replies to an objection that has surely occurred to the reader by now. The possible worlds account of counterfactuals has not been shown to be "viciously circular or of no theoretical interest," but "it does follow that we cannot as a rule *discover* the truth value of a counter-factual by asking whether its consequent holds in those worlds most similar to the actual in which its antecedent holds."[60]

We have seen that the possible worlds account of counterfactuals of freedom is not inconsistent with the true versions of the claim that many persons might have acted out of character. Thus, we may continue to use that account in thinking about these matters. In the next section we resume our discussion of objections to the doctrine of middle knowledge.

7. The Not True Soon Enough Objection

Another objection posed by Adams is that "on the possible worlds theory, the truth of the crucial conditionals cannot be settled soon enough to be of use to God."[61] This is not strictly an objection

60. Ibid.
61. Adams, "Middle Knowledge and the Problem of Evil," p. 113.

to the doctrine of middle knowledge—it does not deny that there are true counterfactuals of freedom or that God knows them. Rather, it denies that God's knowledge of counterfactuals of freedom can play any role in God's decision to actualize the world. The same objection is urged by Kenny. He holds that "prior to God's decision to actualize a particular world those counterfactuals cannot yet be known: for their truth-value depends . . . on which world is the actual world."[62] Here is how Adams argues for the point:

Consider a deliberative conditional,

[(46)] If I did x, y would happen.

Is [(46)] true? According to the possible worlds explanation, that depends on whether the actual world is more similar to some world in which I do x and y happens than to any world in which I do x and y does not happen. That in turn seems to depend on which world is the actual world. And which world is the actual world? That depends in part on whether I do x. Thus the truth of [(46)] seems to depend on the truth or falsity of its antecedent.[63]

If we apply these claims to a counterfactual of world-actualization, say,

(47) If God were to strongly actualize $T(W)$ then there would be a balance of good over evil,

we have the following argument:

(48) The truth of (47) depends on whther a world in which God strongly actualizes $T(W)$ and there is a balance of good over evil is more similar to the actual world than any world in which God strongly actualizes $T(W)$ and there is not a balance of good over evil.

(49) That a world in which God strongly actualizes $T(W)$ and there is a balance of good over evil is more similar to the actual world than any world in which God strongly actualizes $T(W)$ and there is not a balance of good over evil depends on which world is the actual world.

62. Kenny, *The God of the Philosophers*, p. 70.
63. Adams, "Middle Knowledge and the Problem of Evil," pp. 113–114.

(50) Which world is the actual world depends on whether God strongly actualizes *T(W)*.

Therefore,

(51) The truth of (47) depends on whether its antecedent is true.

But if the truth of (47) depends on whether its antecedent is true, God cannot rely on his knowledge of (47) in deciding whether to strongly actualize *T(W)*.

This argument clearly requires that the relation expressed here by 'depends on' be transitive, but, as Plantinga points out, that relation is not transitive.[64] To show this Plantinga provides the following example:

(52) The truth of *The Allies won the Second World War* depends on which world is actual.

(53) Which world is actual depends on whether I mow my lawn this afternoon.

Therefore,

(54) The truth of *The Allies won the Second World War* depends on whether I mow my lawn this afternoon.

Since (52) and (53) are true but (54) is false, the relation expressed by 'depends on' is not transitive; hence, this argument by which Adams attempts to show the uselessness of middle knowledge (and which, presumably, is also intended by Kenny) does not succeed.

8. Another No Grounds Objection

William Hasker has presented some intricate arguments against the doctrine of middle knowledge. Like Adams, Hasker holds that if counterfactuals of freedom are true, something "*brings it about* that these propositions are true."[65] Hasker's argument is quite complex. He first considers the suggestion that if a counterfactual of freedom

64. Plantinga, "Replies to My Colleagues," p. 376.
65. Hasker, "A Refutation of Middle Knowledge," p. 547.

involving a certain agent is true, then it is the agent himself who makes the counterfactual true. Hasker then argues that an agent cannot make his own counterfactuals of freedom true. Finally Hasker argues that if counterfactuals of freedom are true and they cannot be made true by their agents, then agents are not free. Accordingly, Hasker rejects the assumption that counterfactuals of freedom are true.

We do not have to consider all of Hasker's arguments here.[66] It is sufficient for our purposes to examine Hasker's contention that agents do not bring about the truth of their own counterfactuals of freedom or, to put it in Adams's terms, that an agent's action is not an adequate ground of the truth of such propositions.

Hasker begins by rejecting the suggestion that God brings about counterfactuals of freedom, and then he asks: "But if God does not bring it about that [a] counterfactual of freedom is true, then who does? The answer which is in fact given is that it is the agent named in the counterfactual who brings it about that the counterfactual is true. More precisely, it is the agent who brings this about *in those possible worlds in which the antecedent is true* [original emphasis]."[67] Two initial qualifications ought to be made. First, if Saul makes

(1) If David were to remain in Keilah, Saul would (freely) besiege the city

true, it is not by besieging Keilah in *every* world in which the antecedent of (1) is true. Surely it is enough that Saul besiege Keilah in the sufficiently close worlds in which David remains in Keilah. But even with this emendation, the proposal is implausible. If (1) is true, there is some world *W* sufficiently similar to the actual world which is such that (i) in *W* David remains in Keilah and Saul besieges the city and (ii) there is no more similar world in which David remains in Keilah and Saul does not besiege the city. But the proposal Hasker considers seems to be the claim that Saul's besieging Keilah

---

66. See David Basinger, "Middle Knowledge and Human Freedom: Some Clarifications," *Faith and Philosophy* 4 (1987):330–336, for criticism of an argument of Hasker's that we shall not discuss here. Cf. Freddoso, "Introduction."

67. Hasker, "A Refutation of Middle Knowledge," p. 548. Hasker cites conversations with defenders of the doctrine of middle knowledge as the source for this proposal.

in W brings about the truth of (1) in the actual world. But how can Saul's action in some other world have any consequences in the actual world?[68] Nevertheless, there is some initial plausiblity to the view that Saul's besieging Keilah in W makes (1) true *in W* at least; but Hasker's argument, if correct, refutes even this more modest claim. Accordingly, let us consider Hasker's argument.[69] Perhaps we will, in the process, discover something about what is required to bring about the truth of a counterfactual of freedom.

Hasker considers the case of Elizabeth, a graduate student in anthropology, who might receive a grant to conduct a potentially risky study of a tribe of reformed cannibals. Hasker thus considers

(55) If Elizabeth were offered the grant she would accept it.

He begins by considering a general principle

(56) For any event e and proposition p, if e brings it about that p is true then if e were to occur p would be true and if it were the case that e does not occur then p would be false.

Now Hasker realizes that in this unrestricted form, (56) is false. To see why, suppose that in fact e brings it about that p is true but that if e had not occurred some other event sufficient for the truth of p would have occurred.[70] But Hasker thinks that the following substitution instance of (56) is true:

(57) If Elizabeth's accepting the grant brings it about that (55) is true then if Elizabeth were to accept the grant (55) would be true and if it were not the case that Elizabeth accepts the grant then (55) would be false.

(Hasker accepts (57) while rejecting (56) because he believes that nothing other than Elizabeth's accepting the grant could make (55)

68. On David Lewis's rather different theory of possible worlds, it is analytic that no event occurring in one possible world has an effect in another world. See his *On the Plurality of Worlds* (Oxford: Basil Blackwell, 1986), p. 2. I hope that this claim, if not analytic, is at least obvious.

69. A subsequent remark (Hasker, "A Refutation of Middle Knowledge," p. 549) suggests that in fact it is this more modest claim that Hasker is out to refute.

70. Recall the Frankfurt-style examples discussed in Section 4 of Chapter 3.

true. This is an assumption we examine below.) Since the proposal under consideration is that an agent makes his or her own counterfactual of freedom true in at least some sufficiently similar world in which its antecedent is true, Hasker assumes that Elizabeth is offered the grant and that (55) is true. He then attempts to show that the antecedent of (57) is false. He concedes, of course, that if Elizabeth were to accept the grant (55) would be true, but he denies that

> (58) If it were not the case that Elizabeth accepts the grant, then (55) would be false.

If (58) is false then so is the consequent of (57), and it would then follow by *modus tollens* that Elizabeth's accepting the grant does not make (55) true.

But why think that (58) is false? Hasker notes that Elizabeth's not accepting the offer is not the same as her rejecting it, since it could be that she does not accept if it is not offered, but she could reject it only if it were offered. But then Hasker claims that a world in which Elizabeth does not receive the offer is more similar to the actual world (where, by hypothesis Elizabeth receives and accepts the offer and (55) is true) than is any world in which she receives the offer but rejects it. Accordingly, Hasker thinks that if it were the case that Elizabeth does not accept the offer, (55) would (still) be true.[71]

Here we should recall that sentences expressing counterfactuals are often ambiguous, owing to the fact they can be differently interpreted if different relations of similarity are assumed. David Lewis cites Quine's examples

> (59) If Caesar had been in command [in Korea] he would have used the atom bomb

and

> (60) If Caesar had been in command [in Korea] he would have used catapults

---

71. Since Hasker does not himself believe that counterfactuals of freedom are true, he perhaps means to claim here that *according to the standards of the defender of middle knowledge* (55) would be true if Elizabeth were not to accept.

and recommends that we

call on context . . . to resolve part of the vagueness of comparative similarity in a way favorable to the truth of one counterfactual or the other. In one context, we may attach great importance to similarities and differences in respect of Caesar's character and in respect of regularities concerning the knowledge of weapons common to commanders in Korea. In another context we may attach less importance to these similarities and differences, and more importance to similarities and differences in respect of Caesar's own knowledge of weapons. The first context resolves the vagueness of comparative similarity in such a way that some worlds with a modernized Caesar in command come out closer to our world than any unmodernized Caesar. It thereby makes the first counterfactual true. The second context resolves the vagueness in the opposite direction, making the second counterfactual true.[72]

With these ideas in mind we can see that one relation of similarity relevant to (58) emphasizes Elizabeth's actual willingness to accept the grant and discounts the fact that the grant has already been offered. Another relation of similarity emphasizes the fact that Elizabeth has received the offer, and it discounts her willingness to accept. But which, if either, is appropriate to evaluating the truth of (58)? (Alternatively, which proposition does (58) express in the present context? one to whose truth the former relation of similarity is relevant, or one to whose truth the latter relation of similarity is relevant?) Now (58) arises in the context of (57), a proposition that purports to specify some necessary conditions of Elizabeth's accepting the grant bringing it about that (55) is true. We have assumed that Elizabeth has been offered the grant (since the hypothesis in question is that an agent can bring about the truth of one of her counterfactuals of freedom in a world in which the antecedent of the counterfactual is true by performing in that world the action specified by the consequent of the counterfactual.) But it seems clear that if we are wondering whether there is something Elizabeth can do, having received the offer of the grant, to make (55) false, the appropriate interpretation of (58) for this purpose involves a similarity relation that keeps Elizabeth's having received the grant fixed. That

72. Lewis, *Counterfactuals,* p. 67.

is, we have assumed that the offer of the grant has been made and we are asking what would happen if *it* were not accepted. In this case, the hypothesis that Elizabeth did not receive the offer is clearly a greater departure from reality than is the falsehood of the counterfactual *if Elizabeth were to be offered the grant she would accept it*. Accordingly, under this interpretation (58) seems true, and the consequent of (57) has not been shown to be false. Hence, it has not been shown that Elizabeth's accepting the grant does not make (55) true.[73]

We saw above that Hasker accepts (57) while rejecting (56) of which it is an instance because he holds that nothing other than Elizabeth's accepting the grant could make (55) true. We left that

73. By means of an example involving a causal law (p. 551) and in a long footnote (pp. 556–557) Hasker attempts to defend his claim that a similarity relation emphasizing the counterfactual *if Elizabeth were offered the grant she would accept it* and discounting the fact that Elizabeth has been offered the grant is the appropriate one. Hasker claims that according to the doctrine of middle knowledge "the very same counterfactuals of freedom are true *in all the worlds God could actualize*" and, hence, that "counterfactuals of freedom are considerably more fundamental . . . than the laws of nature; *a fortiori*, they are more fundamental than particular facts such as that Elizabeth is offered the grant" (p. 557). But, in the first place, it is not part of the doctrine of middle knowledge that the same counterfactuals of freedom are true in all the worlds God could actualize; even if that doctrine is incorporated into an account of God's actualizing the world (see Section 2 above) this assumption might not be true. Rather, what seems to be presupposed by the account of God's actualizing the world is that the same *counterfactuals of world-actualization* are true in every world God could have actualized. (The Free Will Defense [see Section 3 above] presupposes that it is *possible* that *some* counterfactuals of freedom are true in every world God could have actualized, for example, such propositions as *if Saul were created he would go wrong with with respect to at least one morally significant action*. But even the Free Will Defense does not presuppose that *all* the same counterfactuals of freedom are true in every world God could have actualized.) Moreover, even if counterfactuals of freedom are out of God's control in the way Hasker suggests, it does not follow that they are more fundamental than causal laws unless they are *also* out of the control of *their agents*—but that is exactly what Hasker is trying to show. Hence, he is not entitled to appeal to this claim in the endeavor to show that agents do not bring about their own counterfactuals of freedom.

Note also that, on Hasker's preferred relation of similarity, (57) has no plausibility; for according to the resulting interpretation (57) would seem to require that in order for Elizabeth to bring about (55) it would have to be the case that if she were not to receive the grant (55) would be false—but that is an unreasonable requirement.

assumption unchallenged, but it will prove instructive to examine it. Hasker argues for this assumption as follows:

> How might it be possible for the agent to bring it about that a given counterfactual of freedom is true? It would seem that the only possible way in which the agent might do this is by performing that action specified in the consequent of the conditional under the circumstances specified in the antecedent. In order to bring it about that the counterfactual is true, the agent must do something which excludes the possibility of her failing to perform that action under those circumstances. But if she were to perform some other action which would guarantee that the specified action would be performed . . . then this other action would deprive her of freedom with respect to the specified action. . . . In the case of a genuinely free action the only way to guarantee the action's being done is by doing it.[74]

Hasker thus seems to assume that

> (61) An agent S brings about a counterfactual of freedom $(A > C)$ only if S performs an action B such that it is not possible that (A and S performs B and $\sim C$).[75]

And Hasker holds that for any counterfactual of freedom the only action B satisfying (61) (and which is such that the agent's performing B is consistent with the consequent of the counterfactual) is the action specified by the consequent of the counterfactual. Thus, Hasker holds that nothing other than Elizabeth's accepting the grant could make (55) true.

It seems to me, however, that (61) imposes an exceptionally stringent condition on bringing about a counterfactual. Consider first an analogue for bringing about states of affairs generally:

> (62) S brings about a state of affairs A only if S performs an action B such that it is not possible that ($\sim A$ and S performs B).

74. Hasker, "A Refutation of Middle Knowledge," p. 548.

75. I have not attributed to Hasker the result of strengthening (61) to a biconditional because that would allow an agent to bring about a counterfactual of freedom simply by doing something inconsistent with the truth of its antecedent.

Now I can bring it about that there is water in the sink, for example, by turning on the faucet, despite the fact that it is logically possible that I turn on the faucet and there be no water in the sink. So (62) seems to be false. What is relevant here is that if I were to turn on the faucet I would do so in circumstances (including there being water in the pipes and there being sufficient water pressure) such that if I were to turn on the faucet in those circumstances there would be water in the sink. In other words, I can bring it about that there is water in the sink in virtue of the fact that there is something I can do, namely, turn on the faucet, which is such that if I were to do it there would be water in the sink. Thus,

(62′)   S brings about a state of affairs A only if S performs an action B which is such that S *performs* B counterfactually implies A *occurs*.

It might be thought, however, that even if (62′) holds for bringing about states of affairs generally, (61) nevertheless imposes a correct condition for bringing about counterfactual conditionals; but this, too, seems wrong. Consider first a counterfactual that is not a counterfactual of freedom. By putting shoe polish on the telephone receiver I can bring it about that if you were to use the phone your ear would become dirty, despite the fact that it is possible that you use the phone, I put shoe polish on the receiver, and your ear does not become dirty. (It is possible that you use the phone without touching it to your ear, and it is possible that you clean the receiver before using the phone.) In this case, as before, what seems to be relevant is that I am in circumstances such that if I were to put shoe polish on the receiver, then if you were to use the phone your ear would become dirty. That is,

(61′)   An agent S brings about a counterfactual of freedom (A > C) only if S performs an action B such that S *performs* B counterfactually implies (A > C).

Note that (61′) is just a special case of (62′). Note also that according to both (61′) and (62′), if one brings about a counterfactual of freedom then one weakly actualizes it.

To say that one brings about a counterfactual of freedom by weakly actualizing it is not to foist an unreasonable interpretation on the proposal Hasker is considering. To see this we need to switch examples because Hasker's example has a feature not shared by all counterfactuals of freedom, namely, its consequent entails its antecedent. (Elizabeth could not accept the grant unless it had been offered to her.) So consider instead

> (55′) If Elizabeth were offered the grant she would travel to San Luis Obispo.

(Suppose that is where the reformed cannibals live.) Recall that the proposal Hasker considers is that an agent can bring about the truth of a counterfactual of freedom by performing the action specified by its consequent. Suppose, then, that Elizabeth travels to San Luis Obispo. There certainly seems to be no causal connection between her trip and (55′). And, clearly enough, Elizabeth's traveling to San Luis Obispo does not entail (55′); for it is possible that she disapproves of the organization sponsoring the grant and in order to disassociate herself from it, would travel to San Luis Obispo only if she does *not* receive the grant. How then could Elizabeth's traveling to San Luis Obispo bring about the truth of (55′)? The most natural answer seems to be that it would if it is an action that if she were to do it, (55′) would be true. But that is just to say that Elizabeth brings about (55′), if she does, by weakly actualizing it.[76]

But if weakly actualizing a counterfactual of freedom is also sufficient for bringing it about—and I cannot see why not—then agents may well be able to bring about a counterfactual of freedom in other ways than by performing the action specified in its consequent in the circumstances described by its antecedent. Thus, for example, Elizabeth may bring it about that if she were offered the grant she would accept it, by resolving to accept the grant if offered and by declining all other sources of income (thereby giving herself great incentive to accept it). And if Elizabeth can bring about (55) in this way without

---

76. In saying that Elizabeth brings about (55′) by weakly actualizing it, I do not not mean that (55′) is not true *before* Elizabeth weakly actualizes it. This is analogous to the familiar point that if I bring it about, for example, that there is water in the sink at *t*, the proposition that there is water in the sink at *t* has always been true.

actually accepting the grant, then presumably someone else could bring about (55), too. Suppose that Elizabeth is undecided about whether to accept the grant if it is offered, but that if she were offered a supplement of $30,000 to accept the grant, she would then accept it. Suppose that I know this and am in a position to make sure that if she is offered the grant she is also offered the requisite supplement. In effect, then, I can ensure that the nearest worlds in which Elizabeth is offered the grant are worlds in which she is also offered the enticing supplement, and those are worlds in which she accepts the grant. Accordingly, I can do something such that if I were to do it, it would be true that if Elizabeth were to be offered the grant she would accept it. Thus, I, too, can bring about the truth of (55).[77]

A further consequence of the fact that counterfactuals of freedom can be brought about in this way is that an agent can bring about a counterfactual of freedom even in a world in which its antecedent is not true. Thus, if Elizabeth resolves to accept the grant were it to be offered, then she might bring about (55) even if she is not offered the grant. Usually, of course, it will not be simple acts of resolution that bring about an agent's counterfactuals of freedom. Rather, agents make a series of choices and decisions in a variety of circumstances that shape their characters and, thus, bring about counterfactuals of freedom. We can thus see the importance of the proposal, discussed in Section 5 above but unfortunately rejected by Adams, that an agent's intentions, desires, and character provide a basis for the truth of some of an agent's counterfactuals of freedom. To the extent that

77. This case and the previous one can be used to construct a counterexample to (56), the principle Hasker thinks applies to bringing about counterfactuals of freedom. Suppose Elizabeth's resolving to accept the grant and her declining all other sources of support bring about the truth of (55). Suppose also that I am in close contact with Elizabeth and resolve to put into effect my plan of supplementing the grant with an extra $30,000 if Elizabeth does not herself resolve to accept the grant if offered. We have the following instance of (56):

> (56') If Elizabeth's resolving to accept the grant and declining all other sources of support brings it about that (55) is true, then if Elizabeth's resolving to accept the grant and declining all other sources of support were to occur (55) would be true, and if Elizabeth's resolving to accept the grant and declining all other sources of support were not to occur (55) would be false.

In this case, however, the antecedent is true, but the right conjunct of the consequent is false.

intentions, desires, and character are shaped by an agent's own choices and actions, the agent brings about various counterfactuals of freedom.

In typical cases, of course, agents are not alone in contributing to their counterfactuals of freedom. An example may make this point clearer. As a parent I may nurture my children in ways that contribute to the development of their characters. Thus, I may place them in circumstances in which they will have to make independent choices or in which they will experience satisfaction in helping others. In so doing, I may well bring about some counterfactuals of freedom involving my children. This is not, I suggest, incompatible with my children themselves, through their actions, also bringing about those counterfactuals. And no doubt there are other contributing factors as well.

On the Christian view, God is related to us in a way analogous to the way a parent is related to a child. Thus, God places us in circumstances intended to mold our characters and to enable us freely to commit ourselves to him. And just as it can happen that no matter how hard their parents try, some children still get into trouble, the contention of the Free Will Defense is that an analogous predicament is a possibility for God. We may conclude, I believe, that the objections to the doctrine of middle knowledge we have considered do not succeed in showing that this is not a possibility for God or that his knowledge does not extend to what free agents would do in alternative circumstances.

9. Alternatives to Middle Knowledge

Given the controversy the doctrine of middle knowledge has engendered, it is not surprising that alternatives to it have been proposed. In this concluding section we examine three such alternatives. I argue that they enjoy no decisive advantage over the doctrine of middle knowledge.

Peter Geach has proposed thinking of God as a chess master:

> God is the supreme Grand Master who has everything under his control. Some of the players are consciously helping his plan, others are trying to hinder it; whatever the finite players do, God's plan will be executed; though various lines of God's play will answer to vari-

ous moves of the finite players. God cannot be surprised or thwarted or cheated or disappointed. God, like some grand master of chess, can carry out his plan even if he has announced it beforehand. "On that square," says the Grand Master, "I will promote my pawn to Queen and deliver checkmate to my adversary": and it is even so. No line of play that finite players may think of can force God to improvise: his knowledge of the game already embraces all the possible variant lines of play, theirs does not.[78]

It may not be obvious that this picture is an *alternative* to the doctrine of middle knowledge. Indeed, Herman Bavinck has presented a similar account in an attempt to give an *exposition* of the doctrine:

> God is ready for whatever may happen. He foreknows and sees all possibilities, and he has made provision for all of them. He knows beforehand what he is going to do if Adam falls, and also if he does not; if David goes to Keilah, and also if he does not; if Tyre and Sidon are converted, and also if they are not, etc. Hence, the knowledge of "future contingent events" precedes the decree concerning "absolutely future events". At every moment man chooses with complete freedom and independence, but he is never able to surprise God or annul his plans, for God in his foreknowledge has taken into account every possibility.[79]

There are two important features of Bavinck's account. The first is that God does not have knowledge of future contingent propositions that depend on the free action of his creatures.[80] As Bavinck puts it, God "indeed foreknows future contingent events as possible; nevertheless, he is dependent on the world for finding out whether or not they were realized. However, for every contingency he knows 'an action that will exactly answer the action of the creature,

---

78. Peter Geach, *Providence and Evil* (Cambridge: Cambridge University Press, 1977), p. 58.

79. Herman Bavinck, *The Doctrine of God*, vol. II of *Gereformeerde Dogmatiek*, 3d ed. (1918), trans. William Hendicksen (Grand Rapids, Mich.: Baker Book House, 1977), p. 191.

80. In this respect Bavinck's account differs from Geach's, for Geach allows that God knows future free actions of creatures *provided that those free actions result from present trends and tendencies* (*Providence and Evil*, p. 53). Given that some future free acts might not satisfy this proviso, it seems clear that Geach would allow that God lacks knowledge of some future contingent truths (though presumably Geach would not say that such propositions are already true). See also ibid., p. 50.

whatever that may chance to be.' He establishes with certainty the
outline of the plan of the universe, but he leaves the filling out of this
outline to the creature."[81] But if God does not know what free
creatures will do, then there are also many counterfactuals of freedom he does not know. For example, if before David withdrew
from Keilah God did not know that he would, then prior to David's
flight God did not know that if he were to create David and place
him in certain circumstances (including being free with respect to
remaining in Keilah, receiving advice from the prophet who con-
sulted the ephod, etc.), then David would withdraw from Keilah. It
would seem, furthermore, that among the counterfactuals God
would not know on this account are some counterfactuals of world-
actualization and their denials. Accordingly, this account is incompatible with the doctrine of middle knowledge as we formulated it
in Section 4 above.

The other important feature of this account is that it does attribute
to God knowledge of some counterfactuals of freedom, namely,
those specifying what *he* would do in various circumstances, for
God knows how he would respond to various possibilities. But then
this account is doubly problematic. For in the first place, by denying
that God has foreknowledge of (some) future contingents, the account does not seem adequate to God's omniscience.[82] And in the
second place, if there is a problem about the ground of counterfactuals of freedom, that problem would remain for those counterfactuals of freedom specifying what God would do in various circumstances. The chess master picture seems to be no improvement over
the doctine of middle knowledge.

A second alternative is proposed by Adams. As we have seen, he
denies that such counterfactuals as

(1) If David were to remain in Keilah, Saul would (freely)
besiege the city

81. Bavinck, *The Doctrine of God*, pp. 191–192.
82. Since Geach thinks the only true future contingent propositions are those
corresponding to current tendencies, he would not mind this consequence (*Providence and Evil*, pp. 50, 53). Both Bavinck (*The Doctrine of God*, p. 193) and Kenny
(*The God of the Philosophers*, p. 59) object on this score.

are true. But he holds that what is true instead are such propositions as

> (63) If David were to remain in Keilah, Saul would probably besiege the city.

Adams elaborates this proposal as follows:

> In proposing [(63)] as an alternative to (1), however, I do not understand it as a claim that (1), or any other proposition, *is* probable. It is rather a claim that
>
> [(64)] Saul will besiege Keilah
>
> *would* be probable, given facts that would (definitely, not just probably) obtain if David stayed in Keilah.[83]

But Adams's proposal seems to suffer from at least two difficulties. The first is that if the ersatz counterfactuals of freedom Adams endorses are an adequate basis for divine decision-making, then at least some nontrivial counterfactuals of freedom are true, after all. According to Adams' proposal, I take it, God can know such propositions as

> (65) If God were to strongly actualize $T(W)$ then it would be probable that there is vastly more evil than good.

But if (65) gives God a good reason for not actualizing $T(W)$, it would seem that

> (66) If God were to know (65) then he would not strongly actualize $T(W)$.

Hence, if (65) provides a good basis for God's decision-making, (66) is a true counterfactual of freedom, despite Adams's contention that such propositions are false.

A second problem with Adams's proposal is that his ersatz counterfactuals of freedom are not plausibly taken to be what is really

---

83. Adams, "Middle Knowledge and the Problem of Evil," p. 115.

meant by those of us who think we believe some counterfactuals of freedom. Consider an example cited by Adams:

(67) If I were to ask the butcher to sell me a pound of meat, he would.

On Adams's view, (67) is false. But suppose that I think it is true. In that case, I do not merely mean that

(68) If I were to ask the butcher to sell me a pound of meat, it would be probable that he would.

For if I were to ask the butcher to sell me a pound of meat and he refused, that would falsify what I think to be true, namely (67). But it would not falsify (68). A single exception on new evidence does not falsify the assessment of probability reported by (68), just as a coin landing on heads after a hundred consecutive tosses in which it landed on tails does not falsify the assessment of probability given by

(69) If in a hundred consecutive tosses this coin were to land on tails, it would be probable that on the next toss it will land on tails.

So the introduction of Adams's ersatz counterfactuals of freedom does not lessen the conviction that some genuine counterfactuals of freedom are true.[84]

A final alternative is suggested by Plantinga. In response to Adams's criticisms of the doctrine of middle knowledge, Plantinga suggests a version of the Free Will Defense that does not presuppose that some counterfactuals are true. He writes: "Perhaps, for example, God had no middle knowledge, but knew that no matter which free creatures he created and no matter how they used or abused their freedom, it would be within his power so to respond that there would be enormously more good than evil."[85] On this proposal, God has no middle knowledge, but he nevertheless knew that regardless of whom he created he would be able to ensure that there is

---

84. For this objection I am indebted to Mariam Thalos.

85. Plantinga, "Replies to My Colleagues," p. 379. Plantinga adds that he hopes "to work out a detailed statement of the Free Will Defense along these lines."

vastly more good than evil. How could God know this? It is clear that if God had middle knowledge, he could know how his creatures would respond to his action, and thus he might know that he could act in ways that would ensure a balance of good over evil; but the present proposal denies divine middle knowledge and so cannot avail itself of this account. Alternatively, if it is not possible for there to be as much evil as or more evil than good, then God could know that he could ensure a balance of good over evil. But it surely seems possible that there be free creatures so perverse that they successfully resist all of God's attempts to transform them or to bring good out of evil. As a result, this attempt to explain God's knowledge does not succeed either. There remains the alternative that God simply knows that he is so much wiser than his creatures that he will always be able to devise a plan to achieve his end, even if he does not know ahead of time what that plan will be.

Perhaps this last account of how God knows that no matter whom he creates there will be a balance of good over evil is sufficient for the purposes of the Free Will Defense, since the attempt to show the logical consistency of God's existence with the existence of evil need not, as we saw in Section 3 above, give a true description of the origin of evil or of God's role in dealing with it. The Free Will Defense need only appeal to logical possibilities. But the proposal that God knows that he can ensure a balance of good over evil simply because he is so much wiser than his creatures seems to be inadequate to requirements of the other traditional role for divine middle knowledge, that of explaining God's providence.[86] (See Section 2 above.) If God does not know what a certain creature would do in response to his action, and if God does not even know what he would do in response to a given action of a creature, then what happens would seem not to be under his direct guidance. If God knows that he will succeed in bringing about a balance of good over evil, but he does not have a plan for doing so, then what happens does not fall under his providence. Accordingly, this alternative to the doctrine of divine middle knowledge also seems to be inadequate.

86. Plantinga, as we saw, introduced this proposal in connection with the Free Will Defense. He does not claim that it is adequate to the requirements of divine providence.

6

Eternity, Timelessness, And Immutability

1. Eternity, Timelessness, and Immutability

Augustine cites several divine attributes in the following passage: "Genuine eternity [is that] by which God is unchangeable, without beginning or end; consequently, He is also incorruptible. For one and the same thing is therefore said, whether God is called eternal or immortal, or incorruptible, or unchangeable."[1] Augustine seems to think that he has referred to a single attribute, variously named, but subsequent philosophers have discerned several distinct properties on Augustine's list. In this chapter I first distinguish and describe some of these attributes and then consider several objections to ascribing them to God.

The first, *being eternal*, received its classic statement at the hands of Boethius in his famous phrase "Eternity . . . is the complete possession all at once of illimitable life."[2] Many later philosophers have embraced this formulation.[3]

1. Augustine, *De Trinitate*, XV, 5, 7, trans. Stephen McKenna (Washington, D.C.: Catholic University Press, 1963), p. 459, quoted by Nelson Pike, *God and Timelessness* (London: Routledge & Kegan Paul, 1970), p. 39.

2. Boethius, *The Consolation of Philosophy*, Book V, Prose 6. An important recent discussion of the concept is given by Eleonore Stump and Norman Kretzmann, "Eternity," *Journal of Philosophy* 78 (1981):429–458. Stump and Kretzmann note that although Boethius's formulation has been especially influential, it has its historical antecedents, particularly in Plotinus (p. 431).

3. See, for example, Anselm, *Monologion*, chap. 24, and Aquinas, *Summa Theologica*, Ia, 10, 4.

By 'eternal' Nelson Pike takes Augustine in the passage above simply to mean 'timeless.'[4] We shall look more closely at this latter concept below; for now I note that, however plausible Pike's suggestion is as exegesis of Augustine, it seems to ignore something about the concept of eternity as it has traditionally been understood since Boethius. Eleonore Stump and Norman Kretzmann identify three additional elements in the concept of eternity: possessing life, being illimitable, and having duration. "The life of an eternal being cannot be limited; it is impossible that there be a beginning or end to it. The natural understanding of such a claim is that the existence in question is infinite duration, unlimited in either 'direction'."[5]

The concept of infinite but timeless duration is exceedingly difficult to comprehend;[6] it is therefore also difficult to be sure that the concept of eternity includes it. I am inclined to think, however, that the phrase "complete possession all at once" does introduce an element in addition to timelessness; perhaps that element is what is often put by saying that the life of an eternal being is *present to it* all at once.[7] Thus, Augustine says (speaking of God), "For He does not pass from this to that by transition of thought, but beholds all things with absolute unchangeableness; so that of those things which emerge in time, the future, indeed, are not yet, and the present are now, and the past no longer are; but all of these are by Him comprehended in His stable and eternal presence."[8] On this suggestion, then, an eternal being, in addition to being timeless, has a certain unusual perspective, a perspective from which all things are present at once. To see that although eternity *includes* timelessness, it is not *included by* timelessness, we ought next to consider the latter concept.

The *locus classicus* in recent thought for the doctrine of timelessness—perhaps it is rather the *locus recens*—is Pike's *God and Timelessness*. Pike offers the following definition of timelessness:

4. Pike, *God and Timelessness*, p. 50.
5. Stump and Kretzmann, "Eternity," p. 432.
6. Cf. Paul Fitzgerald, "Stump and Kretzmann on Time and Eternity," *Journal of Philosophy* 82 (1985):260–269, and Stump and Kretzmann, "Atemporal Duration: A Reply to Fitzgerald," *Journal of Philosophy* 84 (1987):214–219.
7. Maybe this just is what Stump and Kretzmann mean by timeless duration.
8. Augustine, *The City of God*, XI, 21, trans. Marcus Dods (New York: Modern Library, 1959), P. 364.

> (1) x is timeless if and only if x lacks temporal extension and x lacks temporal location.[9]

By 'temporal extension' Pike means temporal duration, and he offers the following explanation: "To have duration is, simply, to occupy a number of consecutive temporal positions."[10] By 'temporal positions' Pike apparently means *instants*—he speaks in this context of moments, which he describes as the temporal counterparts of Euclidean points—and to occupy a temporal position is presumably to exist at that instant. But now a minor problem arises; time is often thought to be dense, that is, between any two instants there is another instant. If it is, however, there are no consecutive instants and, a fortiori, nothing that exists at consecutive instants. So perhaps Pike should be interpreted as intending something like

> (2) x has temporal extension if and only if there are distinct times t_1 and t_2 such that x exists at t_1 and x exists at t_2 and for every time t_3 between t_1 and t_2, x exists at t_3.

Pike's explanation of the remaining concept employed in (1), that of temporal location, requires considerably more development. Summarizing his contention that there are two elements in timelessness, Pike says that on this view "God is not to be qualified by temporal predicates of any kind—neither time-extension predicates (such as, e.g., 'six years old') nor time-location predicates (such as, 'before Columbus')."[11] The appeal here to "time-location predicates" suggests that

> (3) x has temporal location if and only if some time-location predicate applies to x.

9. Pike, *God and Timelessness*, p. 7. I have represented Pike as offering a general definition, but in fact he explicitly considers only the claim that *God* is timeless; moreover, Pike is aware that the condition that 'x lacks temporal extension' is redundant, an undesirable feature in a definition. On the other hand, Pike's talk of "conceptual elements" suggests that he intends to provide an *analysis* here. For our purposes it will be sufficient if (1) and its immediate successors state necessary and sufficient conditions.

10. Ibid., p. 8.

11. Ibid.

The problem with this proposal is that time-location predicates of the kind Pike suggests (e.g., 'before Columbus') apply to events rather than to individuals. If all time-location predicates are like this, no individual has temporal location.[12]

There seem to be two ways of repairing this defect. The first, which is attempted by Nicholas Wolterstorff,[13] involves introducing the requisite events as the objects of time-location properties (and as the relata of time-location relations). Thus, Wolterstorff holds that for each individual there is a class of events ("aspects" of the individual) involving that individual and that there is a unique class of events ("the temporal array") which bear temporal ordering relations to one another. He then suggests that an individual is eternal just in case no aspect of it is a member of the temporal array.[14] Obviously, this is a project of considerable complexity. It requires appeal to a theory of events and delineating the right ones to count as aspects. It involves establishing that there is a unique temporal array. And, presumably, it requires a rationale for allowing such events as, for example, God's being worshiped by Saint Paul, to bear temporal relations without God being thereby non-eternal.

A second approach involves recasting the definition of temporal location in terms of the possession of properties at times. In effect, this proposal preserves Pike's claim that the predicates applying to an individual determine whether it is eternal by rejecting Pike's example of a time-location predicate. The idea is that if God is eternal, then his actions and his acts of knowing, for example, do not occur at any time. Instead of appealing to events, we could put

12. Stephen Davis's presentation of Pike's account shares this flaw. Davis considers the claim that "temporal terms have no significant application to [God]" but then gives the following list of temporal terms: "'past', 'present', 'future', 'before', 'after', . . .'simultaneous', 'always', 'later', 'next year', 'forever', 'at 6:00 P.M.',", none of which applies to individuals. Davis, *Logic and the Nature of God* (Grand Rapids, Mich.: Eerdmans, 1983), p. 10.

13. Nicholas Wolterstorff, "God Everlasting," in *God and the Good: Essays in Honor of Henry Stob*, ed. C. Orlebeke and L. Smedes (Grand Rapids, Mich.: Eerdmans, 1975), rpt. in *Contemporary Philosophy of Religion*, ed. Steven Cahn and David Shatz, (New York: Oxford University Press, 1982), pp. 77–98. Page references are to the latter volume.

14. Ibid., pp. 80–81.

this point by saying that God's properties, for example, *creating Abraham* or *knowing that South Bend is north of Kokomo*, are properties he has without having them at any time.[15] More generally,

> (3′) x has temporal location if and only if there is a property P
> and a time t such that x has P at t.

We could, if we wished, follow Pike and take (1) to provide necessary and sufficient conditions for being timeless, with (2) and (3′) explaining the key concepts employed in (1). Or, more simply, we could take timelessness to be specified by

> (4) x is timeless if and only if x lacks temporal location,

noting that anything that has no properties at any time does not have the property of existing throughout some interval of time. Hence, anything that lacks temporal location lacks temporal extension, and, accordingly, (4) is equivalent to (1).

Presumably being eternal includes being timeless in the sense specified by (4). But, on the supposition that it is possible for something to be timeless, it is at least conceivable that something could be timeless without being eternal. A being that was timeless but not limitless, or timeless without having everything present to it all at once, would not be eternal.

Another property mentioned by Augustine is that of being unchangeable. (I pass over immortality and incorruptibility.) *Being unchangeable* (or immutability) is clearly a modalized version of the property of being unchanging. Perhaps, then,

> (5) x is immutable if and only if x is essentially unchanging.

In other words, a being is immutable just in case it is not only unchanging but also not possibly such that it changes.

We should therefore consider what it is for something to change. Intuitively, a thing changes just in case it has a property at one time

15. Depending upon the theory of events employed, this approach may turn out to be not all that different from the approach of the previous paragraph. In particular, it may be that a thing has a property at a time if and only if a relevant event involving it is included in the temporal array.

that it lacks at another. For example, the door on my house was white and now it is red. This change in color is naturally thought of in terms of a change in the door's properties. My door used to have the property of being white, and now it lacks that property. But not every change in properties involves a real change. Acquiring the property of being an uncle, for example, did not signal any real change in me, although it was related to a real change in my sister. Recent literature has called such pseudo-changes "mere Cambridge changes," but the problem is an old one.[16] Thus Anselm asked, "But what is the inconsistency between susceptibility to certain facts, called *accidents*, and natural immutability, if from the undergoing of these accidents the substance undergoes no change?"[17]

Anselm's response is to distinguish two classes of properties:

> For, of all the facts, called accidents, some are understood not to be present or absent without some variation in the subject of the accident—all colors, for instance—while others are known not to effect any change in a thing either by occurring or not occurring—certain relations, for instance. For it is certain that I am neither older nor younger than a man who is not yet born, nor equal to him, nor like him. But I shall be able to sustain and lose all these relations toward him, as soon as he shall have been born, according as he shall grow, or undergo change through divers qualities.
>
> It is made clear, then, that of all those facts, called accidents, a part bring some degree of mutability in their train, while a part do not impair at all the immutability of that in whose case they occur. Hence, although the supreme Nature in its simplicity has never undergone such accidents as cause mutation, yet it does not disdain occasional expression in terms of those accidents which are in no wise inconsistent with supreme immutability; and yet there is no accident respecting its essence, whence it would be conceived of, as itself variable.[18]

Anselm's idea, then, is that properties are divided into those which are *change-relevant* and those which are not.[19] It is not easy to see,

16. The term derives, I believe, from Peter Geach's "Cambridge criterion of change." See his "What Actually Exists," *Proceedings of the Aristotelian Society*, Suppl. vol. 42 (1968):7–16.

17. Anselm, *Monologion*, chap. 25, in *Saint Anselm: Basic Writings*, ed. S. N. Deane, 2d ed. (La Salle, Ill.: Open Court, 1962), p. 84.

18. Ibid., pp. 84–85.

19. I borrow this term from Wolterstorff, "God Everlasting."

however, exactly how this distinction can be made precise. Since we are hoping to explain *being unchanging* in terms of change-relevant properties, it will not do, as Anselm seems to do in this passage, to define change-relevant properties as ones that cannot be acquired or lost without changing. On the other hand, there does seem to be an intuitive difference exemplified in the difference between *becoming red* and *becoming an uncle*. And no doubt *being over six feet tall* is in the former category, and *being worshiped by Saint Paul* is in the latter. So let us proceed without making this distinction more exact.

I suggest, then, that *being unchanging* be understood as follows:

(6) x is unchanging if and only if there are no times t_1 and t_2 and change-relevant property P such that x has P at t_1 and x lacks P at t_2.

An interesting consequence of (4) and (6) is that anything that is timeless is unchanging. This is because a timeless being has no properties at any time at all; hence, a timeless being does not have any change-relevant properties at one time that it lacks at another. The converse does not hold, however. A being could be constant in its change-relevant properties while nevertheless having its properties at times.

We have distinguished in this section four traditionally ascribed divine attributes: eternity, timelessness, immutability, and being unchanging. Moreover, we have seen that these concepts are related in some interesting ways. Anything that is eternal is timeless, and anything that is timeless is unchanging. Hence, whatever is eternal is unchanging. Finally, being unchanging is required by immutability. The relationships holding among these concepts will prove to be important for the arguments to be discussed in Sections 3 and 5 below.

2. Some Reservations

There is no doubt that the attributes we have discussed thus far in this chapter have long been ascribed to God. Moreover, this ascription continues to have its adherents. Nevertheless, it has in recent years come in for a good deal of criticism. In this section I express some misgivings about the origin, application, and scriptural basis of attributing these properties to God. I describe them as misgivings and reservations because, unless they are supplemented by historical research and scriptural interpretation that goes considerably beyond the scope of this book, they do not begin to constitute objections to attributing these properties to God. In Sections 3 and 5 below we examine in detail some more strictly philosophical objections to this cluster of concepts.

Several authors have argued that the doctrines of divine eternity and immutability have their source in Greek and neo-Platonic philosophy.[20] Plotinus is an especially important source of the doctrine.[21] In particular, eternity is often derived from another philosophical doctrine, that of divine simplicity. This source is evident in Aquinas's treatment of divine attributes in the first part of his *Summa Theologica*. In his question on eternity he claims that "the notion of eternity follows immutability."[22] Aquinas had earlier offered three arguments for divine immutability, two of which appeal explicitly to the doctrine of divine simplicity.[23] We shall not investigate the doctrine of divine simplicity; I have nothing constructive to say about it. Let us merely note that it, too, has its origin in Greek philosophy.

A second reservation about eternity and changelessness is that there is scant scriptural justification for ascribing these properties to God.[24] Indeed, some writers contend that the picture of God presented in Scripture is incompatible with divine eternity and immutability. Some claim that Scripture depicts God as acting in history, and that such involvement with the world is incompatible with his being unchanging.[25] The contention that divine action is inconsis-

20. See, for example, William Kneale, "Time and Eternity in Theology," *Proceedings of the Aristotelian Society* 61 (1960–61):87–108. Authors following him include Richard Swinburne, *The Coherence of Theism* (Oxford: Oxford University Press, 1977), pp. 215–219, and Wolterstorff, "God Everlasting."

21. For some details see Stump and Kretzmann, "Eternity," who do not regard the philosophical origin of the doctrine as a defect.

22. Aquinas's *S.T.* Ia, 10, 2. This is a dubious assumption, given our understanding of these concepts.

23. The arguments for immutability are in *S.T.* Ia, 9, 1. Simplicity, the first attribute Aquinas discusses, is the subject of Question 3. Cf. Anselm, *Monologion*, chap. 24, and *Proslogion*, 18.

24. See, for example, Oscar Cullman, *Christ and Time*, trans. Floyd Filson (London: SCM Press, 1951).

25. Ibid. Cf. also Wolterstorff, "God Everlasting."

tent with divine changelessness *is* a philosophical claim, and we will need to examine it in Section 6 below. But explicit scriptural discussion of these issues is difficult to find. Stump and Kretzmann cite three passages as evidence of scriptural support for the doctrine of divine eternity:

> "I the Lord do not change. So you, O descendents of Jacob, are not destroyed." (Mal. 3:6)

> "I tell you the truth," Jesus answered, "before Abraham was born, I am." (John 8:58)

> Every good and perfect gift is from above, coming down from the Father of the heavenly lights, who does not change like shifting shadows. (James 1:17)[26]

These passages, however, do not clearly affirm the doctrines of divine eternity or immutability. The second, for example, seems compatible with Jesus' being everlasting rather than eternal. And the changelessness mentioned in the first and third passages may be the changelessness of God's mercy, the constancy of his promises, rather than the complete or metaphysical changelessness described by (6). This is particularly clear in the case of the first passage, which is part of a speech the prophet attributes to God, the point of which is that God remains faithful in his promises to those who return to him and keep his decrees.

The considerations we have raised thus far in this section are, it seems to me, inconclusive. Even if the doctrines of divine eternity and changelessness are of Hellenistic and philosophical origin, it does not follow that they are mistaken or alien to theistic or Christian belief.[27] And given the lack of interest biblical writers display in philosophical issues, it would not be surprising that they neglect to affirm divine eternity and immutability, even if these doctrines are correct.

There remain the questions whether these doctrines really are coherent and whether there are any powerful reasons for thinking

---

26. Translations from the New International Version.

27. Try to imagine how the doctrine of the Trinity—a doctrine clearly essential to Christianity—could have been formulated without borrowing from Greek thought.

that they are true. These are questions I cannot answer.[28] Rather, I assume that since these views have been widely held, it is of some interest to see whether there are persuasive philosophical objections to them. We consider two such objections, both claiming that these doctrines are inconsistent with other tenets of theism in general and of Christianity in particular. The first, the subject of Section 3, holds them to be inconsistent with divine omniscience; the second, to be discussed in Section 6, claims that they are incompatible with divine action.

3. Temporal Indexicals and Immutability

In a variety of manifestations a familiar argument purports to show that divine omniscience is incompatible with one or more of the cluster of concepts we have been investigating in this chapter. In Kretzmann's influential presentation, omniscience is held to be incompatible with *immutability*.[29] In Wolterstorff's formulation, the argument is supposed to establish the incompatibility of divine omniscience and divine *eternity*.[30] Stephen Davis takes the argument to show the incompatibility of omniscience and *timelessness*.[31] In fact, if the objection is sound, it counts against *all* of the concepts we are currently scrutinizing. Let us first look at what the objection alleges and then see how it applies to these concepts.

An omniscient being knows all true propositions, but in the view of these critics, some propositions, in particular those expressed by sentences containing such temporally indexical elements as tenses or the word 'now,' vary in truth over time; accordingly, what an omniscient being knows varies over time. Hence, an omniscient being—or at least one who exists for more than an instant—must also vary over time.[32]

28. We saw in Section 6 of Chapter 4 that one reason sometimes given in support of the doctrine of divine eternity—that it is required to reconcile divine foreknowledge and human free action—is not a good reason.

29. Norman Kretzmann, "Omniscience and Immutability," *Journal of Philosophy* 63 (1966):409–421.

30. Wolterstorff, "God Everlasting."

31. Davis, *Logic and the Nature of God*, p. 29.

32. There is a large literature discussing this objection. It was considered by Aquinas, *S.T.*, Ia, 14, 15, and defended by Franz Bretanno, *Philosophische Unter-*

Thus stated, it is clear that the objection is not merely an objection to divine immutability. Immutability, we saw, is the property of being essentially unchanging. However, this objection does not hold that there is a special problem with being *essentially* unchanging, conceding that God might be unchanging as long as he is not essentially so. Rather, the objection makes the stronger claim that an omniscient being is not unchanging at all, neither essentially nor accidentally. Of course, it will follow that if God is not unchanging, then he is not essentially unchanging or immutable either. But it is important to be clear about the exact target of the objection. It is also important to recall the other connections we discerned at the end of Section 1, namely, that anything that is eternal is timeless and that anything that is timeless is unchanging. For it follows, then, that if this objection shows that God is not unchanging, he is not timeless or eternal either. It is for this reason, therefore, that this objection, if sound, counts against all of the attributes we are currently discussing.

Let us turn, then, to a consideration of the objection. Here is how Franz Brentano puts it: "If anything changes, then it is not the case that all truths are eternal. God knows all truths, hence also those which are such only for today. He could not apprehend these truths yesterday, since at that time they were not truths—but there were other truths instead of them. Thus he knows, for example, that I write down these thoughts; but yesterday he knew not that, but rather that I was going to write them down later. And similarly he will know tomorrow that I have written them down."[33]

---

suchungen zu Raum, Zeit, und Kontinuum, ed. Stephan Korner and Roderick M. Chisholm (Hamburg: Felix Meiner Verlag, 1976), p. 105. Recent defenders of the objection, in addition to Kretzmann, Wolterstorff, and Davis, include Arthur Prior, "The Formalities of Omniscience," *Philosophy* 37 (1962):114–129, rpt. in his *Papers on Time and Tense* (Oxford: Oxford University Press, 1968); Anthony Kenny, *The God of the Philosophers* (Oxford: Oxford University Press, 1979); and Patrick Grim, "Against Omniscience: The Case from Essential Indexicals," *Noûs* 19 (1985):151–180. Critics of the argument include Hector-Neri Castañeda, "Omniscience and Indexical Reference," *Journal of Philosophy* 64 (1967):203–210; Pike, *God and Timelessness,* pp. 89–95; Richard Swinburne, *The Coherence of Theism* (Oxford: Oxford University Press, 1977); and Kretzmann himself, in Stump and Kretzmann, "Eternity." My criticism of the objection will differ from that of these critics.

33. Brentano, *Philosophische Untersuchungen,* quoted by Roderick M. Chisholm in "Objects and Persons: Revisions and Replies," *Grazer Philosophische Studien* 7/8 (1979):347.

In holding that not all truths are eternal, Brentano opposes what until recently has been the dominant view, namely, that propositions do not vary in truth value over time. This thesis was stated by Frege (who means by 'thought' ['*Gedanke*'] what we mean by 'proposition') in the following passage:

> But are there not thoughts which are true today but false in six months time? The thought, for example, that the tree there is covered with green leaves, will surely be false in six months time. No, for it is not the same thought at all. The words 'this tree is covered with green leaves' are not sufficient by themselves for the utterance, the time of utterance is involved as well. Without the time-indication this gives we have no complete thought, i.e. no thought at all. Only a sentence supplemented by a time-indication and complete in every respect expresses a thought. But this, if it is true, is true not only today or tomorrow, but timelessly.[34]

This view is often interpreted, at least by its critics, to hold that a sentence such as

(7) "Ronald Reagan is now president"

written or uttered on February 27, 1987, expresses the same proposition as

(8) "Ronald Reagan is president on February 27, 1987,"

that is, the proposition that

(9) Ronald Reagan is president on February 27, 1987.

Despite what I think is the obvious implausibility of this claim, there have been some rather unconvincing arguments directed against it. Thus Stephen Davis, for example, takes the following as a necessary condition for two sentences S_1 and S_2 to express the same proposition (or "report the same fact," in Davis's phrase):

34. Gottlob Frege, "The Thought," trans. A. M. Quinton and Marcelle Quinton, in *Philosophical Logic*, ed. P. F. Strawson (Oxford: Oxford University Press, 1978), p. 37.

(C1) S_1 and S_2 always have the same truth value, i.e. there is no conceivable state of affairs where one is true and the other is false.[35]

Davis then applies this criterion to (7) and (8) and claims that "we can easily conceive of states of affairs in which [(7)] is false and [(8)] is true. This will doubtless be the case in the twenty-first century, for example. Ronald Reagan will not then be president (i.e. it will be false for a twenty-first century philosopher to say, 'Ronald Reagan is now president'), but it will still be true (because it will always be true) that 'Ronald Reagan is president on [February 27, 1987].'"[36] But, of course, the fact that it will be possible in the twenty-first century to use (7) to express a proposition other than (9) is completely irrelevant to whether (7) as used on February 27, 1987, expresses (9). As Frege said, "the same words, on account of the variability of language with time, take on another sense, express another thought; this change, however, concerns only the linguistic aspect of the matter."[37]

Wolterstorff also has an unpersuasive argument for the conclusion that sentences such as (7) do not express eternal propositions. He considers, using a slightly different example, the suggestion that (7) asserted today (on February 27, 1987, let us suppose) expresses the same proposition as

(10) "It is, was, or will be the case that Ronald Reagan is president on February 27, 1987."

Wolterstorff then asserts that "the proposition asserted with the former [i.e., (7)] entails that [Reagan's being president] is something that *is* occurring, *now, presently.* But the latter [i.e., (10)] does not entail this at all."[38] So according to Wolterstorff, (7) today does not express the eternal proposition expressed by (10) because the former, unlike the latter, entails that Reagan is president *now.* But what proposition is that? What proposition is expressed by

35. Davis, *Logic and the Nature of God*, p. 28.
36. Ibid., p. 29.
37. Frege, "The Thought," p. 37.
38. Wolterstorff, "God Everlasting," p. 87.

(7) "Ronald Reagan is now president"

now (on February 27, 1987)? Without an account of which proposition that is, it is hard to be sure that (10) does not entail it. Indeed,
according to the proposal I defend below, (7) now *does* express a
proposition distinct from (10) that is, nevertheless, entailed by (10).
So Wolterstorff's argument that (7) and (10) express different propositions seems to me inconclusive.

Despite the failure of these arguments to show that (7) and (8) [or
(7) and (10)] express different propositions, it is clear that they do.
For someone who thought it was still 1985 could know that Reagan
is president now without knowing or even believing that Reagan is
president on February 27, 1987. And someone reading today's
newspaper while under the mistaken impression that it is last week's
paper could know that Reagan is president on February 27, 1987,
without knowing, or even believing, that Reagan is president
now.[39] Analogous considerations show that (7) and (10) do not
express the same proposition.

From the fact that (7) does not express the eternal propositions we
have considered, it does not follow, however, that (7) does not
express *any* eternal proposition. The suggestions we considered are
indeed implausible. Why should anyone have thought that the time-
indication provided either explicitly by the word 'now' or implicitly
by the use of the present tense would just be one of the twenty-four
hour periods referred to by our date terms? But can we do better? Is
there a more reasonable construal of what we know when we know
that something is happening now, that is, of what we might call
knowledge *de praesenti*? An affirmative answer to this question will
enable us to reply to the objection to divine unchangingness.

We may concentrate in this way on knowledge expressed by
sentences with a *present* time indication, because the knowledge expressed by sentences whose verbs are in the past or future tense is
best understood as knowledge that fundamentally involves the present. Thus, what we know when we know, for example, that it
rained is that it rained *before now*. And what we know when we

39. In addition to the argument of his that we discussed, Davis, in *Logic and the
Nature of God*, gives an argument like this one that appeals to what people can know.

know that it will rain is that it will rain *later than now*. In other words, knowledge that something is past or future is always knowledge that is relative to the present.

What we have seen so far is that knowledge *de praesenti* is not akin to knowledge *de dicto*, at least if the *dictum* involved is one expressed by a dated sentence. Then is knowledge *de praesenti* instead a kind of knowledge *de re*? Is it, in other words, knowledge *de re* with respect to the present time? It is not. Suppose that at a certain time, *t*, the president is speaking at a news conference, and suppose that the news conference is being televised with a digital display of the current time in a corner of the screen. Then a person who is ignorant whether the news conference is being broadcast live or whether it was previously recorded may come, given appropriate evidence about the reliability of television news coverage, to know *de re* with respect to *t* that the president is (tenselessly) speaking then, without knowing what would be expressed at that time by saying "The president is speaking now." So it seems possible to have knowledge *de re* with respect to a present time without having knowledge *de praesenti*.[40]

Is knowledge *de praesenti* analogous to knowledge *de se*? I think that in fact the analogy is quite exact, and so I want to explore the proposal that knowledge *de praesenti* can be construed along the lines of knowledge *de se*.[41] As we saw in Chapter 2, belief *de se* can be thought of as belief in one of one's own first-person propositions. More precisely,

> (11) A person, *S*, believes *de se* that he himself or she herself is *F* just in case there is a haecceity *E* which is such that *S* has *E*

40. Grim, "Against Omniscience," pp. 157–158, has used a somewhat more fanciful video example to make substantially the same point.

41. Ernest Sosa has noticed the analogy, although he rejects the haecceitist account of both sorts of knowledge. See his "Consciousness of the Self and of the Present" in *Agent, Language, and the Structure of the World*, ed. James Tomberlin (Indianapolis: Hackett, 1983), pp. 131–143, and his "Propositions and Indexical Attitudes," in *On Believing*, ed. Herman Parret (Berlin: Walter de Gruyter, 1983), pp. 316–332. Richard Feldman has also noticed a parallel between first-person and present-time assertions, though he too, inexplicably, declines to endorse the account I am proposing. See his "On Saying Different Things," *Philosophical Studies* 38 (1980): 79–84. Cf. John Perry, "Frege on Demonstratives," *Philosophical Review* 86 (1977):474–497, especially p. 491.

and S believes a proposition entailing$_c$ the conjunction of E and F,[42]"

Alternatively, we may prefer to speak more literally of propositions having haecceities and other properties as constituents, thus avoiding the circumlocution of propositions entailing$_c$ properties. A first-person proposition, for a given person, is a proposition having that person's haecceity as a constituent. Then we could recast (11) as

> (12) A person, S, believes *de se* that he himself or she herself is F just in case there is a haecceity E which is such that S has E and S believes a proposition having E as a constituent and which attributes *being F* to whomever has E.

If we think of belief *de praesenti* in an analogous way, we should hold that moments of time also have special individual essences or haecceities. Then we could say that

> (13) A person, S, believes *de praesenti* at a time t that it is then the case that p just in case there is a haecceity T such that t has T and at t S believes a proposition entailing$_c$ the conjunction of T and *being such that p*."

Alternatively, we could adopt

> (14) A person, S, believes *de praesenti* at a time t that it is then the case that p just in case there is a haecceity T such that t has T and at t S believes a proposition having T as constituent and which attributes *being such that p* to whatever time has T.

Propositions entailing$_c$ or containing the special individual essence of a person we called "first-person propositions." Let us call those propositions that entail$_c$ or contain the haecceity of a time "present-time propositions." Then we can describe the view presented in (13) (or (14)) as the claim that belief *de praesenti* is belief in a

---

42. Recall that p entails$_c$ the property of being F if and only if (i) necessarily if p is true then something has the property of being F, and (ii) necessarily anyone who believes p believes that something is F. The subscript stands for 'Chisholm.'

present-time proposition. Knowledge *de praesenti* is then, naturally enough, knowledge of a present-time proposition.

The proposition that (7) expresses on some occasion of assertion on February 27, 1987, is a present-time proposition that entails$_c$ or contains the haecceity of that time of assertion. A person can believe it without believing the propositions expressed by such dated sentences as (8), (10), or

> (15) Ronald Reagan is president at 4:35 P.M. E.S.T. on February 27, 1987.

And a person can believe one of these "dated" propositions without believing or even grasping the present-time proposition expressed by (7) at 4:35 P.M. E.S.T. on February 27, 1987.

The time of a present-time proposition is the time that has the haecceity entailed$_c$ by or contained in the proposition.[43] Just as none of us grasps the first-person proposition of another, we grasp no present-time proposition before its time. Nor, I think, do we ever grasp one after its time, either. But this limitation on our ability is not essential to the account. For the reduction of belief *de praesenti* to belief *de dicto* to succeed, all that is required is that whenever a person believes a present-time proposition at its time, that person has a *de praesenti* belief.

It should be clear, then, that there is no reason why God cannot believe all true present-time propositions, just as he believes all true first-person propositions. And just as his belief in a first-person proposition does not give him a belief *de se* unless it is a belief in his own first-person proposition, so a belief in a present-time proposition does not give him belief *de praesenti* unless he believes that proposition at its time.

It is not my intention to take a stand on the question of *when* God has his beliefs, on whether he is in time or outside of time. But it is evident, I think, that facts about the objects of our knowledge and belief do not settle the question whether an omniscient being changes over time (and, accordingly, is neither immutable, timeless, or eternal) or whether it can be that an omniscient being is changeless. This is because those objects of knowledge and belief which are

---

43. I am ignoring the possibility that a present-time proposition entails$_c$ or contains more than one temporal haecceity.

expressed by sentences containing temporally indexical elements need not be construed as objects that vary in truth over time.

4. Some Objections

Roderick Chisholm has written that "if we. . .take tense seriously, we will be prepared for the fact that there will be 'vehicles of truth'—propositions, states of affairs, judgments, sentence-types, or sentence-tokens—which will be variable in truth value."[44] No doubt there are sentences whose truth-value varies over time; but "taking tense seriously" does not require that the truth-value of objects of belief change over time. If we are to take tense seriously because it indicates that our perspective is in time, it will be sufficient that *we* change over time, coming to believe propositions we formerly did not even grasp and ceasing even to grasp propositions we formerly believed.

The view of belief *de praesenti* I have been developing has seemed to some to be objectionable. Ernest Sosa, for example, writes:

> The problem with time is . . . one of discernibility. To believe of time *t* as the present time that it is a time when it rains is to accept the proposition that *t** is a time when it rains. [This is Sosa's way of indicating a present-time proposition.] Such a proposition involves a special concept *t** corresponding to *t*, one that contains no "extrinsic" individuating properties of *t*—such as being the time today when the sun is straight overhead or the time today when the clock strikes twelve. For I might be ignorant of all such extrinsic properties of the present time while *still* believing that it rains now. But then we must be able to distinguish t_1* and t_2* without appealing to a difference in extrinsic properties and simply by reference to some "intrinsic" features of t_1 and t_2. And I for one find myself unable to distinguish moments of time by reference to any such supposed intrinsic features. Moments of time seem indiscernible on the basis of intrinsic features.[45]

Sosa claims that

(16) If belief *de praesenti* is belief in a present-time proposition, then we are able to distinguish two temporal haecceities by discerning their intrinsic features,

44. Chisholm, "Objects and Persons: Revisions and Replies," p. 347.
45. Sosa, "Propositions and Indexical Attitudes," p. 319.

but

    (17) We do not discern the intrinsic features of temporal haec-
           ceities.

It follows, of course, from (16) and (17) that belief *de praesenti* is not
belief in a present-time proposition. But, as far as I can see, Sosa
gives us no reason to accept (16). In particular, since we never do
grasp present-time propositions of different times simultaneously,
we are never in the position of having to discern the intrinsic features that insure that a pair of temporal haecceities t_1^* and t_2^* are
distinct.

    Another objection is due to Arthur Prior. He considers the sug-
gestion that God's knowledge is limited to eternally true propositions, and he says, "God could not, on [this] view. . . , know that
the 1960 final examinations at Manchester are now over; for this
isn't something that He or anyone could know timelessly, because it
just isn't true timelessly. It's true now, but it wasn't true a year ago
(I write this on August 29th, 1960)."[46] Prior adds: "So far as I can see
all that can be said on this subject timelessly is that the finishing date
of the 1960 final examinations is an earlier one than August 29th,
and this is *not* the thing we know when we know that those exams
are over. I cannot think of any better way of showing this than one
I've used before, namely, the argument that what we know when
we know that the 1960 final examinations are over can't just be a
timeless relation between dates because this isn't the thing we're
pleased about when we're pleased that the exams are over."[47] The
proposition that Prior expressed on, say, noon of August 29, 1960,
by uttering,

    (18) "The 1960 final examinations are over"

is, according the view I have presented, a proposition entailing the
conjunction of the haecceity of that time and the property of *being
such that the 1960 exams have finished before then*. This proposition is

    46. Prior, "The Formalities of Omniscience," p. 116.
    47. Ibid. Prior refers to his "Thank Goodness That's Over," *Philosophy* 34
(1959):12–17.

timelessly true, and Prior did not believe it before noon on that day. As we have seen, however, there is no reason to think that God was so limited. Moreover, Prior's example concerning what we are pleased about seems not to establish his claim that if God's knowledge is limited to eternally true propositions then he could not know that the exams are now over. For even if we concede that the objects of pleasure, or at any rate the objects of that about which we are pleased, are the same as the objects of belief and knowledge, it does not follow that the object about which we are pleased is not a timelessly true proposition. We can be pleased that now is a time at which the exams are over or, better, now is a time after which we will never have to take (or grade) those exams. On the view we have considered, these are eternal propositions, but since we have never grasped them before, we cannot have been pleased about them earlier; hence, they are not disqualified from serving as that about which we are pleased.

Finally, it might be objected that this account makes three implausible assumptions: that there are times, that times have haecceities, and that we grasp (some of) the objects of our beliefs only instantaneously.[48] It is true that this view involves quantifying over times, but it seems clear that many other claims we endorse do so, too. Thus, such claims as *Whenever I run I perspire* or *There was a time when there were dinosaurs* seem to involve quantification over times. Of course, it might happen that someone will sometime (another presumptive reference to time) succeed in showing how all such talk may be eliminated in favor of talk that does not require quantification over times. If that happens and we decide as a result that our talk of times is not to be taken literally, then we should see whether the proposed translation involves individuals whose haecceities can play the role haecceities of times play in the present account. But an objection based on the possibility that we will someday come to think that there are no times cannot really be sustained or refuted unless we actually have a concrete proposal for eliminating reference to times. Until then, I shall continue to assume that there are times. But if there are times, then they have haecceities (at least if any things have haecceities, and I believe that *we* do).

---

48. These objections have been raised by a number of people who have heard me give papers on these topics.

But are the objects of our belief really entities that we grasp only instantaneously, and do our beliefs really change as time goes by, even if we appear not to be changing? The first thing to note is that this is a question about our beliefs, but our primary concern here is God's beliefs. Hence, if there are haecceities of times and thus true propositions entailing$_c$ or containing them, then God, if he is omniscient, must know those propositions. So such propositions are the objects of God's knowledge. The real question is whether that gives him the knowledge we have when we have *de praesenti* knowledge. It is somewhat tempting to think that we can grasp the same (temporal) proposition throughout an interval of time and not merely at an instant. But the view we have been discussing can easily be expanded to allow for present-time propositions where the time in question is an interval and not an instant. Exactly which such propositions are the objects of our knowledge would seem to require empirical information about human psychology, information that I do not have. It seems clear, however, that if our account needs to be embellished in this way, there would still be nothing to prevent such eternal propositions from being what we know when we have knowledge *de praesenti* as well as the objects of God's eternal knowledge.

Thus, to draw a conclusion at this point, I hope to have shown that there is a reasonable way of construing the objects of knowledge and belief according to which the doctrine of divine omniscience is not inconsistent with the attributes of eternity, timelessness, changelessness, and immutability. Recognizing, however, that not everyone will be satisfied with this approach, we turn in the next section to an alternative account.

5. An Alternative Account of Omniscience

In Chapter 2 as well as in the two preceding sections of this chapter, I have defended an account of omniscience according to which the objects of God's knowledge are classical propositions. By describing propositions as classical, I mean in part that they do not change in truth-value over time. Developing this view to take account of first-person and present-time indexicals has required the introduction of propositions that have haecceities—both of individuals and of times—as constituents. As we have seen, however, some philosophers reject the claim that there are such entities. Moreover, this approach runs counter to one that has attracted many adherents in recent years. So rather than insist on what is likely to be a controversial account of omniscience, I shall explore in this section an alternative account. I think that the haecceitist approach can be defended, but I do not want resistance to the details of that view to detract from the central thesis of this chapter, which is that facts about the nature of knowledge and belief, despite widespread opinion to the contrary, do not by themselves have any interesting bearing on the difficult questions whether God is eternal, timeless, unchanging, and immutable.

Let us abandon the assumption that propositions are always true if they ever are (and always false if they ever are). Then the proposition that I am sitting, for example, will be true now, but it was false last night at midnight.[49] But whatever reasons there are for thinking that such propositions vary in truth-value over time would seem to be a reason for thinking that some propositions vary in truth-value over persons, as well.[50] So the proposition that I am sitting would be true for you now, if you are sitting, but it would be false for someone who is in the middle of a marathon. We can put this idea somewhat more precisely as follows. Let us say first that a *perspective* is a pair, $\langle S, t \rangle$ of a person and a time. The present proposal, then, is that some propositions are true at some perspectives and false at others.[51] To continue with the same example, the proposition that I

49. This seems to be the view of Wolterstorff and Davis.

50. Richard Feldman has shown that this holds in the case of the reasons that David Kaplan and John Perry give for thinking that propositions can vary in truth value over time. See Feldman, "Saying Different Things." See also Kaplan, "Demonstratives," (University of California, Los Angeles, mimeo. 1977) and Perry, "The Problem of the Essential Indexical," *Noûs* 13 (1979):3–21. The view to be presented here owes much to the work of Kaplan. Perry considers a similar view, but he does not recognize the distinction, to be made below, between believing that a proposition is true at an index and believing at an index that a proposition is true. On this point, see Feldman.

51. I prefer Perry's term 'new-fangled propositions' for those propositions whose truth value is in this way relative to an index, but using it only encourages Richard Feldman to call classical propositions 'old-fashioned.' Accordingly, I follow Ernest Sosa in describing these new-fangled propositions as *perspectival propositions*. See his "Consciousness of the Self and of the Present." I shall not consider the question whether the indices should include additional items, for example, location, audience, or possible world.

am sitting is true at ⟨me, now⟩, but it is false at ⟨me, last night at midnight⟩. In addition, the same perspectival proposition can also be true at ⟨you, now⟩ but false at, say, ⟨Joan Benoit, now⟩.

We should distinguish believing that a proposition is true at a perspective from believing at a perspective that a proposition is true. Consider the perspectival proposition,

(19) I am sitting.

There is a difference between believing

(20) *I am sitting* is true at ⟨me, 3:00 P.M. E.S.T. on May 7, 1987⟩

on the one hand, and believing (19) at the perspective of ⟨me, 3:00 P.M. E.S.T. on May 7, 1987⟩, on the other. The former is really just a case of *de dicto* belief in a classical proposition, since (20) is always true if it ever is. But the latter is something new; it involves believing a perspectival proposition while being at a certain perspective. The former is a belief that you and I might both have. In contrast, the latter is a belief that I have but you lack, since I am at the perspective in question whereas you are not.

This theory has a natural application to the cases of *de se* and *de praesenti* belief which have concerned us. An example, analogous to one considered in Chapter 2, is the case of Jones, hospitalized with amnesia, who believes himself to be in a health spa but learns at *t* from reading the newspaper that Jones is in the hospital. Jones then believes

(21) *I am in the hospital* is true at ⟨Jones, *t*⟩.

But inasmuch as he does not believe that he himself is in the hospital, Jones does not then believe the perspectival proposition

(22) I am in the hospital

from his perspective, namely, ⟨Jones, *t*⟩. And the opposite situation could have obtained. If Jones had not read the newspaper but had been apprised of his location, he would have believed (22) at ⟨Jones, *t*⟩, but he would not have believed (21).

We saw in Section 3 above that a person, S, could believe at a certain time t that Reagan is president at t without believing what would be expressed then by "Reagan is president now." In such a case, perhaps S believes that

(23) *Reagan is president* is true at $\langle S, t \rangle$.

But S does not then believe the perspectival proposition

(24) Reagan is president;

that is, S does not believe (24) at the perspective $\langle S, t \rangle$. And, again, the reverse could obtain. If S believed at t that Reagan was then president without S's having any idea of what time it was, S would have believed (24) at $\langle S, t \rangle$ but S would not have believed (23).

Belief *de se*, then, is belief in a first-person perspectival proposition, and belief *de praesenti* at a given time is belief in a perspectival proposition at (or from) a perspective that includes that time.

Since this view explicitly allows that propositions vary in truth-value over time, is it a simple consequence that no omniscient being is unchanging?[52] To answer this question we need to look more closely at the concept of omniscience. With belief thus complicated to allow for belief in perspectival propositions, it will not do to regard omniscience as simply belief in all true propositions. Rather, we should expect to find a corresponding complication in the formulation of omniscience. Thus,

(25) x is omniscient if and only if for any proposition p and perspective $\langle S, t \rangle$ (i) if p is true at $\langle S, t \rangle$ then x knows that p is true at $\langle S, t \rangle$, and (ii) if x is at $\langle S, t \rangle$ and p is true at $\langle S, t \rangle$ then at $\langle S, t \rangle$ x knows p.

Notice, however, that it does not follow from (25) that an omniscient being is not eternal. That would follow only on the assumption that an omniscient being is at some temporal perspective. Theists who hold that God is eternal tend to speak as well of God's

---

52. To forestall an objection, assume throughout this discussion that by 'omniscient being' I mean 'omniscient being who exists for more than an instant.'

eternal perspective.[53] Thus, they would likely deny that God is at any temporal perspective. On the other hand, if God *is* at some temporal perspective, that is, if there is a time t such that God is at ⟨God, t⟩, then it follows straightaway, without any detour through the complexities of omniscience, that God is not timeless. The reason is that if God is at ⟨God, t⟩, then he has the property of existing at t. But if he has the property of existing at t, then, by (4) above, he is not timeless; and if he is not timeless, he is not eternal, either.[54]

So on this interpretation of the objects of belief, it follows from the claim that God is omniscient that he is not eternal only on the assumption that he is at some temporal perspective; but the conclusion that God is not eternal follows from that assumption alone. Is there any reason to accept that assumption? I do not know of any. In the debate about God's eternity, its defense seems to have been neglected. My conclusion, then, is that on the theory of perspectival propositions, omniscience has not been shown to be inconsistent with divine eternity.[55]

53. Although defenders of divine eternity do not usually use this locution, they may be construed as holding that God is at ⟨God, the eternal present⟩. Compare the following passage in which Aquinas can be read as holding that God satisfies condition (i) of (25) from an eternal perspective: "As we said previously, God knows propositions without joining and separating. Just as God knows many different things in the same manner, both when they exist and when they do not, so does He know in the same manner different propositions, both when they are true and when they are false, because He knows each to be true at the time when it is true. For example, He knows this proposition, 'Socrates is running,' to be true when it is true; similarly this proposition, 'Socrates will run,' and so forth. Hence, although it is not now true that Socrates is running but that he has run, nevertheless God knows each because He simultaneously intuits each time when each proposition is true." *Quaestiones disputate de veritate*, q. 2, a. 13, *ad 7*.

54. It is less clear that there is a straightforward argument available here for the conclusion that God changes (and, hence, is not immutable) which does not appeal to claims about omniscience. The assumption, for example, that there are distinct times t_1 and t_2 such that at t_1 God is at ⟨God, t_1⟩ and at t_2 God is at ⟨God, t_2⟩ does not seem strong enough by itself, unless, implausibly, merely existing at different times (in contrast to having different beliefs at different times) is sufficient for undergoing a change in change-relevant properties. So in arguing that God is *unchanging*, appealing to God's omniscience might not be taking a detour. Nevertheless, the requisite additional premise that God is at different temporal perspectives remains unsupported.

55. This is not the place to undertake an exhaustive survey of alternative views on the objects of knowledge and belief. I conjecture, however, that on any reasonable account, the concept of omniscience can be plausibly construed in such a way that

6. Divine Action and Immutability

Considerations about divine action are a second source of objections to the doctrines of divine eternity, timelessness, changelessness, and immutability. As in the case of the objection from omniscience, different formulations of the objection from divine action are directed against one or another of these attributes. Unlike the objection from omniscience, however, the various versions of the objection from divine agency cannot all be construed as attacks on divine changelessness, since at least one of the objectors, Richard Swinburne,[56] concedes that God could be changeless while arguing that he is neither immutable nor timeless. Accordingly, we consider objections to these attributes individually, without trying to relate each to all of the others.

Wolterstorff endorses a version of the objection from divine action. He writes,

> the biblical writers present God as a redeeming God. From times most ancient, man has departed from the pattern of responsibility awarded him at his creation by God. A multitude of evils has followed. But God was not content to leave man in the mire of his misery. Aware of what is going on, he has resolved, in response to man's sin and its resultant evils, to bring about renewal. He has, indeed, already been acting in accord with that resolve, centrally and decisively in the life, death, and resurrection of Jesus Christ.
>
> What I shall argue for is that if we are to accept this picture of God as acting for the renewal of human life, we must conceive of him as everlasting rather than eternal. God the redeemer cannot be a God eternal. This is so because God the redeemer is a God who *changes*.[57]

Wolterstorff identifies such divine actions as God's calling Abraham to leave Chaldea, instructing Moses to return to Egypt, leading Israel through the Red Sea, and sending his Son into the world, and he suggests that they occurred in time. If God's actions occur in time, God acts in time; in that case God is not timeless.

---

omniscience is not inconsistent with divine eternity, timelessness, and the rest (subject to the proviso that divine eternity, timelessness, etc., are not themselves impossible concepts).

56. Swinburne, *The Coherence of Theism*, pp. 214, 221.
57. Wolterstorff, "God Everlasting," pp. 77–78.

Ironically, however, when Wolterstorff comes to argue for these claims, he backs off, noting instead that there is an alternative way of conceiving of God's actions that does not require that they take place in time. Wolterstorff cites the following passage from Aquinas as a source of this alternative view.

> Nor, if the action of the first agent is eternal, does it follow that His effect is eternal. . . . Now, an effect follows from the intellect and the will according to the determination of the intellect and the command of the will. Moreover, just as the intellect determines every other condition of the thing made, so does it prescribe the time of its making; for art determines not only that this thing is to be such and such, but that it is to be at this particular time, even as a physician determines that a dose of medicine is to be drunk at such and such a particular time, so that, if his act of will were of itself sufficient to produce the effect, the effect would follow anew from his previous decision, without any new action on his part. Nothing, therefore, prevents our saying that God's action existed from all eternity, whereas its effect was not present from eternity, but existed at that time when, from all eternity, He ordained it.[58]

So Aquinas distinguishes the effects of God's action, which do occur in time, from God's action itself, which, according to Aquinas, does not occur in time. Thus, in the case of the examples cited by Wolterstorff, Aquinas would distinguish God's calling Abraham to leave Chaldea from Abraham's being called by God to leave Chaldea (or Abraham's hearing God's call to leave Chaldea); God's instructing Moses to return to Egypt is to be distinguished from Moses' receiving God's instruction, and similarly for the other examples. In each of these pairs, the former does not occur in time even though the latter does.

Although Wolterstorff does not himself accept this Thomistic reply, he concedes that it is an adequate response to the objection from divine action as it has so far been developed. He then claims that

> to refute the . . . Thomistic theory we would have to do one or the other of two things. We would have to show that some of the temporal-event language the biblical writers use in speaking of God's

---

58. Aquinas, *Summa contra gentiles*, 2, 35, quoted in ibid., p. 89.

actions cannot properly be construed in the suggested way—that is, cannot be construed as used to put forth the claim that God acts in some way with respect to some temporal events. Or, alternatively, we would have to show that some of the actions God performs with respect to temporal events are themselves temporal, either because they are infected by the temporality of the events or for some other reason.[59]

Wolterstorff opts for the second alternative, claiming that "in the case of certain of God's actions the temporality of the event that God acts on infects his own action with temporality."[60]

The actions Wolterstorff cites in support of this claim, however, are God's acts of knowing what we express by tensed sentences. God "knows what is happening in our history, what has happened, and what will happen. Hence, some of God's actions are themselves temporal events."[61] Thus, in defense of the thesis that some of God's actions occur in time, Wolterstorff appeals once again to the claims that tensed sentences (typically) express propositions whose truth-value varies over time and that God knows them; so as Wolterstorff presents it, the argument from divine action is just a version of the argument from omniscience. But that argument we have already rejected. If the view presented in Sections 3 and 4 is correct, sentences with temporal indexicals express eternal propositions (containing haecceities of times), and there is nothing to prevent God from knowing all such truths "at once." On the other hand, if some propositions really do change in truth-value over time, if propositions are thus "perspectival," then omniscience is best thought of as in Section 5. In that case, an omniscient being is required to know a perspectival proposition only if the being is at a perspective at which the proposition is true. But then it cannot be assumed that God knows all true perspectival propositions—all perspectival propositions true in any present perspective—unless it has been shown that he is at some present perspective. But that is one of the things the argument from omniscience (and the argument from divine action) is supposed to show.

Is there a way of arguing that God is not eternal or not immutable

59. Wolterstorff, "God Everlasting," pp. 92–93.
60. Ibid.
61. Ibid., p. 93.

that appeals just to the nature of divine action and not to knowledge involving temporal indexicals? Richard Swinburne offers two such arguments. The first is directed against the claim that God is immutable, and it depends on the assumption that God is a *perfectly free* agent. Swinburne writes:

> It seems to me that although the God of the Old Testament is not pictured as such a being, nevertheless a perfectly free person might act in fact only on intentions which he had from all eternity, and so in a strong sense never change. However, a perfectly free person could not be immutable in the strong sense, that is *unable* to change. For an agent is perfectly free at a certain time if his action results from his own choice at that time and if his choice is not itself brought about by anything else. Yet a person immutable in the strong sense would be unable to perform any action at a certain time other than what he had previously intended to do. His course of action being fixed by his past choices, he would not be perfectly free. Being perfectly free is incompatible with being immutable in the strong sense.[62]

Swinburne apparently intends to give something like the following argument, where S is any person and A is any action:

(26) If S is perfectly free in doing A then A results from S's choice (to do A) and S's choice (to do A) is not brought about by anything else.

(27) If S is immutable and chooses to do A, then S's choice (to do A) is brought about by S's previous intentions.

Therefore,

(28) If S is free in doing A then S is not immutable.

Several comments are in order. First, by *perfect freedom* Swinburne, as he has earlier made clear, means being free and not having one's

---

62. Swinburne, *The Coherence of Theism*, pp. 214–215. Note that by *immutable* Swinburne means *unable to change*, whereas we had taken it to mean *essentially unchanging*. If a being is able to change, there is a possible world in which it does change, since no one is able to do what is impossible. Therefore a being that is able to change is not essentially unchanging. Hence, if God is not immutable in Swinburne's sense, he is not immutable in ours, either. Accordingly, in discussing Swinburne's argument I shall not bother to keep these two sense of 'immutable' distinct.

choices influenced by causal factors such as fatigue or hunger.[63] This is why he accepts (26). According to this conception of perfect freedom, then, if S is perfectly free, S's choice is not caused by antecedent causal conditions or by any other agent.[64] Consequently, the condition in (26) that "S's choice is not brought about by anything else" should be understood as ruling out antecedent causal conditions and the action of other agents; it should not rule out that S's intention is brought about by S himself or herself. Thus understood, (26) seems correct; however, (27) is considerably more problematic. In extracting it from Swinburne's remarks I have replaced his phrase "fixed by S's previous intentions" with "brought about by S's previous intentions." That change seems to be required if (27) is to link immutability with what (26) denies of perfect freedom.

But why should we think that (27) is true? If S is eternal or timeless, none of his or her intentions is (temporally) previous to any other. So (27) seems to be true, if at all, only when 'S' is restricted to beings in time. Accordingly, the argument shows at most that nontimeless, perfectly free beings are not immutable. But then the conclusion of the argument does not apply to God unless he is not timeless. But that God is timeless is one of the theses that is at issue; it surely should not be presupposed at this point. Of course, if God is not timeless, there is very little plausibility to the claim that he is immutable; but unless there is some independent reason to think that he is not timeless, it would seem that this argument cannot be used to show that he is not immutable.

Finally, however, we should note that even if (the universal closure of) (27) is true, the conclusion, (28), seems not to follow. (26) asserts that the free choice of a perfectly free being is not brought about by anything else; and (27) appears to deny that by affirming that the free choice of an immutable being *is* brought about by something else, namely, that being's (prior) intentions. But in our discussion of (26) we saw that the something else in question was either an antecedent causal condition or the action of another agent. Thus, what is intended by (26) is more carefully put as

63. Ibid., pp. 144–145.
64. Cf. ibid., p. 143.

(26′) If S is perfectly free in doing A then A results from S's choice (to do A) and S's choice (to do A) is not brought about by antecedent causal conditions or by the action of another agent.

The condition that (26) places on free choice should not preclude that an agent's free choice is brought about by the agent's *own* intentions. So the claim of (27) that an immutable agent's choice is brought about by his or her own intentions is not incompatible, after all, with that agent being perfectly free. So this version of the argument from divine agency seems unsuccessful.

Swinburne offers a second argument from divine agency, this time for the conclusion that God is not timeless. He writes:

> So many . . . things which the theist wishes to say about God—that he brings about this or that, forgives, punishes, or warns—are things which are true of a man at this or that or at all times. If we say that P brings about x, we can always sensibly ask *when* does he bring it about? If we say that P punishes Q, we can always sensibly ask *when* does he punish Q? If P really does 'bring about' or 'forgive' in anything like the normal sense of the words, there must be answers to these questions even if nobody knows what they are.[65]

This line of reasoning has been presented in somewhat more detail by Stephen Davis, who gives the following argument:

(29) God creates x.

(30) x first exists at t.

Therefore,

(31) God creates x at t.[66]

We should first attend to several items of detail. If 'x' is a variable (as Davis intends), then (29)–(31) are open sentences. Taken as comprising an argument, therefore, they are incomplete. Second, why

---

65. Ibid., p. 221. Swinburne allows that the theist can claim to ascribe action to God in a merely analogical sense, but this is a course he is reluctant to follow.

66. Davis, *Logic and the Nature of God*, p. 11, repeated on p. 13. This argument is similar to one Pike considers in *God and Timelessness*, p. 106.

is (30) taken as a premiss? If its temporal variable '*t*' is bound by an existential quantifier, it should follow from the first premiss. Finally, by changing the tense of the verb in (29) we can take advantage of the fact that the theistic claim is that God *has* created something. Adopting these suggestions results in the following argument.

(29′) There is something *x* such that God has created *x*.

(32) Whatever has been created began to exist at some time.

Therefore,

(30′) There is something *x* and a time *t* such that God created *x* and *x* began to exist at *t*. (29′) (32)

Therefore,

(31′) There is something *x* and a time *t* such that God created *x* at *t*. (30′)

If this argument is sound, then God has created something at a time and is therefore not timeless.

Davis recognizes an ambiguity here, however. He states it by reference to his conclusion (31), but I adapt what he says to our conclusion (31′). There is a difference, Davis notes, between

(31′a) There is something *x* and a time *t* such that God at *t* created *x*,

and

(31′b) There is something *x* and a time *t* such that God created *x* and *x* began to exist at *t*.

Davis then claims that

[(31′a)] clearly cannot be true of God if God is timeless—a being that performs some action at a certain point in time is temporal. So [(31′b)] is the interpretation of [(31′)] that will be preferred by the defender of divine timelessness. Notice that [(31′b)] is . . . indeed entailed by [(29')] and [(30')]. But can [(31'b)] be true of God if God is timeless? Only if we have available a usable concept of atemporal causation, which, as I say, we do not have. Therefore we are within our rights in concluding that [(29'), (32), and (30')] entail that God is temporal.[67]

Davis is certainly correct in thinking that (31'a) is incompatible with God's being timeless. If there is a time at which God creates something, then God's creating something occurs at a time, and God is not timeless. Oddly, Davis does not claim that (31'a) follows from (30'). If it does, he would have a good objection to divine timelessness. But is there any reason to think that it does? It seems, on the contrary, that Aquinas's distinction applies. If God's act of creating occurs in his eternal present, but it has the effect that the thing he creates begins to exist in time, then (30') could be true and (31'a) false. On the other hand, (31'b) does follow from (30'); indeed (31'b) just *is* (30'). Now (31'b) does not appear to preclude God's timelessness, but Davis claims that (31'b) is compatible with God's being timeless only if we have a "usable concept" of atemporal causation. Since Davis denies that we have such a concept, he concludes that (31'b) entails that God is not timeless. But whether (31'b) entails that God is not timeless is surely independent of whether *we* have a usable concept of atemporal causation; perhaps atemporal causation is possible but we are unable to grasp it. Moreover, we do have some concept of atemporal causation, the concept Aquinas had in mind when he claimed that "God's action existed from all eternity, whereas its effect was not present from all eternity, but existed at that time when, from all eternity He ordained it."[68] Thus, I see no reason to think that (31'b) entails that God is not timeless.

So (31'a) entails that God is not timeless, but it has not been shown that the argument establishes it; on the other hand, (31'b) does follow from the premises of the argument, but we have seen no reason for thinking that it entails that God is not timeless. I conclude that this attempt to disprove the doctrine of divine timelessness does not succeed.

A final attempt to show that God is not timeless by appealing to

67. Davis, *Logic and the Nature of God*, p. 13.
68. Aquinas, *S.c.G.*, 2, 35.

the nature of divine action holds that some divine actions are re-
sponses to human actions and thus can only occur temporally later
than the events to which they are a response. Wolterstorff suggests
this line of thinking, but he does not develop it: "Some of God's
actions must be understood as a response to the free actions of
human beings. . . . I think it follows, given that all human actions
are temporal, that those actions of God which are 'response' actions
are temporal as well."[69]

Stephen Davis argues for this view at greater length. He begins by
quoting two biblical passages which attribute actions to God:

> If you obey the commandments of the Lord your God . . . by loving
> the Lord your God, by walking in his ways, and by keeping his
> commandments and his statutes and his ordinances, then you shall
> live and multiply, and the Lord your God will bless you. . . . But if
> your heart turns away, and you will not hear, but are drawn away to
> worship other gods and serve them, I declare to you this day, that
> you shall perish. (Deut. 30:16–18)

> In many and various ways God spoke of old to our fathers by the
> prophets; but in these last days he has spoken to us by a Son. (Heb.
> 1:1–2)[70]

Davis then makes the following claims:

> But the obvious problem here is to understand how a timeless being
> can plan or anticipate or remember or respond or punish or warn or
> forgive. All such acts seem undeniably temporal. To make plans is to
> formulate intentions about the future. To anticipate is to look for-
> ward to what is future. To remember is to have beliefs or knowledge
> about what is past. To respond is to be affected by events that have
> occurred in the past. To punish is to cause someone to suffer because
> of something done in the past. To warn is to caution someone about
> dangers that might lie in the future. To forgive someone is to restore
> a past relationship that was damaged by an offense.[71]

Some of the actions Davis cites here are not mentioned in the passages he quotes: these passages do not affirm that God anticipates

69. Wolterstorff, "God Everlasting," p. 93.
70. Davis, *Logic and the Nature of God*, p. 14. Davis quotes from the Revised
Standard Version of the Bible.
71. Ibid., p. 14.

things or that he makes plans (in contrast to his having a plan). On the other hand, the remaining actions need not be understood in a way that requires that they occur, if at all, in time. Thus, to punish someone is to cause that person to suffer at a time t for an offense that person has committed at a time t' earlier than t. But here Aquinas's distinction applies again. Perhaps in a case of divine punishment God's act, which occurs in his eternal present, has the temporal effect that a person suffers at a particular time; the required temporal element, then, is that the offense precede the punishment, not that the offense precede God's action. Similarly, to warn a person is to bring it about that a person is informed at a certain time of a danger that might occur after that time. But again, we can distinguish between God's warning a person, which may occur in God's eternal present, from the effect of God's act, namely, that the person is warned or receives God's warning.

It might be thought that the most difficult examples for the atemporalist to deal with are ones, such as God's answering a petitionary prayer, in which God's action might seem to be a *response* to a temporal event. Stump and Kretzmann consider this question. They distinguish

> (33) Something constitutes an answer to a prayer only if it is done because of the prayer

from

> (34) Something is done because of a prayer only if it is done later than the praying of the prayer.

They then add: "We think that [(33)] is true; [(34)], on the other hand, seems doubtful even as applied to temporal entities. If at 3:00 a mother prepares a snack for her little boy because she believes that when he gets home at 3:30 he will ask for one, it does not seem unreasonable to describe her as preparing the food because of the child's request, even though in this case the response is earlier than the request."[72] According to Stump and Kretzmann, then, God's

---

72. Stump and Kretzmann, "Eternity," p. 450.

answering a prayer can be a response to a temporal event without occurring later than that event.

This claim does not seem correct, however, and the example employed to support it is unconvincing. It may be that the mother prepares the snack in *anticipation* of the child's request, but it does not seem correct to describe the preparation as a *response* to the request; she has decided how to act before the request is made. The only course open to the atemporalist, it seems to me, is to deny that God's answering a prayer is a response to the prayer. But this is not an implausible position; it is, indeed, the position that someone who holds God to be in time should take, too. For if God is in time, he knows in advance what prayers will be made, and his plans take them into account. Thus, if God is in time, he decides before a prayer is made how he will act. In this respect he is similar to the mother who anticipates the request for a snack. But in neither case do we have an action that is properly regarded as a response. So it remains to be shown that facts about God's action require that he not be timeless.

7

Divine Goodness
And Impeccability

1. Perfectly Good

The claim that God is good can be taken in two ways. In the first, it attributes a certain status to God. Aquinas, for example, holds that "the essence of goodness consists in this, that it is in some way desirable," and he adds that "a thing is desirable only in so far as it is perfect."[1] Aquinas then claims that "to be good belongs pre-eminently to God" because of his "desirableness" and that God is the highest good because "all desired perfections flow from Him as their first cause."[2] In this sense, then, the claim that God is good is an ontological, or perhaps even an aesthetic, claim.[3]

On the other hand, the claim that God is good may be taken instead to express a moral judgment: God is morally good or morally perfect. It is this thesis which I am interested in exploring in this chapter. However, I shall not attempt to define the concept of being morally good, in contrast to many of the other attributes we have examined. I am not confident that this can be done.[4] Nevertheless,

1. Aquinas, *S.T.*, Ia. 5, 1.
2. Ibid., Ia, 6, 1 and 2.
3. Cf. Norman Kretzmann, "Goodness, Knowledge, and Indeterminacy in the Philosophy of Thomas Aquinas," *Journal of Philosophy* 80 (1983):353–382.
4. For an attempt to define the concept of *omnibenevolence*, see William Mann, "The Divine Attributes," *American Philosophical Quarterly* 12 (1975):151–159. I have criticized Mann's proposal in "Intrinsic Maxima and Omnibenevolence," *International Journal for Philosophy of Religion* 10 (1979):41–50.

we have some intuitions about what such goodness consists in, and it clearly involves doing no wrong. According to Richard Swinburne, "in claiming that God is by nature morally perfectly good, the theist means that God is so constituted that he never does actions which are morally wrong."[5] This is surely part of moral goodness, but it is not all of it. For one thing, the theist may hold that what is wrong is determined by God; it is that of which God disapproves. In that case, however, there must be more to God's goodness than merely that he never does anything of which he disapproves—that would seem to have little moral value. In the second place, being morally good, at least in the case of finite beings, seems to require more than performing right actions. Imagine a malicious but thoroughly misinformed person who, unintentionally, manages to do what is right while trying to wreak incredible havoc. So it seems that intentions, and perhaps also traits of character, are relevant to being morally good. Moreover, the Christian tradition has identified various virtues that seem to be involved in God's moral perfection. These include, among others, the virtues of being loving, merciful, just, and faithful. I assume, therefore, that the exercise of such virtues is part of what is required to be morally good, but for simplicity of exposition I focus on the property of doing no wrong.

Theists agree that God is good. Two related theses are often, though not universally, accepted. The first is that God is *essentially* good, that is, that it is not possible that he not be good or that he do evil. The second is that God is impeccable. Literally understood, impeccability is the inability to sin. However, sin is sometimes taken to be alienation from God;[6] but if it is impossible for anyone to be alienated from himself, it would, on this interpretation, be trivial that God is impeccable. So let us understand impeccability as the inability to do what is morally wrong. In that sense, impeccability follows from essential goodness; if it is impossible for someone to do what is wrong, he or she is unable to. The converse is not obviously true, however. If a person is unable to do what is wrong, it does not follow that it is impossible for him or her to do wrong.

The problem of evil is frequently thought to constitute the leading challenge to the doctrine that God is good. In its standard for-

5. Richard Swinburne, *The Coherence of Theism* (Oxford: Oxford University Press, 1977), p. 179.
6. See Vincent Brümmer, "Divine Impeccability," *Religious Studies* 20 (1984):203.

mulation, the problem of evil is the claim that the existence of evil is incompatible with the existence of an omnipotent, omniscient, perfectly good God; however, this is as much a challenge to the doctrines of divine omnipotence and divine omniscience as it is to the doctrine of divine goodness. Moreover, the problem of evil is too large an issue for me even to begin to discuss it here. Suffice it to say that I do not believe that anyone has succeeded in showing an incompatibility between the existence of evil and the existence of an omnipotent, omniscient, perfectly good God.[7] Accordingly, I concentrate, with one exception, on objections to the theses that God is essentially good and that he is impeccable. In the next chapter we shall consider the claim that morality depends upon the will of a perfectly good being.

2. Goodness and Omnipotence

We saw in Chapter 1 that various classical theists denied that God could do wrong. Thus Anselm said that God "cannot be corrupted or tell lies,"[8] and Aquinas said that to sin is to fall short in action and "to be able to fall short in action is repugnant to omnipotence."[9] However, Nelson Pike has presented an argument for the incompatibility of divine omnipotence and perfect goodness to which he thinks the proper response is that God is able to do wrong.[10] Pike claims that to be omnipotent, a being must be able to bring about morally reprehensible states of affairs. Pike tries to reconcile this ability with being perfectly good by distinguishing between the role or office of being God and the occupant of that office. According to Pike, it is not possible for someone to hold the office of God and also bring about a morally reprehensible state of affairs; in this sense, then, God is unable to do wrong. But any occupant of the office of God has the ability to do wrong. So, according to Pike, the person who is God is not essentially perfectly good.

Pike's outrageously unorthodox response to this puzzle is surely not required to resolve it. We saw in Chapter 1 that a being's essen-

7. See the discussion of the Free Will Defense in Section 3 of Chapter 5 above.
8. Anselm, *Proslogion* 7.
9. Aquinas, *S.T.*, Ia, 25, 3 *ad* 2.
10. Nelson Pike, "Omnipotence and God's Ability to Sin," *American Philosophical Quarterly* 6 (1969):208–216.

tial properties may properly limit what it must be able to do in order to be omnipotent, at least if omnipotence is to be understood in a way that accords with what classical theism has said about God's abilities. Hence, an essentially good being need not be able to bring about a morally reprehensible state of affairs in order to count as omnipotent.

W. R. Carter has attempted to take Pike's contention a step farther. Carter believes Pike has shown that omnipotence requires that the person who is God is not essentially morally good; Carter's innovation is to claim that God cannot be accidentally or contingently good, either.[11] Carter's argument is contained in the following passage (following Pike, Carter uses the Hebrew name of God, 'Yahweh,' as a proper name of the individual who occupies the position of God—a position Carter refers to as 'D'):

> Let us suppose. . .that Yahweh (a hypothetical occupant of D) is not *essentially* sinless, even though *in fact* Yahweh never sins. It is a corollary of this assumption that there are possible worlds in which Yahweh *does* sin. Let 'W_S' designate such a world and 't' designate a time, in the history of 'W_S', at which Yahweh acts in a sinful way. (If you deny that there is such a possible world as 'W_S' then you are committed to saying that Yahweh is essentially sinless.) . . . The trouble is the present model cannot be correct. For consider the position of Yahweh at $t - 1$, a minute (say) before he acts sinfully. Since Yahweh occupies D at $t - 1$, Yahweh is at $t - 1$ omnipotent, omniscient, and without sin. Being all-knowing at $t - 1$, Yahweh must then realize that he is about to act sinfully and so is about to vacate his office. Being omnipotent at $t - 1$, Yahweh has it within his power to see that things do not turn out this way. After t Yahweh can be charged with having foreseen that he was about to commit a sinful action— one that was in his power not to perform. In light of this, I doubt that Yahweh can be sinless at $t - 1$, and so doubt that he can occupy D at $t - 1$. One surely is guilty of *some* sort of moral failing in the event that one realizes that one is about to act maliciously (say), it is within one's power not so to act, and yet one proceeds to act maliciously. . . . Accordingly, I am sceptical of the idea that there is such a possible world as 'W_S', in which an individual ceases by way of a moral failing

11. W. R. Carter, "Omnipotence and Sin," *Analysis* 42 (1982):102–105. This way of viewing Carter's project is influenced by Thomas Morris, "Impeccability," *Analysis* 43 (1983):106–112, who rejects Carter's argument for reasons similar to those given below.

to occupy the divine office. No possible world is such that one of its inhabitants sins at t but is also omnipotent, omniscient, and 'wholly good' at $t - 1$.[12]

So Carter apparently believes that the demands of omnipotence and omniscience together require that God cannot be contingently or accidentally wholly good.

Carter's argument does not establish this claim, however. The most it shows is that an omnipotent, omniscient, wholly good being cannot *lose* its perfect goodness; it does not follow from this that any such being is not *accidentally* wholly good. Put in terms of the concept we employed in Section 6 of Chapter 1, what Carter's argument suggests is that *being wholly good* is *enduring* for any being who is omnipotent and omniscient. But that leaves it open that *being wholly good* is also accidental for such a being. Carter begins his argument by assuming that Yahweh occupies the divine office and is contingently sinless. From this assumption it does follow that there is a world W_S and a time t such that in W_S Yahweh sins at t. But then when Carter asks us to consider the position of Yahweh at $t - 1$, he says, "since Yahweh occupies D at $t - 1$, Yahweh is at $t - 1$ omnipotent, omniscient, and without sin," and he adds, "Yahweh must then realize that he is about to act sinfully and so is about to vacate his office." Thus, Carter assumes both that Yahweh is omnipotent, omniscient, and wholly good, and that at $t - 1$ Yahweh is about to sin. But he is not entitled to both of these assumptions. It follows from his assumption that Yahweh occupies the divine office that Yahweh is *in fact* omnipotent, omniscient, and wholly good. And it follows from the claim that in W_S Yahweh sins at t that *in W_S* Yahweh is about to sin at $t - 1$. But it does not follow from Carter's assumptions that Yahweh is omnipotent, omniscient, and wholly good in W_S at $t - 1$. So Carter's argument does not yield the conclusion that Yahweh does not sin in W_S, and hence it does not show that Yahweh is not accidentally wholly good.

I have no objection, of course, to Carter's claim that God is not accidentally wholly good. It is only in conjunction with Pike's discredited thesis that God is not essentially good that Carter's claim has any real force against theism, for the two claims together entail

12. Carter, "Omnipotence and Sin," p. 105.

that God is not wholly good *simpliciter*. I wish to maintain here only that Carter's argument does not succeed in showing that God is not accidentally good.

3. Goodness and Freedom

A second source of objections to the theses that God is impeccable and essentially wholly good derives from claims about the nature of free action. For example, Wesley Morriston claims that certain features of free action central to the Free Will Defense can be used to show that God is not essentially morally good.[13]

According to the Free Will Defense,[14] it is possible that God so values creatures who freely choose to do what is right in circumstances in which they are significantly free that he created such creatures even though they would sometimes do what is wrong and, as a result, add moral evil to the world. It is possible, in other words, that the moral goodness of properly exercised significant freedom outweighs the moral evil resulting from its abuse. 'Significant freedom' here is a technical term, which Alvin Plantinga introduces as follows. He first says that "an action is *morally significant*, for a given person, if it would be wrong for him to perform the action but right to refrain or *vice versa*."[15] Then he adds that "a

---

13. Wesley Morriston, "Is God 'Significantly Free'?" *Faith and Philosophy* 2 (1985):257–264. The precise targets of Morriston's criticism are the the Free Will Defense as Plantinga develops it in *God, Freedom, and Evil* (1974; rpt. Grand Rapids, Mich.: Eerdmans, 1977), pp. 7–64, and what Plantinga in the same work (pp. 111–112) calls a sound ontological argument. This version of the ontological argument is an attempt to prove the existence of a being who is, among other things, essentially wholly good.

In the first section of this Chapter, I distinguished between God's goodness in an ontological sense and God's goodness in a moral sense. It is clear, I think, that in attributing essential goodness to God, Plantinga has in mind *moral* goodness. These two sorts of goodness are not always distinguished in Anselm's thought. Thus he asks, "What goodness could be wanting to the supreme good, through which every good exists? Thus You are just, truthful, happy, and whatever it is better to be than not to be—for it is better to be just rather than unjust, and happy rather than unhappy." *Proslogion* V, trans. M. J. Charlesworth (Notre Dame: University of Notre Dame Press, 1979), p. 121. Justice and truthfulness pertain to moral goodness, but happiness and whatever it is better to be than not seem more appropriate to ontological goodness.

14. See Section 3 of Chapter 5 above.

15. Plantinga, *God, Freedom, and Evil*, p. 30.

person is *significantly free*, on a given occasion, if he is then free with respect to a morally significant action."[16] Finally, Plantinga holds that "if a person is free with respect to a given action, then he is free to perform that action and free to refrain from performing it; no antecedent conditions and/or causal laws determine that he will perform the action, or that he won't."[17]

Wesley Morriston claims that these presuppositions of the Free Will Defense are incompatible with God's being essentially morally perfect. Morriston says that if God is essentially morally perfect, then

> God is *morally perfect in every possible world*. Since moral perfection is incompatible with wrongdoing, it follows that there is no possible world in which God performs a wrong action. In other words, God's nature is such that it is logically impossible for Him to perform a wrong action. He is determined—in the strongest possible sense of 'determined'—not to perform any wrong actions. Thus it seems that, on Plantinga's analysis of significant freedom, God is not significantly free. And since *moral* goodness presupposes significant freedom, it also follows that God is not morally good, which is as near as makes no matter to saying that God is not morally perfect![18]

Morriston seems to me correct in holding that God is not significantly free. If an agent S is significantly free at a certain time t with respect to an action A, then two conditions hold. First, either S's performing A is morally right and refraining from performing it is morally wrong, or S's performing A is morally wrong and refraining from performing it is morally right. Second, no antecedent conditions at t determine either that S perform A or that S refrain from A. We can put this latter point, employing the idea of an initial segment of a possible world,[19] by saying that the initial segment up until t is compatible with S's performing A and it is compatible with

16. Ibid.

17. Ibid., p. 29. In my review of *Alvin Plantinga*, ed. James Tomberlin and Peter van Inwagen (Dordrecht: D. Reidel, 1985), in *Faith and Philosophy* 5 (1988):214–219, I suggest that Plantinga can relax this strongly incompatibilist condition. It is sufficient for the purposes of the Free Will Defense that *God* cannot cause another's free actions; it is immaterial whether, say, the beliefs and desires of the agent can cause an agent's free actions.

18. Morriston, "Is God 'Significantly Free'?" p. 258.

19. See Section 3 of Chapter 1.

S's refraining from A. It follows, then, that whether it is the performing or the refraining that is wrong, there is a possible world in which S goes wrong with respect to A. So if an agent is significantly free with respect to an action, it is possible that the agent do what is morally wrong. Hence, if God is essentially morally perfect, since it then is not possible that he do what is wrong, there is no action with respect to which he is significantly free.

Morriston regards this as a serious shortcoming. He says, as we have seen, that "since *moral* goodness presupposes significant freedom, it also follows that God is not morally good."[20] But here, I believe, Morriston betrays a serious confusion. As the term 'moral goodness' is used in the context of the Free Will Defense, it is true that the existence of moral goodness presupposes that someone has significant freedom. But it does not follow that significant freedom is required for being morally good as we are using the term in this chapter. To see this, we should look more closely at the Free Will Defense.

Both the person who propounds the problem of evil as an objection to theism (the "atheological objector") and the person who replies by giving the Free Will Defense presuppose that some things are intrinsically valuable, that other things are intrinsically disvaluable, and that the balance of what is valuable over what is disvaluable in a given world is, or ought to be, a relevant factor in God's decision whether to actualize that world. What is intrinsically valuable is good, and what is intrinsically disvaluable is evil. Both the atheological objector and the free will defender agree, furthermore, that the actual world contains a large amount of evil, including, for example, the pain and suffering of sentient creatures. The free will defender, however, claims that it is possible that this evil is *moral* evil, where *moral evil* is defined as evil that results from significantly free actions. Correspondingly, some or all of what is good is *moral* good, where that is simply intrinsic good resulting from significantly free action. The free will defender claims, furthermore, that such moral good is a very great good; it is so great that enough of it can outweigh a very large amount of evil.[21] So the kind of moral

20. Morriston, "Is God 'Significantly Free'?" p. 258.
21. It is sometimes unappreciated just how much evil can be outweighed, according to this view, by moral good. Christian doctrine affirms, however, that for the sake of moral good God was even prepared to suffer himself. See Alvin Plantinga,

goodness that figures in the Free Will Defense is a species of intrinsic value—it is that goodness which is produced by significantly free actions. It should be clear, then, how "moral goodness presupposes significant freedom"; moral goodness is by definition goodness that results from significantly free action.

In contrast, the moral goodness that we have been discussing is the goodness involved in always doing what is morally right, having morally proper motives, and exercising the moral virtues. From the fact that God is not significantly free it does not follow that he is not morally good in this sense. Moral goodness, in this sense, does not presuppose significant freedom, and Morriston's argument that God is not significantly free does not show that God is not essentially morally perfect.

Is there, perhaps, a way of arguing that doing what is morally right requires being significantly free? Eleonore Stump and Norman Kretzmann present (without endorsing) the following principle:

> (1) A person P in a world W_1 is morally good in deciding to perform an action x at time t only if there is some possible world W_2 like W_1 in all respects up to t, but at t in W_2 P does not decide to perform x but decides instead to do something evil.[22]

(1) precludes the existence of an essentially morally good agent, at least if it is impossible to be morally good without ever being morally good in deciding to do something, since, according to (1), if an agent is morally good in deciding to perform an action, it is possible that the agent decide to do something evil instead. But is there any reason to accept (1)?

It is plausible to think that if an agent is morally good in performing an action, then the agent does the action freely. Moreover, if an agent does an action freely, then there is something the agent could have done differently. As we saw in Section 4 of Chapter 3, it is a

---

"Self-Profile," in Tomberlin and van Inwagen, *Alvin Plantinga*, p. 46, and Nicholas Wolterstorff, "Suffering Love" (unpublished). Nevertheless, the Free Will Defense need not hold that moral good is the highest good or that it is such a great good that God must be able to produce it directly, without the aid of free creatures.

22. Eleonore Stump and Norman Kretzmann, "Absolute Simplicity," *Faith and Philosophy* 2 (1985):359.

delicate matter to say exactly what the agent of a free action could have done instead. Perhaps we can summarize our earlier discussion by saying that if an agent does an action freely, then the agent could have refrained from causing his or her performing that action. Thus, it is plausible to think that

(2) If a person *P* is morally good in performing an action *x* in a world W_1 at a time *t* then there is a world W_2 such that (i) W_1 and W_2 share an initial segment up to *t*, and (ii) in W_2 *P* does not cause *Ps performing x at t.*

According to (2), if a person is morally good in performing an action at a certain time, then it is possible, given what has happened up to that time, that the person does not cause the action; this seems to be a reasonable claim. However, (2) does not preclude there being an essentially morally perfect being. God can satisfy (2) if, whenever he is morally good in performing an action, there is another (perhaps equally good) action which it is possible that he perform instead; it need not be possible for him to do an evil action instead.

Now (1) is a considerably stronger principle than (2). In order for an agent to be morally good in performing some action, according to (1), it is not enough that the agent do the action freely; rather, it must be possible for the agent to do something evil instead. This is a claim, however, that cannot be defended simply by appealing to considerations of what is required for free action, and I see no reason to think that it is true. Accordingly, facts about freedom do not seem to show that God is not essentially morally good.

4. Impeccability and Praiseworthiness

A related claim is that God is not worthy of praise for his moral goodness if he is not able to sin. Stephen Davis endorses this objection to divine impeccability. He writes,

If God is unable to do evil it is no more morally apt to praise him for his goodness than it is apt to praise the refrigerator for keeping the food cold or a spider for refraining from telling lies. Refrigerators are designed to keep food cold; they aren't agents who make choices; it isn't praiseworthy that they keep food cold. Spiders just aren't able to tell lies; it isn't praiseworthy that they don't. If God's nature causes or determines him to do good in such a way that doing evil is not in his power, I would conclude that he is not a free and responsible agent and thus not a fit object of the praise and thanks of his people.[23]

Davis's remark that if God were unable to do evil then he would not be free suggests that this objection is a version of the one we considered in the last section.[24] If it is, then our response to that objection applies. God's freedom requires that he be able to do alternatives to what he does; it does not require that these alternatives be evil.

On the other hand, is there something about being morally praiseworthy that requires the ability to do evil? John Calvin's response to this question was to write, "Suppose some blasphemer sneers that God deserves little praise for his own goodness, constrained as he is to preserve it. Will this not be a ready answer to him: not from violent impulsion but from his boundless goodness comes God's inability to do evil?"[25] Of course, by quoting this passage I do not mean to accuse Davis of blasphemy or even of sneering. But why could not God be praiseworthy for goodness so boundless it is not so much as possible for him to do evil? It is worth noting that being *essentially* good does not make God more *morally* praiseworthy than he would be if he were merely contingently good; his goodness in other possible worlds does not add to his goodness in the actual world. But his goodness in other worlds might, nevertheless, contribute to his overall *greatness* and thus provide additional grounds for praise. So I am not convinced that divine impeccability detracts from God's praiseworthiness.

23. Stephen T. Davis, *Logic and the Nature of God* (Grand Rapids, Mich.: Eerdmans, 1983), p. 95. Cf. Pike in "Omnipotence and God's Ability to Sin," who writes: "If an individual does not have the creative power necessary to bring about evil states of affairs, he cannot be praised (morally) for failing to bring them about."

24. Anthony Kenny lumps the two together in his remark, "Only a few eccentrics have argued that it must be possible for God to do something wicked, since otherwise he would not be a free agent and his goodness would not be a matter for praise." *The God of the Philosophers* (Oxford: Oxford University Press, 1979), p. 110.

25. John Calvin, *Institutes of the Christian Religion*, II, iii, 5, ed. John T. McNeill, trans. Ford Lewis Battles (Philadelphia: Westminster Press, 1960), p. 295.

[8]

The Source of Moral Obligation

1. God and Morality

Norman Kretzmann has recently written that "if there is goodness itself, as there is if there is an absolutely perfect being, then obviously it is and must be the sole criterion of moral rightness and wrongness."[1] Whether it is *obvious* that God is the sole criterion of right and wrong, theists typically do think that there is a close connection between God and morality; it is the nature of the connection that is a matter of dispute.

A range of views on the relation between God and morality is provided by the various versions of the divine command theory of ethics.[2] The strongest version of this theory is definist. It holds that

---

1. Norman Kretzmann, "Abraham, Isaac, and Euthyphro: God and the Basis of Morality," in *Hamartia: The Concept of Error in the Western Tradition*, ed. D. V. Stump et al. (New York: Edwin Mellen Press, 1983) p. 45.

2. Recent interest in the divine command theory has been stimulated by the defenses of two versions of it provided by Robert M. Adams in "A Modified Divine Command Theory of Ethical Wrongness," in *Religion and Morality*, ed. G. Outka and J. Reeder, Jr. (Garden City, N.Y.: Anchor, 1973), pp. 318–347, and "Divine Command Metaethics Modified Again," *Journal of Religious Ethics* 7 (1979):66–79. See also his "Autonomy and Theological Ethics," *Religious Studies* 15 (1979):191–194, and "Moral Arguments for Theistic Belief," in *Rationality and Religious Belief*, ed. C. F. Delaney (Notre Dame: University of Notre Dame Press, 1979), pp. 116–140. These papers are all reprinted in Robert M. Adams, *The Virtue of Faith and Other Essays in Philosophical Theology* (New York: Oxford University Press, 1987).

moral predicates, such as 'is obligatory,' are to be defined in terms
of such theological predicates as 'is commanded by God'; alternatively, moral properties, such as the property of *being obligatory*,
are identical to such theological properties as *being commanded by
God*. Perhaps the most famous defender of this sort of divine command theory is Euthyphro.[3] Plato, of course, is widely regarded as
having refuted Euthyphro's definition of the pious as that which is
loved by the gods. I think, however, that Plato showed merely that
Euthyphro's definition is inconsistent with certain other premisses
Euthyphro accepted but need not have.[4] Nevertheless, definist divine command theories are implausible. The most persuasive consideration against them is the evidence of our linguistic intuitions.
Most persons, including many theists, who have thought about
whether moral and theological predicates are synonymous have
concluded that they are not. And most persons, including many
theists, who have thought about whether moral properties are identical with theological ones have similarly concluded that they are
not.

Perhaps the weakest forms of the divine command theory are
those which assert simply that what God commands is coextensive

---

Other recent work includes Baruch Brody, "Morality and Religion Reconsidered,"
in *Readings in the Philosophy of Religion*, ed. Brody (Englewood Cliffs, N.J.: Prentice-
Hall, 1974), pp. 592–603; Philip Quinn, "Divine Commands and the Logic of
Requirement," presented at the Eastern Division meetings of the American Philosophical Association, December 1976, and *Divine Commands and Moral Requirements*
(Oxford: Oxford University Press, 1978); Richard Swinburne, "Duty and the Will
of God," *Canadian Journal of Philosophy* 4 (1974):213–227, and *The Coherence of
Theism* (Oxford: Oxford University Press, 1977), chap. 11; and Edward Wierenga,
"A Defensible Divine Command Theory," *Noûs* 17 (1983):387–407, and "Utilitarianism and the Divine Command Theory," *American Philosophical Quarterly* 21
(1984):311–318. Two important collections have recently appeared. They are *Divine
Commands and Morality*, ed. Paul Helm (Oxford: Oxford University Press, 1981),
and *Divine Command Morality: Historical and Contemporary Readings*, ed. Janine Marie
Idziak (New York: Edwin Mellen Press, 1979). Finally, two recent issues of *Faith
and Philosophy* are devoted to Christianity and ethical theory: vol. 3 (October 1986)
and vol. 4 (July 1987). The latter includes another paper by Robert Adams: "Divine
Commands and the Social Nature of Obligation," pp. 262–275.
   3. Plato, *Euthyphro*, 9D.
   4. The best reconstruction of Plato's argument with which I am familiar is by S.
Marc Cohen in "Socrates on the Definition of Piety: *Euthyphro* 10A–11B," *Journal of
the History of Philosophy* 9 (1971):1–13, rpt. in *The Philosophy of Socrates*, ed. G.
Vlastos (Garden City, N.Y.: Anchor, 1971), pp. 158–176.

with what is right. On this view, God's commands provide a reliable guide to morality, but they do not determine it.[5] Other weak versions of the theory have also been proposed. According to Richard Swinburne, for example, God can bring about the obligation that we obey certain of his commands by placing us in the circumstances of having been created and sustained by him or of being allowed to use his property.[6] But according to this theory, some of God's commands merely reinforce obligations we would have anyway, and many moral truths are entirely independent of God's will or commands. And one of the versions of the divine command theory presented by Philip Quinn holds that "divine commands, were they to be imposed, would suffice to impose indefeasible requirements."[7] This theory does not, however, include the claim that God *has* issued any commands, and it leaves open the possibility that any requirement imposed by a command of God is also imposed by something else.

I attempt to develop a formulation of the command divine theory which is not as strong, or as implausible, as the definist version but which is not as weak as those versions which allow for moral obligations that are not dependent upon God's will or commands. In the next two sections I present some of the details of such a theory, and in the section following I show how the theory can be defended against a variety of initially impressive objections.

2. The Divine Command Theory

According to the divine command theory, God is a moral authority, in the sense not merely that he is a reliable source of information about moral matters but that he determines morality. The moral status of actions depends upon God. To make this more precise we need to make some assumptions. I shall assume that there are such basic moral properties as *being obligatory*, *being permissible*, and *being wrong*. These properties are related to one another in the following

5. Richard Mouw appears to endorse such a view in "The Status of God's Moral Judgment," *Canadian Journal of Theology* 16 (1970):61–66.
6. Swinburne, "Duty and the Will of God," and *The Coherence of Theism*, chap. 11. A similar view is presented by Brody in "Morality and Religion Reconsidered."
7. Quinn, "Divine Commands and the Logic of Requirement." Cf. *Divine Commands and Moral Requirements*, chap. 4.

way: it is possible to define any two of them in terms of the remaining one. Thus if we begin with the property of *being permissible*, we may say that an action is obligatory just in case it is not permissible not to do it, and an action is wrong just in case it is not permissible to do it. I shall also assume that there are such theological properties as *being commanded by God* and *being forbidden by God*, but in contrast to the definist versions of the divine command theory, the theory I shall present does not assume that the basic moral properties are identical to, or can be defined in terms of, any such theological properties.

The fundamental task for a theory of normative ethics is to provide necessary and sufficient conditions for an action's possessing these moral properties. Given the equivalences just noted, this task can be accomplished by providing necessary and sufficient conditions for just one of these properties. Moreover, such necessary and sufficient conditions must be conditions upon which the moral properties *depend*, or to use a familiar but not entirely clear term, *supervene*. It would be desirable to have a clear account of this crucial notion, but since this is a problem for any normative ethical theory, and not only for the divine command theory, it will not matter if we rely on our intuitive grasp of this relation.

I have spoken thus far of the moral status of *actions*, but we need not add an additional category to our ontology at this point. We can simply take the basic moral properties to apply to an agent's bringing about a state of affairs. Let us turn, then, to a statement of the theory, which includes the following principles:

> (P1) For every agent x, state of affairs S, and time t, (i) it is obligatory that x bring about S at t if and only if God commands that x bring about S at t, and (ii) if it is obligatory that x bring about S at t, then by commanding that x bring about S at t God brings it about that it is obligatory that x bring about S at t.

> (P2) For every agent x, state of affairs S, and time t, (i) it is permissible that x bring about S at t if and only if God does not forbid that x bring about S at t, and (ii) if it is permissible that x bring about S at t, then by failing to forbid that x bring about S at t God brings it about that it is permissible that x bring about S at t.

(P3) For every agent x, state of affairs S, and time t, (i) it is wrong that x bring about S at t if and only if God forbids that x bring about S at t, and (ii) if it is wrong that x bring about S at t, then by forbidding that x bring about S at t God brings it about that it is wrong that x bring about S at t.

The left conjuncts of these principles assert the coextension of the basic moral properties and the respective theological ones. The right conjuncts are intended to express the stronger condition that the possession of these moral properties depends upon, or holds in virtue of, God's activity.

An omnipotent, omniscient, and perfectly good being never commands an action that he also forbids, and I also assume that if such a being commands an action, then he also forbids that it not be done.[8] Accordingly, these principles preserve the interdefinability of our three basic moral concepts.

A question can arise about (P2), because it requires that in order for an action to be permissible, God's *failing* to forbid makes it permissible. Accordingly, (P2) is open to the objection that a failing cannot make something the case. However, I am not persuaded by this objection, because in many instances a failing *can* make something the case. My failing to restrain my companion can make me an accomplice, or my failing to vote in two successive elections can make me ineligible to vote (without reregistering). Moreover, God's failing to forbid an action is never a mere oversight; actions that he fails to forbid are ones of which he is aware but which he *declines* to forbid. Nevertheless, someone who objects to (P2) on this ground may wish to delete its right conjunct. Such a revision would accept what Philip Quinn calls "Karamazov's Thesis," namely, that if God did not exist, then everything would be permitted.[9]

3. Divine Commands and Divine Will

I have spoken of God's commands and prohibitions, and I have called this theory a divine command theory, but although this name

---

8. Cf. Calvin: "If [God] commands this, he forbids the opposite; if he forbids this, he enjoins the opposite." *Institutes*, II, viii, 8.

9. Quinn, *Divine Commands and Moral Requirements*, p. 30.

is customary, it can be misleading. For, as even the theist is likely to concede, more things are obligatory or wrong than the actions covered by God's explicit commands or prohibitions. Elsewhere I have suggested that the divine command theory is best formulated in terms of God's will or in terms of his approval.[10] This is contrary to the view of Robert Adams, who writes,

> Theists sometimes speak of wrong action as action contrary to the 'will' of God, but that way of speaking ignores some important distinctions. One is the distinction between the absolute will of God (his 'good pleasure') and his revealed will. Any Christian theology will grant that God in his good pleasure sometimes decides, for reasons that may be mysterious to us, not to do everything he could to prevent a wrong action. According to some theologies nothing at all can happen contrary to God's good pleasure. It is difficult, therefore, to suppose that all wrong actions are unqualifiedly contrary to God's will in the sense of his good pleasure. It is God's *revealed* will—not what he wants or plans to have happen, but what he has told us to do—that is thought to determine the rightness or wrongness of human actions.[11]

So if nothing can happen contrary to God's will—what Adams calls God's 'absolute will'—the divine command theory should not be understood to hold that an action is wrong if and only if it is contrary to God's will, for it would then follow that no one ever does anything wrong. On the other hand, if we frame the theory in terms of God's commands, we are left with the problem that God's explicit commands fail to apply to many moral situations.

The solution requires distinguishing God's explicit commands (his *commandments*, let us say) from his implicit commands. This was Calvin's approach to the Ten Commandments, about which he says, "the commandments and prohibitions always contain more than is expressed in words."[12] He interprets God's prohibition against killing, for example, to enjoin giving "our neighbor's life all the help we can,"[13] and he says that by "half-commandments" God

10. Wierenga, "A Defensible Divine Command Theory," p. 390.
11. Adams, "Divine Command Metaethics Modified Again," pp. 76–77. It will become clear below that my disagreement with Adams is more apparent than real.
12. Calvin, *Institutes*, II, viii, 8.
13. Ibid., II, viii, 9.

signifies through synecdoche, rather than expresses, what he wills.[14]
Let us extend Adams's term 'revealed will' to include what Calvin
thus takes God's commandments to signify. A similar approach to
biblical interpretation is adopted by Richard Mouw, who writes
that "we will miss some of the commands to be 'found' in the Bible
if we attend only to sentences which are grammatically impera-
tive."[15] Mouw, too, is interested in God's revealed will, and his use
of the term 'command' to refer to it suggests a resolution of our
problem. We can continue to interpret the divine command theory
as basing morality on God's commands, provided that we understand God's commands not as commandments but as statements of
his revealed will.

4. Some Objections

Although the divine command theory is embodied in much of
popular piety, it is difficult, with some notable exceptions, to find a
responsible philosopher or theologian who accepts it, at least in the
relatively strong formulation we have been discussing. This is due, I
believe, to the fact that most people who have reflected on the
divine command theory have concluded that it is subject to decisive
objections. In this section we examine some of those objections, as
well as some new ones. I argue that they do not succeed in refuting
the theory.

A. The "Anything Goes" Objection

Perhaps the most widely held objection to the divine command
theory is given by Ralph Cudworth. He writes that

> divers Modern Theologers do not only seriously, but zealously con-
> tend . . . , *That there is nothing Absolutely, Intrinsically, and Naturally
> Good and Evil, Just and Unjust, antecedently to any positive Command of
> God; but that the Arbitrary Will and Pleasure of God,* (that is, an Om-
> nipotent Being devoid of all Essential and Natural Justice) *by its Com-
> mands and Prohibitions, is the first and only Rule and Measure thereof.*
> Whence it follows unavoidably that nothing can be imagined so

14. Ibid., II, viii, 10.
15. Richard Mouw, "Biblical Revelation and Medical Decisions," *Journal of Medicine and Philosophy* 4 (1979):371.

grossly wicked, or so foully unjust or dishonest, but if it were supposed to be commanded by this Omnipotent Deity, must needs upon
that Hypothesis forthwith become Holy, Just and Righteous.[16]

Consider some foully unjust state of affairs S—an innocent child's
suffering gratuitous cruelty, for example. Presumably Cudworth's
claim is that it follows from the divine command theory that

> (1) If God were to command someone to bring about S, then
>   it would be obligatory for that person to bring about S.

In this Cudworth is correct; for (1) appears to be a straightforward
consequence of (P1). However, merely pointing out that (1) is a
consequence of (P1) does not constitute an objection to (P1), unless
it can be shown that (1) is false. But is it? William of Ockham is
sometimes taken as an example of someone who would accept (1).
He seems to have held that if God were to order fornication, for
example, then fornication would be not only licit but meritorious.[17]
He made similar remarks about hatred of God, stealing, and adul-
tery.[18] And he apparently thought that God could at any time
change the moral order.[19]

Perhaps, however, Cudworth could point to a difficulty in accepting (1). He might argue that (1) is incompatible with some
obvious and incontrovertible fact, perhaps with

> (2) There is no possible world in which someone's bringing
>   about S is obligatory.

Now (2) does have an air of incontrovertibility about it, and I am
willing to concede that it is true. But this does not yet give us a

16. Ralph Cudworth, *A Treatise Concerning Eternal and Immutable Morality* (1731;
rpt. New York: Garland, 1976), pp. 9–10.

17. William of Ockham, *Super quattuor libros sententiarum*, III, 12, AA, in vol. 4 of
his *Opera plurima* (1494–96; rpt. Farnsborough, England: Gregg Press, 1962).

18. Ibid., II, 19, o.

19. William of Ockham, *Opus nonaginta dierum*, c. 95, in vol. 1 of *Opera plurima*.
There is some reason to doubt that these snippets accurately represent Ockham's
views, however. See Marilyn McCord Adams, "The Structure of Ockham's Moral
Theory," presented at the 1986 NEH Summer Institute in Philosophy of Religion.

reason to reject (1), for (2) is compatible with (1). We could use (2) to discredit (1) if we also accepted

(3) There is a possible world in which God commands someone to bring about S.

But why should a divine command theorist be willing to concede (3)? He or she might believe that God is essentially wholly good. As we saw in the last chapter, doing what is right is part of being morally good, but so is having the proper traits of character and exercising the moral virtues. Thus, the divine command theorist might hold that certain features of God's character, for example, that he is essentially just and that he is essentially loving, place constraints on what God would command.[20] In particular, bringing about a foully unjust state of affairs such as S is incompatible with being loving and just; so then is commanding someone else to bring S about. Accordingly, since these are essential features of God's character, they preclude his commanding that someone bring about S in any possible world.

The divine command theorist who holds that God is essentially loving and just has a straightforward response to Cudworth's objection. He or she should concede that (1) is a consequence of the theory but hold that since there is no world in which God commands someone to bring about S, the antecedent of (1) is impossible. According to the leading theories of counterfactual conditionals, a counterfactual conditional with an impossible antecedent is (trivially) true.[21] Thus, the divine theorist can accept (1) but insist that it is true. So Cudworth's objection does not refute the divine command theory.

B. The "Depriving God of Goodness" Objection

Another standard objection to the divine command theory holds that if God determines what is right and wrong, then he cannot

20. Rather than hold that God is essentially loving, Adams suggests that an ethical statement of a believer "*presupposes* that certain conditions for the applicability of the believer's concepts of ethical right and wrong are satisfied. Among these conditions is . . . that God loves His human creatures." Adams, "A Modified Divine Command Theory of Ethical Wrongness," p. 323.

21. See Robert Stalnaker, "A Theory of Conditionals," in *Studies in Logical Theory*, ed. N. Rescher (Oxford: Basil Blackwell, 1968), pp. 98–112, and David Lewis, *Counterfactuals* (Oxford: Basil Blackwell, 1973).

properly be described as good. According to this objection, if to be morally good is to do no wrong, and if what is wrong is what is forbidden by God, then to say that God is good is just to say that he never does what he forbids himself to do. But there is no *moral* value in never doing what one forbids oneself to do; so the divine command theorist is unable to maintain that God is good. Leibniz endorses a version of this objection in his *Theodicy*: "Those who believe that God establishes good and evil by an arbitrary decree . . . deprive God of the designation good,"[22] and he cites as his reason, "what cause would one have to praise . . . [God] for what he does, if in doing something quite different he would have done equally well?"[23]

We have anticipated this objection in our discussion, in the last chapter, of God's goodness. There we noted that never doing what is wrong is only part of what is involved in being morally good. Exercising the moral virtues, for example, being loving, just, merciful, and faithful, is also part of moral goodness. Thus, the theist can concede that there is little moral value in merely refraining from what one forbids oneself to do[24] but add that God is good in virtue of being loving, just, merciful, and faithful. Moreover, the divine command theorist might well value these attributes independently of God's commands. This would allow an account of how by ascribing goodness to God a divine command theorist not only describes God but also typically expresses approval—the relevant attributes are ones the divine command theorist values.[25]

Finally, the divine command theorist who holds that God has these virtues essentially has available a reply to Leibniz which parallels the response to Cudworth. It is true that whatever God were to do would be good, but given the constraints that the essential possession of these virtues places on what God *could* do, the range of "whatever God were to do" includes no actions for which God would not be praiseworthy.

22. Leibniz, *Theodicy*, para. 176, ed. Austin Farrer, trans. E. M. Huggard (London: Routledge & Kegan Paul, 1952).

23. Ibid.

24. Of course, the divine command theorist can hold that in doing what he commands himself to do, God is good *to us*, and that provides a reason to praise him.

25. I am here influenced by Adams, "A Modified Divine Command Theory of Ethical Wrongness," pp. 337–341.

C. The "Redundancy" Objection

In a recent article John Chandler has clearly described how several versions of the divine command theory, including the version I have proposed, appeal to God's love in order to reply to our first two objections.[26] Chandler claims that these theories are committed to what he calls the "co-extensiveness thesis," namely, that *being loving* is coextensive with *being right*. He then poses a dilemma: "If the co-extensiveness thesis is true, God's will becomes redundant, and the D.C.T. [divine command theory] is abandoned, since independent factors (even if not directly moral ones) constrain His will in detail, and by virtue of the transitivity of these constraints, constrain Him to will whatever is required by independent moral principles; if it is false, we are left with the traditional form of the D.C.T. with all its problems."[27] Fortunately for the defender of the divine command theory, both horns of this dilemma are mistaken. To see this, let us examine Chandler's claims.

Chandler argues that the divine command theory is committed to the "co-extensiveness thesis" as follows. He asks, "What must be the case in order for love to play its intended role in countering the. . .objection, that evil acts would become right if commanded by God? It will have to be maintained that, although the properties of being loving (unloving), as possessed by actions or types of actions are not identical with the properties of being morally right (wrong), they are co-extensive. . . . For if they are not, it is possible that an action which is loving, and such as would be commanded by a loving being, is (in one's judgment) wrong."[28]

According to our version of the divine command theory, God is loving, indeed, essentially loving. But what is it for an *act* to be loving? Chandler nowhere explains this concept. Perhaps an act is loving just in case it is done in a loving manner or from a loving motive. But there is no reason to suppose that the divine command theory is committed to holding that all and only right acts are loving in this sense, for an act that causes unnecessary suffering can be done in a loving manner or from a loving motive. In particular, the claim

26. John Chandler, "Divine Command Theories and the Appeal to Love," *American Philosophical Quarterly* 22 (1985):231–239.

27. Ibid., p. 238.

28. Ibid., p. 236.

that all and only right acts are loving in this sense does not seem to follow from the claim that God's loving nature ensures that he will not command an evil act such as, for example, inflicting gratuitous suffering; for having a loving nature seems compatible with willing or commanding an act that, though it is neither motivated by love nor performed lovingly, nevertheless brings about something good.[29] But suppose we look at whether accepting the coextensiveness thesis is damaging to the divine command theory.

Chandler claims that it is by arguing that

> if it is true that (i) *a* is a loving act iff God commands *a* and if it is true that (ii) God commands *a* iff *a* is right (obligatory), then it follows directly that: *a* is a loving act, iff *a* is right (obligatory). This is an interpretation of the traditional objection that if God has a reason for commanding an action, we can have the same reason for performing the action and regarding it as right. . . . If an action's being loving is a good (or compelling) reason for a loving God to command it, it must be an equally good reason for us to perform it insofar as we are loving in our limited way. That loving actions are commanded by God, may be an additional reason for believers to perform them; but there is already sufficient (justificatory) reason. It would also appear that God's will is so constrained by the requirement of love as to leave him little if any discretion in what He commands *qua* loving being. The content of the moral code can in principle be read off from the knowledge of which acts are loving, without reference to God. . . . The divine characteristics which are relevant are love, kindness, forgiveness, omniscience, etc., and what matters is what these characteristics themselves require, not the fact that they are divine.[30]

It is not clear what the point of the initial argument in this passage is, for the conclusion is the coextensiveness thesis for which Chandler has already argued, and the first premiss, (i), is given no defense at all. But granting, for the moment, the coextensiveness thesis, why

---

29. Alternatively, perhaps an act is loving just in case it has as a consequence an increase of love in the world, or better, if it results in at least as large an increase in the world's love as does any alternative act open to the agent. (The second formulation is perhaps that intended by Joseph Fletcher, who I take to be a kind of act-utilitarian, in *Situation Ethics* [Philadelphia: Westminster Press, 1966].) But unless (i) love is the *only* thing of intrinsic value, and (ii) God's commands aim at maximizing intrinsic value, the coextensiveness thesis remains implausible.

30. Chandler, "Divine Command Theories," p. 236.

should it be thought to reveal God's *reason* for his commands? There are many properties of actions which are distinct from but coextensive with (even necessarily coextensive with) the property of being right, for example, *being such that anyone who thinks it is wrong is mistaken*, but these properties do not all provide God with a reason to command those actions possessing them. On the other hand, even if God commands loving actions because they are loving, that we are *morally* required to perform such actions might still depend upon their being commanded by God, rather than on their being loving. To use a familiar if ill-understood term, the property of *being right* can *supervene* on the property of *being commanded by God* even if those properties are correlated with the property of *being loving*.

Turning to the other horn of Chandler's dilemma, we should ask whether, if the coextensiveness thesis is false, the divine command theory succumbs to the traditional problems. The traditional problems Chandler has in mind are, presumably, specifying in a nontrivial way how God is good and dealing with the objection that if God commanded something evil, the theory would entail that it was right. I have already suggested that if a loving act is either one motivated by love or one performed in a loving manner, then the coextensiveness thesis is false, for acts having these properties can fail to be right. Moreover, the claim that God's loving nature ensures that he does not will any "evil" act requires at most that any act that God wills is such that his willing it is compatible with his being loving. The claim does not require that every act that God wills *be* loving or that God will *every* loving act. Accordingly, the coextensiveness thesis can be false, while the property of being loving both constrains God's actions and provides a reason for ascribing goodness to him.

D. The "For Believers Only" Objection

It is sometimes objected that if the divine command theory is true, then only religious believers, or only persons informed of God's commands, could tell right from wrong. Eric D'Arcy puts the point this way: "If immoral actions are immoral merely because God so wills it, merely because God legislates against them, it would be sheer coincidence if someone who knew nothing of God or his law happened to adopt the same view about particular actions as God did."[31] It should be clear that this objection does not apply to our formulation of the divine command theory. According to this theory, there are both moral and theological properties, and the exemplification of the former depends upon the exemplification of the latter. But it is no part of this theory that a person can recognize that an action has a moral property only by first discerning that it has the corresponding theological property. In short, out theory does not purport to give an account of moral knowledge.

E. The "Irrelevant" Objection

The objector may regard the reply to the last objection as providing grounds for another objection: if what is right or wrong can be recognized independently of knowing anything of God's commands, the divine command theory is simply irrelevant. We should concentrate on finding which actions have the moral properties of *being obligatory*, *being permissible*, and *being wrong*, however that can best be done, and not worry about trying to discern God's commands. There are two things that may be said in reply. First, there is clearly a place for a theory of morality which is of theoretical interest and not, primarily, of practical interest. It would be theoretically interesting to learn that what makes actions obligatory is that they are commanded by God, regardless of the practical difficulties in discovering God's commands, just as it would be of theoretical interest to learn that utilitarianism is true, regardless of the practical difficulty of calculating and comparing the values of the consequences of all of our alternative actions.[32] Second, the divine command theorist need not be so pessimistic about the practical relevance of God's commands, for presumably the divine command theorist believes that God has revealed them. Indeed, the divine command theorist might believe that, at least in some cases, it is

31. Eric D'Arcy, "Worthy of Worship: A Catholic Contribution," in Outka and Reeder, *Religion and Morality*, p. 194.
32. Compare G. E. Moore, "Whether [utilitarianism] is of any practical importance is, indeed, another question. But, even if it were of none whatsoever, it certainly lays down propositions of so fundamental and so far-reaching a character that it seems worthwhile to consider whether they are true or false." *Ethics* (London: Thornton Butterworth, 1912), p. 68.

easier to discern God's commands than to detect whether an action has the corresponding moral property. William Paley, who thought that we could discern God's will directly in scripture and indirectly by inquiring into "the tendency of the action to promote or diminish the general happiness," advocated the former approach in the following passage: "An ambassador, judging by what he knows of his sovereign's disposition, and arguing from what he has observed of his conduct, or is acquainted with his designs, may take his measures in many cases with safety; and presume, with great probability, how his master would have him act on most occasions that arise: but if he has his commission and instructions in his pocket, it would be strange not to look into them."[33] If Paley is right, if we do have a commission and instructions, then the divine command theory is of practical as well as theoretical interest.

F. The "No 'Ought' from 'Is'" Objection

Some philosophers apparently believe that the divine command theory violates the Humean dictum "No 'Ought' from an 'Is.'" In discussing the claim "that certain religious beliefs entail certain ethical beliefs, and that the latter can be logically inferred from the former," William Frankena appeals to Hume's slogan and remarks that "properly construed, it is a perfectly correct dictum. By the ordinary canons of logic a conclusion containing the term 'ought' or 'right' cannot be logically derived from premises which do not contain this term, except in such cases as 'It is raining, therefore either it is raining or we ought to be kind to animals,' which can hardly afford aid and comfort to theologians who [claim to derive ethical conclusions from theological premises] or even to those who advocate kindness to animals."[34] Let us say that an argument is *formally valid* just in case its corresponding conditional is a theorem of the predicate calculus, and let us say, somewhat less precisely, that an ethical claim is *interesting* just in case it is not like the claim that either it is raining or we ought to be kind to animals. If we suppose that there is a clear distinction between purely factual state-

33. William Paley, *Principles of Moral and Political Philosophy*, 4th American ed. (Boston: John West, 1819), pp. 61–62.
34. William K. Frankena, "Is Morality Logically Dependent on Religion?" in Outka and Reeder, *Religion and Morality*, p. 300.

ments and ethical or evaluative ones, we can say, then, that a formulation of Hume's dictum suggested by Frankena's remarks is the claim that *no formally valid argument whose premisses are jointly consistent and purely factual has an interesting ethical conclusion.* So construed, Hume's dictum does seem to be supported by the "ordinary canons of logic," but the divine command theory is not incompatible with it. Let *S*, as before, be the state of affairs of an innocent child's suffering gratuitous cruelty. In order to deduce an ethical conclusion such as

> (4) It is wrong for anyone to bring about *S*,

from the sort of factual premiss endorsed by the divine command theorist, say,

> (5) God forbids that anyone ever bring about *S*,

we would need to employ some additional evaluative premiss such as,

> (6) For every agent *x*, state of affairs *S*, and time *t*, it is wrong that *x* bring about *S* at *t* if and only if God forbids that *x* bring about *S* at *t*.

The divine command theory does not entail that (4) is deducible from (5) alone; so the divine command theory does not run afoul of this version of Hume's dictum.

There is a second formulation of Hume's dictum suggested by Frankena's remarks, since he was discussing the view "that certain religious beliefs *entail* certain ethical beliefs [emphasis added]." One proposition entails another just in case it is not possible that the first be true and the second false. Now one proposition can entail another without there being a formally valid argument from the first to the second, so it might be that a principle framed in terms of entailment will differ from one framed in terms of deducibility. A second interpretation of Hume's principle, then, is that *no consistent set of purely factual premisses entails a contingent, interesting ethical conclusion.* In the argument above, the conjunction of (5) and (6) entails the conclusion (4). Moreover, the divine command theorist presumably holds that (6) is a necessary truth, since (6) is a consequence of (P3). If (6) is a necessary truth, then (5) alone entails (4). So this version of the divine command theory licenses a violation of the second formulation of Hume's dictum. However, I know of no reason to think that this second formulation of Hume's dictum is true—unlike the first version, it cannot be defended by a simple appeal to the "ordinary canons of logic." So this objection, too, seems to me to be unpersuasive.

G. The "No Changes" Objection

A final objection has not, as far as I know, actually been made against the divine command theory, but it is a natural application of recent work on the formulation of act-utilitarianism. According to Lennart Åqvist, the moral status of an action may change over time.[35] It might be alleged, however, that there is no way to incorporate this feature into our version of the divine command theory. God is often thought to be immutable, and his commands and prohibitions must on that view remain constant. Hence, according to our theory, the moral status of actions, which is dependent upon those commands and prohibitions, must also remain constant.

Why should we think that the moral status of an action can change with the passage of time? Fred Feldman has constructed the following example to show that it does.

> Suppose a patient is ill, and that his doctor can choose between two main courses of treatment. He can either give the patient medicine A today, and then give him medicine A again tomorrow, or he can give him medicine B today and again tomorrow. Suppose the course of treatment with B would cure the patient, but would produce some unpleasant side effects, while the course of treatment with A would cure the patient without any unpleasant side effects. Suppose, finally, that mixing the treatments would be fatal to the patient, a delightful person who spreads cheer wherever he goes. In this case, let us agree, prior to the time at which he gives any medicine, it is right for the doctor to give A on the first day, and it is right for the doctor to give A on the second day. Suppose, however, that the doctor fails to do what is best. For whatever reason, he gives the patient B on the first

35. Lennart Åqvist, "Improved Formulations of Act-Utilitarianism," *Noûs* 3 (1969):299–323.

day. It seems clear that is is no longer right for him to give A on the second day—that would kill the patient. Once the doctor has failed to do his duty, and has given B on the first day, the rights and wrongs of the case seem to change.[36]

To assess this case, let us suppose that t_0 is some time before the treatment is begun, t_1 is the time at which the first dose is given, and t_2 is the time at which the second dose is given. Then we can summarize Feldman's claims about this case as follows:

(7) At t_0 it is right to give medicine A at t_1.

(8) At t_0 it is right to give medicine A at t_2.

(9) At t_2 it is not right to give medicine A at t_2.

Taken together (8) and (9) entail that the moral status of an action changes between t_0 and t_2. Now (9) is beyond dispute. But why should we accept (8)? One might try to support it by claiming that what is right at t_0 is the complete course of treatment. Thus,

(10) At t_0 it is right to give A at t_1 and to give A at t_2.

And (10), it might be alleged, entails (8). However, Feldman's example can equally well be taken to show that (10) does not entail (8) and that (8) is false. Presumably it was true all along that the doctor would give medicine B at t_1; in particular, this was true at t_0. But if it was true at t_0 that the doctor would give medicine B at t_1, then it was also true at t_0 that it would be wrong to give medicine A at t_2, since it is wrong to give A to a patient who has previously been treated with B. At t_0 we might be ignorant of the doctor's impending poor choice at t_1; hence, we might be justified in believing at t_0 that giving medicine B would be wrong at t_2. God, however, being omniscient, would always have known that medicine B would be administered on the first day of treatment. Hence, he would have been careful to command that B also be given on the second day. Thus, this case

36. Fred Feldman, "World Utilitarianism," in *Analysis and Metaphysics: Essays in Honor of R. M. Chisholm*, ed. Keith Lehrer (Dordrecht: D. Reidel, 1975), p. 267. Feldman notes that this example is based on one given by Åqvist.

does not clearly show that the moral status of an action can change over time.

It might be objected that this way of viewing the doctor's dilemma requires that we say, counterintuitively, that it was a good thing the doctor did not perform all of his obligations. For if the doctor had done what was right at t_1 and given medicine A then, and he had done what was right at t_2 and given medicine B then, he would have killed a delightful person instead of curing him. The objector's premisses are

(11) If the doctor had done what was right at t_1, he would have given medicine A then,

and

(12) If the doctor had done what was right at t_2 he would have given medicine B then.

We may concede that (11) and (12) are both true. It does not follow, however, that if the doctor had done what was right on both occasions he would have killed the patient. For that the objector needs

(13) If the doctor had done what was right at t_1 and the doctor had done what was right at t_2, then he would have given medicine A at t_1 and he would have given medicine B at t_2.

But (13) does not follow from (11) and (12), and, furthermore, it appears to be false. If the doctor had done what was right on both occasions, he would first do what is right at t_1, namely, give A then. If the doctor *had* does what was right at t_1, what would have been right at t_2 would have been different—it would then have been right to give A at t_2. So if the doctor had done what was right on both occasions, he would have given A each time. Thus, we have not found a reason for thinking that the moral status of an action can change over time. Hence, it is no defect if the divine command theory, at least if it is coupled with the doctrine of divine immutability, does not admit such change.

I have argued that the divine command theory can be stated in such a way that it can be defended against seven initially impressive objections. Showing that it is thus defensible does not, of course, provide a reason for thinking that it is true. But if these objections fail to refute the divine command theory, then rejection of the theory is premature and further discussion of it is appropriate.

5. Utilitarianism and the Divine Command Theory

There are some interesting connections between the divine command theory and utilitarianism. Some divine command theorists have held that we can discover God's will by appealing to utilitarianism. Paley, for example, writes that we can discern God's will by his express declarations in scripture as well as by "what we can discover of his designs and dispositions from his works, or as we usually call it, the light of nature." Paley goes on to explain that this second "method of coming at the will of God concerning any action by the light of nature, is to enquire into 'the tendency of the action to promote or diminish the general happiness.' This rule proceeds upon the presumption, that God Almighty wills and wishes the happiness of his creatures; and consequently, that those actions, which promote that will and wish, must be agreeable to him."[37] And John Gay writes that "the Will of God is the immediate Criterion of Virtue, and the Happiness of Mankind the Criterion of the Will of God; and therefore the Happiness of Mankind may be said to be the Criterion of Virtue, but *once* removed."[38]

Elsewhere I have noted a different parallel between utilitarianism and the divine command theory.[39] Many of the objections raised against the divine command theory are closely analogous to objections that can be raised against utilitarianism. Moreover, the replies to these objections which are open to the divine command theorist are at least as strong as the corresponding replies open to the utilitarian. Thus it is hard to justify the contemporary attitude that takes utilitarianism seriously but dismisses the divine command theory out of hand. Accordingly, I advocated renewed attention to the divine command theory by arguing that it was no worse than utili-

37. Paley, *Moral and Political Philosophy*, pp. 61, 63.
38. John Gay, "A Dissertation Concerning the Fundamental Principle and Immediate Criterion of Virtue," in William King, *An Essay in the Origin of Evil* (London: W. Thurlborn, 1731), p. 19.
39. Wierenga, "Utilitarianism and the Divine Command Theory."

tarianism. That no doubt struck some as faint praise. But for those for whom utilitarianism is, in William James's phrase, a live hypothesis, I want in this final section to suggest two respects in which the divine command theory is superior to utilitarianism. If I am correct, then, *pace* Paley and Gay, utilitarian considerations are not by themselves a guide to the will of God.

Utilitarianism presumably includes some principles analogous to our (P1)–(P3). For simplicity, let us merely note that it is committed to something like

(U1)   For every agent x, state of affairs S, and time t, it is obligatory that x bring about S at t if and only if x's bringing about S at t has greater utility than any alternative open to x at t.[40]

The utility of an action is the total amount of good that would be produced if the action were performed minus the total amount of evil that would be produced. Classical utilitarians were hedonistic; that is, they held that pleasure is the only good and pain the only evil. But that is unreasonable. It is plausible, for example, that justice is intrinsically valuable.[41] So, too, is persons loving each other. And aesthetic contemplation, friendship, and having certain traits of character have also been proposed as intrinsically valuable.[42] But at this point a problem arises for utilitarianism.

According to hedonistic utilitarianism, determining whether an action is obligatory requires determining whether it would produce a greater balance of pleasure over pain than any alternative open to the agent. That task is daunting enough, but the prospect of calculating with multiple kinds of good seems hopeless. It will not do to retreat to the position, noted above in Section 4, that utilitarianism is of theoretical and not of practical interest. For if there are diverse values, there is no guarantee that there is even a theoretical

40. A complete statement of this principle will, like (P1), include a condition indicating that an action's being obligatory *depends* upon its utility. Also, to avoid certain puzzles, more would need to be said about what is to count as an *alternative* to an action. We can safely ignore these complications here.

41. See Fred Feldman, *Doing the Best We Can* (Dordrecht: D. Reidel, 1986), pp. 50–52.

42. See the discussion in Richard Brandt, *Ethical Theory* (Englewood Cliffs, N.J.: Prentice-Hall, 1959), pp. 340–352.

answer to the question whether a given action produces a greater balance of good over evil than any of its alternatives. Maybe the various goods are incommensurable; perhaps there is no way of comparing love and happiness or pleasure and a just distribution of goods. If this is a possibility, utilitarianism would fail to yield a judgment on what is obligatory in any situation in which incommensurable goods would be produced by alternative actions.[43] For if two alternatives produce incommensurable goods, it is not the case that one produces a *greater* balance of good over evil than the other. But the divine command theory faces no such problem. For even if there is no objective ranking of goods produced by alternative actions, God could, nevertheless, command one action rather than another. In such a case, God's command might even be taken to determine that one good outweighed another, although apart from God's decision, the goods are incommensurable.

A second advantage the divine command theory has over utilitarianism will be recognized by those who accept the Free Will Defense. As we have seen in Chapters 5 and 7, the Free Will Defense holds that it is possible that God values creatures doing what is right in circumstances in which they are significantly free. But given that what is valuable is a matter of necessity, if it is possible that God values significantly free right action, significantly free right action *is* valuable. But it is difficult to see how utilitarianism could accommodate this claim. According to utilitarianism, the rightness of an action depends upon the utility that would be produced if it were performed as compared to the utility of performing any alternative. But if part of what is valuable in performing a certain action, and hence part of its utility, is that performing the action is a case of freely doing what is right, then its utility cannot be determined prior to determining that it is right. It would be circular if in trying to find a right action by comparing the value of the consequences of our alternatives, we had to take into account that part of the value of doing one (or another) of these alternatives is that we would be freely doing what is right. The divine command theory, by not requiring that the value of an action's consequences determines its moral status, avoids this problem.

43. Ibid., p. 350.

6. Conclusion

In the course of this book we have examined a variety of divine attributes. We have seen that omnipotence can be defined in a way that allows the limitations on ability recognized by classical theism to be compatible with omnipotence and that can be defended against philosophical objections. Omniscience, as we have seen, is knowledge of all truths, and it extends to knowledge *de re* and *de se*. Moreover, omniscience includes foreknowledge, and there is no reason to fear that foreknowledge restricts human free action. And omniscience includes middle knowledge, as seems to be required by the doctrine of divine providence and the Free Will Defense. Eternity, timelessness, and immutability are closely related but distinct properties; and although it has become controversial to ascribe them to God, it is a mistake to think that facts about God's knowledge or his action require abandoning them. In addition, God is good, and arguments against his impeccability and essential goodness ought to be rejected. Finally, the thesis that morality depends upon the commands of God can be given a strong formulation and defended against the objections often thought to refute it.

Index

Library of Congress Cataloging-in-Publication Data

Wierenga, Edward R., 1947–
    The nature of God.

    (Cornell studies in the philosophy of religion)
    Includes bibliographical references and index.
    1. God—Attributes.   I. Title.   II. Series.
BT130.W54   1989   212'.7   88-47929
ISBN 0-8014-2212-4 (alk. paper)